TITANIC ADVENTURE

TITANIC ADVENTURE
One Woman's True Life Voyage
Down to the Legendary Ocean Liner

By
JENNIFER CARTER
and JOEL HIRSCHHORN

Foreword by William F. Buckley, Jr.

Requests for permission should be addressed to:
New Horizon Press
P.O. Box 669
Far Hills, NJ 07931

Carter, Jennifer and Hirschhorn, Joel
        Titanic Adventure
        Foreword by William F. Buckley, Jr.

Interior Design: Susan Sanderson

Library of Congress Catalog Card Number: 98-66221

ISBN: 0-88282-170-9
New Horizon Press

Manufactured in the U.S.A.

2003 2002 2001 2000 1999 / 5 4 3 2 1

The most casual student of history knows that, as a matter of fact, truth does not *necessarily vanquish. What is more, truth can* never *win unless it is promulgated. Truth does not carry within itself an anti-toxin to falsehood. The cause of truth must be championed, and it must be championed dynamically.*

WILLIAM F. BUCKLEY, JR.

AUTHOR'S NOTE

These are my actual experiences and history, and this book reflects my opinion of the past, present, and future. The personalities, events, actions, and conversations portrayed within the story have been reconstructed from my memory, tape recordings, documents, press accounts, photographs, video footage, and the memories of participants. In an effort to safeguard the privacy of certain individuals, I have changed their names and in some cases, altered otherwise identifying characteristics and locations. Events involving the characters happened as described.

ACKNOWLEDGEMENTS

Titanic Adventure could never have been written without the tremendous help and support of many people. Thanks to Ralph White and Emory Kristof who got the dream rolling; Dr. Robert Ballard and Jean-Louis Michel for being trailblazers, the pioneers who found the *Titanic* and for paving the way for so many others to know her; P. H. Nargeolet and George Tulloch for preserving the ship's artifacts and devoting their lives to caring for the legend; P. H. Nargeolet and Yann Keranflech for giving me their love and support; Adam Jahiel, Mark Burnett, Randy Wimberg, Peter Pilafian and Bobby Keyes for being the best, most capable and most delightful crew anyone could ever work with; all the men aboard the *Abeille* and the *Nadir*; Don Lynch and Ken Marschall for doing the *Titanic* full justice in their writing and their art; John Joslyn and Doug Llewelyn for giving me the opportunity to become expedition leader; Miriam Bass for being, as always, so wonderful and encouraging; and Nick Noxon for being my mentor and teaching me everything I know.

Deepest admiration and gratitude to Stephen Low for his consummate talent, his loyalty and his genius at recreating the *Titanic's* history on IMAX; Peter Serapiglia, a great producer, for his integrity and his willingness to stand up for a friend in the face of adversity; Howard Hall for being the most talented and innovative cameraman a producer could ever have; Edwina Troutt MacKenzie for encouraging me to fulfill my dream; Linda Reavely for her belief and support; P. H. Nargeolet for showing me everything a Captain should be; and Captain Rowarch for teaching me how to stand firm. Love and appreciation to Robert Wagner, Linda Alvarez, Andy Gellis, Emily Tompkins Carter, Jennifer Frasier, Candace Smilow, Sam Raymond, Rich Mula, John Weisman, Dr. John E. McCosker, Linda Konnor, Peter Filichia, Alan and Margaret Abrahams, Madeleine and Richard Des Jardins, Evelyn Hirschhorn, Dimitri Logothetis, Warren and Judy Levine, my wonderful mother Peggy Dlouhy, my brother Chris—who we all deeply miss—my sister-in-law Marlene and my sisters Cindy, Pam and Charmaine.

We can't find words strong enough to express thanks to historians that gave us information and guidance and insured our accuracy: John P. Eaton, Charles A. Haas, Wyn Craig Wade, Walter Lord, and the Titanic Historical Society, for making sure that the great ship, its history and its people are remembered and cherished.

Bouquets to the remarkable William F. Buckley, Jr., who is—beyond a superb sailor and a brilliant writer—a fine human being and friend, who brought immeasurable joy to everyone aboard the *Abeille* and the *Nadir*.

Finally, thanks to our publisher/editor Dr. Joan Dunphy for believing in *Titanic Adventure* from the beginning and for helping us to develop, tighten and polish it with extraordinary care, encouragement and skill; and to Rebecca, JoAnne and Shannon, for making the process so enjoyable and productive.

CONTENTS

FOREWORD

When the invitation came to join the *Titanic* exploratory group, I asked my host how much time it would require and he answered: Ten days. That doesn't sound like a great deal of time, measured against the seasons when whalers and such went for as many as thirty-six weeks without sighting land. But if your time is heavily mortgaged, ten days is like an entire season. But the lure of the *Titanic* was such that I grabbed a machine gun and shot it through every appointment I had for the necessary fortnight.

But then I faced the question: What shall I do when I am not actually in the little submarine, diving down to the quarry? It isn't easy, when fully grown and accustomed to the voluptuarian comforts of the comfortable, to face the prospect of ten days in a tiny cabin without your library, your computer, your files and your music.

When with my companions I came aboard the mother vessel, I felt almost exactly as I had felt fifty years earlier when deposited at an English boarding school. Everything seemed foreign and somehow out of reach. That was when I was introduced to the expedition leader, Jennifer Carter.

She is one of those presences who instantly emit what the lonely stranger most wants: Warmth, and competence. As the days went by, she would unfold her spellbinding adventures, here fully related: diving with sharks and whales, producing for National Geographic Society, travels from Alaska to Zimbabwe and becoming the first woman to dive down to view the *Titanic*.

After delicious meals, she would be there for a drink and conversation. The whole of the male company of two dozen adventurers and entrepreneurs were here for her to manage, placate, comfort. It was of course a very exciting time, when the turn came for your own dive. Notwithstanding that there was one such every day, initiating a fresh and enduring experience for the adventurer, Jennifer Carter managed to greet every emerging guest-diver as if he had just come in from the moon. Her excitement, affability, enterprise, and charm were such that when the day we had thought to welcome—the day when the ship would take us back to dry land and to an airplane and back home—the happy prospect of returning to one's own hearth was sharply reduced: It would mean saying goodbye to Jennifer.

This book alleviates that pain. I hope she will be persuaded to do a book tour, to give hundreds and thousands some exposure, however brief, to her loveliness. Read this book with the admiration it justifiably evokes, and know that the author of the book is rare and utterly wonderful company.

WILLIAM F. BUCKLEY, JR.
May 1, 1998

PROLOGUE

The waves of the North Atlantic, 453 miles southeast of Newfoundland, were pitching violently on the morning of August 9, 1987. I grabbed the rail to keep my footing.

It was almost time to make my long-awaited dive to the *Titanic*.

Our expedition was a jointly backed French-American venture. The Americans had leased two French ships (*Nadir* and *The Abeille Supporter*), and a bright yellow submersible, *The Nautile*—named after Jules Verne's *Nautilus* from *20,000 Leagues Under the Sea*. The goal was to recover and preserve artifacts from the legendary ship.

Because of my eight year background as documentary filmmaker for the National Geographic Society, I had been hired to produce and direct our two month adventure at sea for a television special, plan the dive schedules and negotiate between French and Americans—a potentially explosive situation, since rivalries were thick and national pride was at stake.

My dive, originally scheduled for six in the morning, had been delayed due to a malfunction. "Battery problems," said Paul Henri Nargeolet, Captain of the *Nautile*. Nargeolet, known to friends as P. H., resembled a French Mel Gibson. He was a man of magnetic personality and intelligence, but his charm didn't defuse the impact of the word 'malfunction.' I tried not to show how apprehensive I felt. I was the only woman on board and the all-male crew couldn't resist teasing me for invading their territory.

Nargeolet knew I was a veteran of dozens of ocean expeditions and an accomplished scuba diver, but it was his duty to point out the life-and-death hazards that lay ahead. Handing me liability waiver forms, which absolved the company of any responsibility if I died, he pointed out, "Jennifer, your air supply is good for only seventy-two hours. If the umbilical cord on the remote vehicle gets caught on the *Titanic* wreckage, and the air in the sub runs out, there's no way you can be rescued. Remember, there are only two other submersibles that are designed to reach such a depth, and it would take them seven days to make the trip by sea. By then you'd have no more air."

"What else?" I asked, digesting this unsettling information.

"There could be a spark in the electrical equipment. That would cause a flash fire, just like what happened in the space capsules because your oxygen content is so high."

"What about the fireproof suit I'm wearing? Won't that protect me?"

He shrugged. "You have to wear it. It's part of regulations. But no, it won't help at all."

Cautioning me to dress warmly, P. H. said, "the heat will be intense. Ninety-five degrees and eighty percent humidity on the surface, but you have to dress like you're going to the North Pole because when you arrive at the bottom, the temperature will be freezing and you'll remain at that temperature for over seven hours. There's no heating or air conditioning in the *Nautile*."

P. H. reiterated an earlier warning. "I hope you didn't drink or eat anything for the last twenty-four hours." No one had to tell me that; it's the first thing anyone thinks of because there are no bathroom facilities.

He concluded, "If there's even a pin leak in the Titanium hull, the sub would instantly implode. The pressure at that depth is over 6,500 pounds per square inch. That's enough to immediately crush any human flesh or bones."

Faced with so many life-and-death possibilities, I wondered aloud if I was insane to attempt this dive.

"Maybe," he smiled. "But you'll be the first woman to film the *Titanic*, and to see it up close. You'll be setting a world record. Not only as the first woman to dive to the *Titanic*, but the first woman to reach that depth."

Hours and hours passed. Still the malfunctions weren't fixed. And as the time dragged on, my fears multiplied. Was this a bad omen, alerting me that something fatal might happen on the sub? Could these be my last hours alive? Just as I was ready to give up the chance of a lifetime, P. H. came in and told me it was time to go. Climbing a ladder to the top of the sub, I quickly crawled through the tiny hatch, feeling like Alice in Wonderland, tumbling down the rabbit's hole into a completely different world. The world of the *Nautile* was a miracle of modern technology—a twenty-five million dollar vehicle weighing twenty tons, equipped with mechanical arms that could gather artifacts from the bottom of the sea.

The interior of the bathosphere was completely filled with electronics, including VCRs which recorded everything that happened at the bottom. Video cameras, still cameras and halogen lights with the power of 3,000 watts were attached to the outside of the submersible, all specially designed to withstand extraordinary pressures, as well as two manipulating arms that made the submersible look like a giant crab. At the end of one arm was a pincer that could rotate in every direction imaginable, giving it the flexibility to work just like a human hand. The other arm had a rubber suction device attached to a vacuum which allowed the pilot to safely pick up fragile items such as first class china and Baccarat crystal without breaking them.

The yellow shell of the vehicle was slightly over twenty-six feet long, but the Titanium bathosphere enclosed within it made up only a small portion of the submersible. The rest of the shell contained the batteries, a propellor allowing the sub to go up to a speed of two-and-a-half knots when on the bottom, and lead weights which had to be perfectly balanced with the weight of the interior and the people going down so it could descend and ascend to the surface with no problem.

P. H. and Jean-Paul, his co-pilot, fired up all the sub's systems while I struggled to find a comfortable position. I tried to lie on my back, but the metal bar beneath my spine made it impossible. When I attempted to lie on my stomach, I had to bend my knees and hold my feet in the air so as not to hit the electrical equipment.

I was encapsulated in a four inch thick Titanium sphere, only six feet in diameter on the interior. The digital readout showed eighty-five degrees and eighty percent humidity. P. H. had warned me about the heat, and I had to ignore the fact that my body—covered with two sweaters and a fireproof suit—was soaked in sweat. But I was ready to handle whatever happened. Two hours from now, after dropping 12,500 feet through a pitch-black ocean, I would finally be face to face with the *Titanic*.

Chapter 1

Sea Connection

My initiation began when I first saw *Titanic,* a Robert Wagner-Clifton Webb movie which depicted the fatal collision and provided enough sketchy details to pique my interest. I didn't know then that the characters were completely fictionalized and the ending—when Webb's son joined him and the two went down with the ship—was invented to humanize the plot and bring tears to the eyes of its viewers. It didn't matter if the little boy was an actual person. As a child, I identified with his plight. I cried as he stood on the collapsing bridge with his father and bravely waited for the *Titanic* to sink. From that moment on, the legendary ship haunted me.

Even before I became aware of the *Titanic,* I had become fascinated by the ocean. That same year, my mother had exposed me to *The Sea Around Us,* a prizewinning documentary based on Rachel Carson's book. The film version of *Kon Tiki,* Thor Heyerdahl's account of his raft trip from Peru to Tahiti, set my imagination on fire. I pictured myself at the center of all these adventures. I discovered the Santa Monica pier in California. There were amusement park rides on the pier—roller coasters, carousels, shooting galleries, fun houses—but I didn't care about them. All I wanted to do was venture out to the end of the pier and take what the management called "a bathysphere ride to the bottom of the sea." *See live sharks,* the signs proclaimed. *See a giant octopus.*

The bathysphere carried me down and I screamed with delight as the bottom of an octopus pressed against the porthole, its suction cups clinging to the porthole glass. A shark whipped its tail in my face, and a grey nurse shark with long and sharp pointed teeth seemed as if he were going to crash right through the bathysphere and swallow me up. There were giant turtles, starfish, sting rays, crab, lobsters, and an enormous grouper that looked as though it weighed over a hundred pounds. When these creatures loomed up before me, I became Captain Nemo in the *Nautilus*, diving 20,000 leagues beneath the sea.

Every time I rose to the surface, in a euphoric state, I begged my mother to let me go another time. And I did—again and again. The steel bathysphere—which descended thirty feet and held eight people—felt more like a home than any place I'd ever been on land.

Somehow, I thought, if I went down enough times, I would turn into a mermaid, or be transported to a different world—a world of vast, endless ocean.

Given my powerful psychic connection to the sea and my exposure to the *Titanic* story at an early age, I was a ripe candidate for *Titanic* fever. Though the fever was, at this point, low grade, it's a fever that continued to burn as I grew up.

My family couldn't understand this fascination with the sea, the *Titanic*, or any underwater creature. Their world functioned within what we children called the castle—a house my father had built on top of a mountain in

Hollywood. My father—whom my sisters, brother, and I were told to call Francis—was an architectural engineer, and he designed and built the house himself, using the Mediterranean villas and castles he had seen in the South of France and Prague as models. The house was a curiosity; it stood out bizarrely within the colonial, cape cod and ranch-style homes that were popular during that period. The exterior was painted peach-pink, and it had an orange tile roof typical of mediterranean homes. The house had battlements, a rounded tower room that extended up to the top, and balconies all around the living room and dining room that rose so high that when you walked out onto them, you felt you were on top of the pine trees outside. Our castle gazed out over Beverly Hills, Hollywood, and the Pacific Ocean, and on a day after rain cleared the air you could see all the way to Catalina Island, twenty-six miles away.

The strangely distinctive, expensive looking exterior gave no indication of what the rooms were like inside; the furnishings were threadbare, drapes had been worn from years of exposure to sunlight and five children and a myriad of cats had taken their toll on the couches and chairs which at one time had been elegant, covered in tapestried fabric.

In spite of the daily deterioration, nothing was ever replaced because my father dreaded spending money. As a result, my family lived in genteel poverty, and I was so ashamed that I never dared invite any friends over for fear of ridicule.

My three sisters, my brother and I were all placed in the tower room as newborns directly after arriving home from the hospital. It made for a fanciful, fairytale kind of existence. As children, my sisters pretended to be Sleeping Beauty, Snow White and Rapunzel. My assumed identities were more adventurous; I pretended that the battlements were a ship on the ocean, and I was fighting off deadly pirates.

This early obsession with water was carried to extremes. My brother had a dog named Max and my sisters had cats, but I insisted on turtles and goldfish.

When I made any attempt to share my dreams and fantasies with my father, he was remote, uncommunicative. He was incapable of opening up to people. Except for his appearances at dinner, it was hard to believe he actually lived with us, and he spoke so seldom I can't even recall the sound of his voice.

Despite this, Francis was a brilliant, creative man who had graduated from the University of Prague at nineteen years old. He went through a four-year curriculum in one, but had to wait until the proper four-year time period had elapsed to receive his degree.

Like so many immigrants envisioning fame and fortune in the United States, he traveled west and quickly established himself as a well respected architectural engineer. He designed the Egyptian Theatre and the Pantages in Hollywood, as well as St. John's Hospital, among numerous other important California buildings and landmarks. To relax, he painted portraits of my mother and the castle in Prague where he had grown up.

Fortunately, my mother, Peggy, provided the love and attention I needed. A slim, beautiful redhead with hazel eyes, Peggy helped us with our homework, drove us everywhere and involved us in extracurricular activities. Her children were her life, and she saw to it that I took violin lessons, piano, drama, ballet and swimming.

Peggy had a beautiful singing voice, and she sang all the time—standards like "You'll Never Know," "Bye Bye, Blackbird" and "My Romance." She was also highly imaginative and spiritual. An expert numerologist, she consulted her charts to make sure the names she had chosen for us were lucky. Astrology was another passion, and she used it to determine where we should go to school and when it was the proper time to travel.

Peggy visited psychics regularly and took their predictions seriously. As a result, I've always been torn between believing that I control my own destiny and being deeply affected by those who claim fatalistically they can predict my future. As a child, I often wondered what Peggy would have seen, through her charts and numbers, if she had been asked about the *Titanic* in advance of its sailing.

My father's rigid practicality presented a challenge to Peggy but she always found a way to stretch a dollar so that I had lovely clothes which she often made and I felt as well-dressed as my peers.

Another ally was my grandmother, who lived with us. After her marriage failed, she was left penniless, having pridefully refused a financial settlement from her wealthy, philandering husband. A resourceful woman, she sought to be self-sufficient and studied interior design and earned her real estate license. However, she was unable to find work after the depression struck and had to support herself and my mother in grinding poverty for years. Yet she made up in culture what she lacked in monetary reserves. My grandmother's background included travel all over Europe as well as friendships with Teddy Roosevelt and other heads of state. Her name was Amy Plant, and she was related to the Plantagenets who ruled England and France from Henry II in 1154 through Richard III in 1485.

Amy looked like royalty too. She had stature, a regal bearing, and an aristocratic chin. She was a classic example of someone short in size—only five feet one—but perceived by all as large and powerful. In fact, she was the most powerful member in our house. My mother deferred to her and my father feared her. But none of this bothered me, because she was my champion from earliest childhood. I was her favorite and could do no wrong.

I used to go through her chest of drawers and find exquisitely beaded bags, mother-of-pearl opera glasses, long silk gloves and a fragile lace mantilla made in Spain that she wore on top of a comb to cover her head when she was presented to the king and queen of Spain. Of course, those were from the years when she had all the wealth one could dream of. There were also elegant shoes and hats with huge feathers and an embroidered box with pictures and postcards from all over the world on the shelves of her armoire. I saw her spoon collection from places she had visited throughout the world, and I lived vicariously through her colorful adventures—sailing down the Nile, visiting the Pyramids, meeting royalty. She had pictures of herself with King Alfonso of Spain and the Queen of England. Her uncle's home in New Hampshire was named Luchnow— later made into a tourist attraction above Lake Winnipesaukee in the town of Moultonboro—where Teddy Roosevelt was often a guest.

Best of all, she remembered all the events surrounding the *Titanic*. She was twenty-five when the *Titanic* sank, and she had vivid memories of the horrific headlines, the controversy about guilt and innocence, and the stories of young people her own age who had met untimely and tragic ends. Seeing my fascination with the subject, she told me about a friend of hers who had been aboard with her mother and father.

"You *knew* someone who was on the *Titanic*?" I asked, my eyes opening like saucers. "How amazing!"

"She never got over it. Had nightmares for years after."

"What was her name?"

"Helen Newsom. Her parents had homes in New

York and New Hampshire. Squam Lake, not far from Luchnow. She married a tennis star, Carl Behr. He proposed to her on the lifeboat."

"That's romantic."

"I suppose. After all, if you think you might die, you're apt to make the most of your last hours on earth."

As a result of my mother's devotion and my grandmother's commanding influence, I was able to glide past the fact that my father totally ignored me, my sisters Pam, Cindy, and Shari, and my brother Chris.

Pam, a tall attractive redhead like my mother, was three-and-a-half years younger than I was, a shy ethereal person who developed into an outstanding flutist and later joined the Houston Ballet Orchestra. Lucinda (nicknamed Cindy), two years behind Pam, was effervescent and an optimist. She became a well-known disc jockey in northern California and then moved to Maui where she gained a huge Hawaiian following with her radio show and cable television program. Five years younger than I and the family rebel, Cindy was as outspoken as Pam was conservative. She adored horses, as I did, and was the only member of our family to take up flying.

The youngest of my siblings, Shari had buoyant energy and a sense of humor. I had a wonderful time teaching her to read, and was thrilled when she expressed interest in the sea stories which I preferred.

As the only boy of the house, Chris was catered to. Like us, he was largely ignored by my father, but, unlike us, he was given a room of his own; the girls all had to share bedrooms. He got to watch more television, was given permission to go on trips with his friends, and was, in general, the king of our castle. All these privileges incited tremendous jealousy in me.

"Just because he's a boy doesn't mean he should get *everything*," I complained.

The jealousy grew when he was the only one to get a bicycle. He had a paper route, which I wanted. My mother declared that girls don't have paper routes, an explanation that made no sense to me.

"It's too dangerous. We live on a steep hill," said my mother, disregarding the fact that I was drawn to danger and loved to take chances.

When Chris had his friends over, I was never allowed to play with them because "You are just a girl."

Nobody understood that dolls, from the start, were anathema to me, and I had no use for frills and laces. I preferred books that would take me to faraway lands. I wanted to sail around the world. My favorite book was *Twenty Thousand Leagues Under the Sea*, which I read over and over. When I discovered Jules Verne's biography and found that his favorite books were *Swiss Family Robinson* and *Robinson Crusoe*, I read those too. A hero to me was not the ladylike young waif who won Prince Charming. I didn't want to be Rebecca of Sunnybrook Farm; I wanted to be Amelia Earhart or the unsinkable Molly Brown.

I loved my brother and became very close to him when we grew up, but as children our competitiveness was too strong to overcome. Sibling rivalry reached its height when my father was pressured into taking Chris away for a weekend. Francis owned a tiny cabin he had built himself in northern California's Sequoia National Park, and he often went there to collect rock samples he felt might contain valuable minerals, such as uranium, tantalum, and beryllium. Beryllium was a lightweight, corrosion-resistant, rigid steel grey metallic element used as an aerospace structural material. Uranium contained plutonium, a naturally radioactive element that was used in reactor fuels. Francis felt these minerals could be mined from the areas he had put quitclaims on.

"Can I come along?" I said, sensing an opening, my one and only opportunity to attain recognition from my father.

He didn't even answer. My mother rushed in and took my hand, forcibly leading me from the room.

"A father should be with his *son*," she explained.

"But I can climb, fish, play baseball, swim. I can do anything Christopher can do."

"There's no running water, no bathrooms. There's no stove or refrigerator. It's too *primitive*. There are bears up there, coyotes and mountain lions. It's no place for a girl," she went on as if that explained it all.

Chris taunted me, borrowing a line from *The Wizard of Oz*: "Lions and tigers and bears, oh my." After which I tried to hit him before my mother separated us.

All these supposed negatives—the lack of stoves and refrigerators, the treacherous mountain creatures—only excited me more, but the wilds of the redwood forest and mountains were "no place for a girl." This event made me even more determined to live a life of adventure when I grew up. In the meantime, I pored over *National Geographics* and biographies of adventurers and secretly planned for the future.

At fifteen, I announced plans to sail around the world after high school. My mother nodded patiently and then told me to make a beauty parlor appointment because my hair was getting too long and curly.

My education as a proper young lady continued that September when my mother enrolled me at the Westlake School of Girls where I was an honor student.

After graduation, I took a summer job at City National Bank of Beverly Hills to raise enough money to live at a USC dorm. My father would not finance my living away from home; he was too afraid I couldn't handle men. I was quiet and studious, the perfect stereotyped bank employee. At various times I was a teller, a bookkeeper, a collections clerk, and a foreign exchange manager. And I even met such celebrities as members of the Rat Pack, including Dean Martin, Joey Bishop, Frank Sinatra and Sammy Davis Jr. Other high-profile customers included a surly James Mason and an extremely rude Zsa Zsa Gabor. My favorite was Warren Beatty. Like legions of others, I had a tremendous crush on him. Of course, except for blushing when he was around, I never betrayed my interest.

Groucho Marx and Dean Martin flirted and told me jokes, trying out their material before presenting it on television. They found me a delighted and receptive audience, albeit somewhat shy.

Their jokes were far more fun than figuring out why someone's bank statement was in overdraft, or filing checks for people's accounts. After millions of adventurous dreams, I often worried that I would spend the rest of my life at a teller's window or in a tiny back office with loan applications. Fortunately, I made a wonderful friend—Linda Alvarez, who was destined to become one of California's leading newscasters. Like me, Linda longed for adventure, and she was willing to take as many risks in life as she did in her imagination.

It seemed, as a diligent bank employee, that I was destined for the sea only in my imagination. I told my next door neighbor, Tom, a portly public relations man who had once been in the Navy, that for my vacation I was taking my first ocean voyage on a cruise ship to Hawaii, and confided in him that I hoped eventually to find some kind of job connected with the sea.

"Don't you know that the sea isn't for women?" he said. "Fishermen for centuries haven't permitted women on their ships. They're bad luck. Women are a jinx around the world."

"Do you consider them a jinx?" I asked him.

"Maybe not, when a girl's as pretty as you."

I colored at his suggestive remark and tried to turn away, but I listened when he told me that most of the women who sailed through history were prostitutes.

This grim portrait of male resistance to seafaring women filled me with resentment, and inwardly I never said an official goodbye to my seafaring dreams or my *Titanic* books. But between my mother's repeated discussions of marriage and the era itself, I fell prey to social pressures that were all powerful in the early 1960s. Nice girls worked, but only till they caught a husband.

Nice girls didn't dream of sailing around the world by themselves.

Perhaps I might have resisted, but then a sudden, life-shattering experience forced me into the stereotypical mold.

It was December 26, 1963, the day after Christmas.

My sisters and I were chattering away, making so much noise that my grandmother was constantly telling us to be quiet. Chris was putting together a model airplane at the table while wolfing down a peanut butter sandwich, and Peggy had begun to wash the mountain of dishes that filled the sink every morning.

"It's not like Francis," Peggy said referring to our father, "to sleep this late."

"He worked all night," said Pam. "I guess he's really tired."

"But it's not like him," Peggy insisted. "He always

leaves for the stock market before you children go to school. Jennifer, go upstairs and see if he's all right."

I finished the last spoonful of cereal and went to my father's room. His door was closed. He always closed it before going to sleep, which was typical—keeping all human interaction away as much as possible.

I opened the door quietly and walked over to the bed. He was strangely still, head facing the ceiling. It was an odd moment. I never spoke to my father and even in this half-darkened room, with no one around, I felt self-conscious about saying a word.

I moved closer and whispered, "Francis?"

There was no response. I touched his forehead. His blue eyes stared sightlessly at me.

"Peggy!" I screamed. "Come up here now. Somebody call a doctor, quick!"

I ran to the living room and picked up the phone, while my mother tried frantically to revive him. But even as I called, I knew it was too late—I knew that he was dead.

It was my first experience with sudden death, a death made more terrifying because no warning had preceded it. A week ago, my father had been examined and pronounced in perfect health.

To my surprise, I burst into wrenching sobs. I cried and cried, and no one could comfort me. My grandmother's arms provided an anchor until I was able to pull myself together again.

Through it all, through the tidal wave of tears, through an overwhelming grief that seemed to rise up from nowhere, I heard myself asking: "Why am I crying?" I had no relationship with Francis. He never spoke to me, never acknowledged anything I did, never saw a school play I was in, or a dance recital.

I was crying for the father I never had.

My mother's belief in psychics increased after my father's death. As a young widow of forty-two, she was grief-stricken and troubled about the prospect of caring for a large family without her husband's help. A friend told her about Grace, a European psychic whose predictions were uncannily accurate. When I heard about Grace, I wanted to visit her too.

Grace's reputation had spread quickly, and I waited for two hours on line with twenty other people. Finally, my turn came. She was in her fifties, with long black hair tied in a bun and a beautifully woven shawl of brilliant lapis blue draped over her shoulders. Her loose skirt flowed down to her ankles. Studying me with dark, kind eyes, she said hello in a gentle voice and reached for my hand.

Staring at my hands carefully, she took them in hers and held them for a while. Then she spoke in a thick middle-European accent.

"I see a caul. You were born with a caul over your head."

"What is that?"

"It's a very fortunate sign. You're a lucky girl. It's a very rare thing, and it means you'll be blessed in many ways and protected from danger."

After a silence she continued, "You have special intuitive qualities and you must always listen to them. Listen to the voices of danger and the voices of your heart. They will not lead you wrong."

Then Grace went over to the other side of the room, picked up a globe and brought it back. She spun the globe and waited until it stopped, then pointed to Egypt.

"You'll be doing something important in this country, and you'll visit it several times. Do you know anyone in Egypt?"

"No, but I'd love to go there."

She told me I'd travel through Europe, through Paris, Italy, England, and Germany. Japan stood out for her, and so did Greece. Then her finger moved to the Atlantic Ocean, to a spot in the Northern Atlantic, not far from New York and Canada.

"I don't know why this spot is so important, because it's not on land, and there's no island there. But this is coming through *very* strongly for me that you will have something of great significance happen here. In fact, you will be in this spot several times during your life."

She talked of Montreal, Toronto, New York, and the East Coast.

"I see you traveling to these areas also. You'll have a job that takes you all over the world." For a moment her face darkened.

"There will be some terrible problems too, but you will have the strength to handle them."

The intensity that charged her words was so powerful that I felt certain she was right. I glided past her reference to problems, concentrating instead on the exciting portrait of travel and adventure she had painted.

That night I told my mother everything Grace had said. Somehow, I sensed she wasn't a fake or a phony, as many psychics were.

I went to see Grace the following week for more advice. I had met a young man named Kurt Johnson, and I wanted to ask her about him. But the doors to her storefront office were closed, and a note said she had gone back to Europe.

Chapter 2

Broken Shell

I first went out with Kurt on a blind date arranged by one of my friends at City National. He was twenty-five, just out of law school, six feet tall, with thick blond hair, horn-rimmed glasses and a rapid-fire, staccato way of speaking. A chain smoker who downed margaritas two at a time, Kurt was also clever, wildly ambitious, and goal-oriented. He had his entire life mapped out, including an early retirement at age forty.

"I'll have a million before I'm thirty," he boasted.

I was attracted to his tenacious attitude, his way of taking over and making all decisions. My father had been so distant, so introverted, that Kurt's dominance gave me a sense of security.

I was also in a weakened state following my father's death. None of my sisters were working—they were younger and still in school—nor my brother, attending the University of Southern California, or my mother. My summer bank job had turned into the sole support of my home. It was too much responsibility for a teenage girl to handle, but I had no choice; we had no funds.

My father's money would be tied up for a year in probate, because he hadn't made a will. Plans I had made to attend USC were put aside. The crushing responsibility of supporting seven people fell on me.

Kurt seemed strong and self-assured, and I was in desperate need of someone to lean on. I didn't know then that the only security comes from depending on yourself and your own resources. The inevitable result was marriage, and I retired from my position at the bank.

A wedding present from my friend, Linda Alvarez, should have alerted me to the trouble ahead. She gave me matching bath towels that were embroidered with the words *Slave* and *Master.*

I soon found out that what I had seen as strength was really tyranny. Nothing I did pleased Kurt. He didn't like my cooking, my clothes, my friends, or even the gifts I chose for his family. He disliked reading and resented it so much when I picked up a book that he forbade me to read in his presence.

Another of his obsessive habits was his compulsive approach to cleanliness.

"There's *dust,*" he would scream, running his finger on the top of a table. "Your mother obviously didn't teach you how to clean. For that matter, she didn't teach you how to cook either. What *did* she teach you?"

When I fixed coffee for Kurt, it had to be the exact temperature he desired. Too cold and it would be thrown out. Too hot and it would be rejected. If it was too hot, I'd have to put ice cubes in it to cool it down, and then he claimed it was *too* cool. This mania about temperature went beyond coffee. Every morning I was expected to kiss him, and he then let me know if my lips were too warm—in which case I had to put an ice cube on my mouth and kiss him again—or if too cold, I had to drink something hot to raise the temperature.

Trying hard to please him, my ego steadily deflated as he tore apart everything I did. He was alternately critical and violent. I worked harder at cleaning and read every cookbook ever published. I begged him for a washing machine and he refused.

"We're not going to throw around money," he shouted.

Not throwing around money meant buying an old car that collapsed almost daily. It startled me to realize that my father's resistance about spending money was exaggerated in Kurt. When I mustered the courage to answer back—which was seldom—he warned me that he had a talent for revenge, and he would make me pay if I ever opposed him.

Then I became pregnant, and the baby was born dead. Never had my heart been so close to breaking.

"Don't worry, my child," said a well-meaning nun, who was sent by a nurse to speak to me immediately after I learned that the infant—at eight months—was stillborn. "It's God's plan. Your child is in heaven now."

"I don't want him in heaven, I want him here," I said, unable to stop the tears.

When Kurt came to take me home, I saw he too was genuinely grief-stricken. His eyes were red. Tragedy brought us together, if only for a brief moment.

I tailspinned into a depression, tormenting myself with questions: why did God make this happen? Was it somehow my fault? I had tried to do everything right, eating properly, exercising regularly, taking vitamins the doctor prescribed.

My mother and grandmother tried to help me conquer my paralyzing depression, but I hardly heard them. I was anxious to conceive again so I could erase what I felt to be my terrible failure. Three sons followed in quick succession—Derek, Brent and Kevin—but motherhood only exacerbated our conflict.

Now, from Kurt's view, I was an inadequate mother, just as I had been an inadequate wife.

When Brent was eighteen months, Kurt decided to add a new addition to our Coldwater Canyon home—a tiled dining room with a whole wall of windows looking out over the back yard.

"We'll do our own painting," he announced. Kurt always announced, never suggested. We had already laid the tile ourselves and now he wanted to paint the walls.

"Let's not use lead paint," I said, remembering articles I'd read that children pulled chips off paint and ate them, sometimes dying from lead poison.

"Paint chips won't happen with brand new paint. That's only in an old building that's been standing for years, where the paint is chipped off. Lead makes it a stronger, better solution for the walls." He gave me every chemical reason why lead was necessary to make the paint last longer.

A violent battle ensued, which Kurt won; he always won, because winning was his goal, and he would fight to the death to come out triumphant.

We were both up on ladders when I turned around and saw Brent standing below. Chubby, blond, and beautiful, with an angel's face and blue eyes, Brent's expression gave no indication of danger—but I instantly noticed the paint dripping from his mouth. He had a paint stick in his right hand and had placed it in his mouth like a lollipop.

I jumped off the ladder and grabbed him, rushing him to the bathroom and trying frantically to clean his mouth of any excess, using paper towels to sop up any residue.

"Why the hell weren't you watching him?" Kurt screamed.

I ignored the unfair accusation, and Kurt called Children's Hospital, insisting that Brent couldn't have swallowed enough paint to hurt himself. But I knew better; Brent was so young that any amount of lead in his system could be fatal. While Kurt and I looked on in horror, his face began to turn pale and then blue. His temperature had dropped and we were petrified.

A doctor at the hospital said, "Bring him in right away. And for God's sake, don't let him fall asleep."

All the way to the hospital, as Brent kept dropping off and I forced him to stay awake, Kurt kept shouting at the top of his lungs, "You killed my son. You killed my son."

It was too insane to merit a response; Kurt had been the one to insist on the lead paint.

The doctors pumped Brent's stomach and did blood tests, trying to measure the quantities of lead remaining in his system. They warned us afterward that he had to be carefully watched for the next year to make sure there was no loss of energy level and mental development. Excessive weakness and exhaustion were signs that the lead poisoning had done brain damage.

Fortunately, as the months passed, it became evident that Brent was not impaired in any way. Later on when he went to school, this good news was reinforced when he took an IQ exam and tested at genius level.

Four more unbearable years went by. The fantasy

of a happy marriage evaporated. Visions of distant voyages and travel faded away. Motherhood nourished me, but I was too tormented by Kurt's incessant criticism and violent outbursts to be able to enjoy staying at home and being a mother. Derek handled the tension at home by rebelling at everything, inciting Kurt's wrath and provoking countless beatings. Brent and Kevin banded together, two musketeers trying to dodge the storms. Brent met them head-on and suffered more blows than Kevin, the baby of the family, who learned to defuse situations with charm, and keep himself comparatively safe.

The idea that a good wife sticks by her husband under all circumstances was still ingrained in me. I prayed I'd die and find release from Kurt's cruelty. I was a shell by then, without any dreams. I didn't even have the energy to fantasize about distant voyages or a safe port for my children and myself.

In June, Kurt's mother and stepfather came over to see their grandchildren. Kurt had recently had a vasectomy against his will, because my pap smears were at a cancerous level. It was necessary for me to discontinue birth control pills.

After his parents left, Kurt exploded, a rage fueled by alcohol and paranoia.

"You told her, didn't you? I told you, under no circumstances, to let on about the operation."

At first I couldn't grasp what he was saying. I hadn't said a thing.

"You're a liar."

"Why would I tell her?"

"I heard you saying I didn't feel well."

"Yes, but I never said you had an operation."

I fled into the bathroom to avoid his ranting, to cut

out the sound of his voice. Turning the shower on full blast, I felt relief that his screaming was obliterated.

My back was to the shower entrance and suddenly I felt two hands grasping my throat, tightening. I tried to scream, but no words came out. It seemed like forever that his hands were on my neck.

As I struggled, I felt certain that he would kill me. However, something—perhaps a realization of what he was actually doing—must have stopped him. As I gasped for breath, he released his hold.

In my dazed and horrified state, I stood there paralyzed with fear, too shocked to move. Then, without even thinking about it, I leapt from the shower and ran out of the bathroom. Alone and locked in my bedroom, I stood cold, wet and shaking. As I gradually calmed down, I found myself gingerly touching my neck to be sure the unbelieveable attack had not been imagined.

The marks on my throat lasted for weeks. The black, blue and red finger imprints remained clear, where all the blood vessels under my skin had broken.

Kurt never apologized, never acknowledged that he had nearly killed me. It was as if the incident had never happened.

I stayed outwardly submissive against the tyranny under which my children and I continued to live, but within me rage simmered. Against his wishes, I enrolled in a woman's consciousness raising course at UCLA. I met dozens of contemporaries as well as women twice my age, who were struggling to define themselves as individuals and escape untenable relationships.

For the first time in nine years, since my wedding, I began to feel hope. Successful career women came as guest lecturers and spoke to us, unveiling for me a new world of possibilities.

An attorney of twenty-seven made a particularly powerful impression. She spoke of being told her entire life, by husband, in-laws, and family, that she was wasting her time concentrating on going to law school. She eventually graduated at the top of her class and opened her own firm. Her obvious pride and joy in her work made me realize there was another life beyond the isolated prison in which I and my children dwelled. I took a slew of tests and personality profiles to determine career capabilities. The tests showed that I really had a high IQ—145—with talents that I could develop and capitalize on. But I had lost all my self-esteem during my marriage. I could hardly believe this personality, outlined clearly in black and white, was me.

I said nothing about all this to Kurt, once again swallowing the hurt, but within me rebellion was igniting.

Our final confrontation came when he screamed once too often about my inability to follow his morning list and do everything on it exactly as he ordered.

"You forgot to pick up my jacket at the cleaners," he screamed.

Kurt's lists were so long that I could never complete them. No matter how hard I tried, there was always some item I missed.

"I'll do it tomorrow," I said wearily.

"I *needed* it tomorrow. You're so goddamn stupid you can't even follow a simple list."

Past caring, past fear, I cried out, "The hell with you and your lists."

"What did you say?"

"You heard me."

The list was still in my hands. I tore it up into dozens of little pieces and threw it on the floor.

"And get a maid to pick up after you," I continued. "I want out. I want a divorce."

"Just try it. You'll never see your kids. You won't get a cent of support. I'll declare bankruptcy."

Believing him, but unwilling to commit suicide or kill him—the only alternatives I could think of—I walked away. I heard him shout, "What do you think you're doing? Where are you going? You can't leave."

When I didn't stop, he added, "You won't survive a week on your own."

No one, I resolved, would ever say that to me again.

Chapter 3

The Sky Above,
The Sea Below

Once I was free, I confronted the bitter, agonizing truth. Through systematic criticism, cruelty and manipulation, Kurt had destroyed my courage and replaced it with fear. I didn't know if I could hold a job, relate to people, or even survive. For weeks I functioned, but only on the most minimal level. My self-confidence was so damaged that I nearly yielded to Kurt's pleas for a reconciliation. I came close to considering it because of that age-old phrase *for the children's sake.* But something—some instinct to stay afloat rather than drown—kept me from succumbing to his perilous promise, *I'll change.* I hadn't prayed since I was a child, but I found myself praying for strength now. My sons Kevin, Derek, and Brent were sharp reminders that I had no right to sink into self-pity or dwell on suicide. I had to create a better life for my children and for me.

I returned to work that December at a savings and loan institution, California Federal. Kurt, true to his word, refused support. I was too emotionally damaged to face him in court, so, not knowing of his viciousness, the court allowed him joint custody. I would make my own way and take care of my children's future needs through my own efforts. I would prove to myself that I didn't need to be dependent. Traveling the world, breaking free of routine and finding adventure would have to wait for the right time.

Strangely, that time began during the most ordinary of events—a visit to my dentist. While filling one of my cavities, he waxed enthusiastically on about his hobby, scuba diving. My dreams of the sea, so long dormant, suddenly sprang to the surface.

A few days later, as if fate took a hand, I saw an advertisement in the local paper for scuba diving lessons at the New England Divers School in Santa Monica. I ripped out the ad and saved it. As I worked and took care of the kids, an idea took hold and wouldn't let go. I was meant to recapture my connection with the sea. I went to the library and got out books about scuba divers—mostly men—and felt a piercing need to acquire the skills. Land had proved so harsh and painful that the ocean held even more allure than in my childhood. Saving up for eight weeks and paying my fee, I felt myself trembling. I knew this was a challenge, one with heavy symbolic freight. But now was the time to move beyond fear and to fling myself headfirst into life again.

When you have a dream—even one embedded in your subconscious that you only sense rather than fully understand—fate often moves you toward that vision without your knowing it. It draws you to people you sense will turn half-formed fantasies into reality.

Ralph White, my scuba instructor, was that kind of man.

Six-foot-four, a former   physical defense and

weapons instructor in the Marine Corps, Ralph had also made a dive through ice to find a sunken ship 123 miles from the North Pole. His legs and arms were disproportionately powerful and muscular in contrast to his slim body. He wore a navy knit watch cap, Jacques Cousteau style, with a dolphin diving medal pinned to the front.

He was also the most confident person I'd ever met, which was underscored when he handed me his card:

> Ralph White
> Professional Adventurer
> *Deep Sea Diver - Ranger - Pilot - Parachutist - Photographer - Skipper - Body Guard - Scout - ObGyn - Chauffeur - Cartographer Ex-Everything*
> Services Rendered
> *Wars Fought - Governments Run - Riots Organized - Uprisings Quelled - Tigers Tamed - Epic Films Produced - Snakes Charmed - Mortals Immortalized - Bars Emptied - Whales Harpooned - Maidens Satisfied - Bad Guys Caught*

He stepped into my life just at the time I was ready to conquer all the fears created by my past.

Somehow, as if he saw my need, I was instantly singled out by him as a protégée. Ralph had a powerful Svengali side to his nature and I struck him—rightly—as a person who had been trapped without air and was now coming alive.

"If you don't learn to do it right *now,* you could die later on," he said repeatedly. "Do you want to just pass, or do you want to be the *best*?"

Ralph's insistence on perfection evoked the memory of my grandmother Amy Plant, and her family connection to the Plantagenets. "As a descendant of the Plantagenets, more is expected of you," she would say. "You must be brave, fight hard and never complain."

But his training—he referred to it with a grin as "torture training"—was extremely rigorous. He was determined to push me to the limits of my ability, shape me, and remold me as his female counterpart. Mixed with my apprehension was an instant, genuine passion for the sport. The large high school pool in Santa Monica where I took lessons was far from an exotic location, but Ralph's approach made me feel I was deep in the Pacific Ocean.

One of his scuba exercises for new trainees was called Ditch and Recover, which meant ditch your tank underwater, come to the surface, re-enter the pool in a different area and recover your equipment. Along with everyone else, I removed all my equipment underwater, dropped my weights, took off my tank—my source of air—still breathing from the regulator while I was on the bottom. Last of all, I removed my mask.

The mask was a lifeline as much as my air, because I couldn't see without the prescription lenses which had been inserted into it. Divers who wear glasses have their masks made with special lenses put in, because there's too much danger of losing contact lenses underwater.

After my scuba gear was removed, I ascended to the surface, exhaling, so I wouldn't get the bends.

Then, as Ralph instructed, I was taken to another part of the pool and pushed in. He told me to make sure I took enough air into my lungs so I'd be able to hold my

breath while finding my equipment. This was a more terrifying task for me than anyone else in my class, because I
alone was doing it without being able to see. I finally found
the regulator—air at last—and struggled into the backpack
attached to the tank.

Ralph had moved my mask. It wasn't next to my
tank and I had to comb the bottom, reaching out sightlessly
and feeling my way until I located it in a totally different
area. I exhaled with force to clear the water from the mask
and rose to the surface.

Since Ralph had added that extra burden of moving the mask, I was the final one up. I swallowed my anger
at him for making me the last one to accomplish my ditch
and recovery.

Another of Ralph's tests took us on a dive boat to
Catalina Island, near the Isthmus. The test required me to
swim underwater into a thick growth of seaweed called
ribbon kelp, which is much tougher than the conventional
bladder kelp. I was made to spin around and around, like
a blindfolded child at a party playing pin the tail on the
donkey. The idea was to make me so dizzy that I didn't
know where I came from, what was up and down and
where I was going.

I became completely disoriented, and the kelp
wrapped itself around my neck, my arms, and legs.

I knew I wasn't supposed to swim on top of the
kelp. Doing that only results in serious entanglement, causing death if a person can't get out of the mass of brown and
rubbery rope-like tentacles. I dropped down, still being
held taut by those underwater vines, searching for a clear
area. I found no opening.

Tightly surrounded by this suffocating seaweed,

I could barely reach the diving knife that was strapped to my right leg. With each movement, more kelp entwined me. I worried that it might yank the regulator hose out of my mouth.

Finally, with a firm grip of my knife, I fought to cut myself loose. I didn't dare slice around my neck, which would have cut the hose open and eliminated all my air. I continued to cut over a seemingly endless period of ten minutes, till I extricated myself from the mass of underwater vines.

A sinewy seal swam up close, eyeing me with tremendous curiosity, before moving back into the kelp beds to find food.

Ralph's response when I completed the exercise was, "What took you so long?"

By the time I did my buddy breathing, I could cheerfully have drowned him. But I was also intent on showing him I could take whatever he dished out. I asked him why he'd chosen me as a scapegoat, and he said, "Because you can do it. You're special."

Proving to him I could buddy breathe meant taking the regulator from my mouth and giving the hand signal to my diving partner—my "buddy"—that I was out of air. I then tapped him on the shoulder and made the "cut" signal (running my index finger across the front of my neck, left to right). At that point, my buddy took one last breath from his regulator and put the regulator into my mouth, whereupon I took two breaths and returned it to him so we could go on sharing the air.

The surf entry exercise, done at Zuma Beach near Malibu, was on a day when the waves were abnormally high. If that's the situation and you're trying to walk with huge rubber fins on your feet, lead weights around your waist that put over twenty pounds on you, a mask on your face that cuts down on your vision out of the water, a tank and backpack that weigh over twenty-five pounds, and a buoyancy compensator on your chest, you're extremely unstable. As you enter the surf, standing up, you have to enter it at exactly the right moment or else the wave will knock you down.

Once you fall wearing so much heavy equipment, it's very difficult to recover. Usually you tumble around off your feet, unable to get your bearings, sometimes losing your regulator and sometimes having to be dragged back out to start the operation over again. It's the same with all new divers. They almost never make it through the surf on the first time out.

Even though I *had* executed it correctly, Ralph didn't see how well I'd done, because he was busy recovering someone else from the surf line who couldn't get up.

"Now it's your turn, Carter."

"I already did it."

"Well, if you did it so well, you won't mind doing it another time."

So he made me repeat the torturous exercise, and this time I was exhausted from the first entry and fell flat on my face when the surf hit, rolling over on my back. Finally recovering, I did it to Ralph's satisfaction.

"I'm giving you a hard time because I like you," Ralph joked. It was the kind of affection I could gladly have done without. By the time my lessons were ended, I had formed a love of scuba diving and a loathing for Ralph.

After getting my NAUI Certification (National Association of Underwater Instructors), my mother, knowing how much I had been through, offered to help out with the children and send me on my first vacation. I would be going to join a scuba diving tour to Cozumel, Mexico. When I mentioned this to Ralph, he said, "Why don't I come along?"

To my complete surprise I said, "Great," and just like that, we became a couple.

Cozumel, an island in the Mexican Caribbean, is a world of shimmering white sand, coconut palms, and coral reefs. There, the warmest, clearest waters in the world have a visibility many times exceeding 200 feet. At thirty-two miles long, it's Mexico's largest island. The reefs around Cozumel, particularly the reef of Palancar, are internationally famous—a scuba diver's paradise.

We were to spend five days in Cozumel and three days at a new resort called Akumal, on the Yucatan peninsula, where some wrecks of Spanish galleons could still be found.

Even though we were with a tour group, Ralph and I snatched as much time as possible by ourselves. We discovered each other among primitive ruins and vast expanses of turquoise blue ocean. I was starved for the affection I'd never had, and we fell in love against breathtaking drops—the top of Mayan pyramids at Chichen-Itza, caves at Tulum, empty beaches, and the insides of stone temples. Even dive-bombing bats swooping down on us in a jungle pool in Merida couldn't cool the fires that this Latin paradise ignited.

Other times, we enjoyed the company of the diving group we'd traveled with from Los Angeles. Everyone tried to outdo each other by relating their most exciting scuba experiences. The night before we were slated to dive on the *Matancero*, a Spanish galleon that had gone down in 1741, the topic of conversation turned to all the other shipwrecks that divers in the group had been part of, and what was still out there to be conquered.

Eventually, as the more experienced talked of deeper and deeper wrecks, the *Lusitania*, the *Britannic* and its sister ship the *Titanic* came up for heated discussion. All three of these famous ships had not been discovered, and everyone in our party expressed the desire to be a part of finding them, even though all of them were too deep for any scuba diver to reach.

"Someday they'll all be found," said Ralph. "And when they are, I'll be there."

To me, Ralph sounded as though he was bragging, but even though his words were outrageous, I secretly hoped I'd be part of it too.

Joined by love, admiration, and a common obsession, Ralph and I continued our Cozumel adventure by making night dives off Palancar reef and deep water dives to retrieve black coral at 170 feet. These carried a haunting danger: beyond 130 feet, divers begin to get raptures of the deep, also known as nitrogen narcosis, which are hallucinations that fuel their desire to go further and further down, beyond the point of survival.

Each day brought a new kind of thrill. Being dropped into the water where the currents run at ten to twenty knots was like the most dangerous roller coaster. The dive boat would have the divers jump in at the point where the current began to pick up, and once you dropped to a level of approximately thirty feet, you were carried with an amazing speed, having absolutely no control. By totally relaxing, you are somersaulted by the water on a wildly fast ride—it's almost like aquatic skydiving. Free falling, but beneath the sea rather than the sky.

The staghorn coral dive brought its own rewards—
and challenges. Staghorn coral resembles a giant massive
crown of thorns underwater. Immediately upon jumping
into the water, as I drifted sixty feet downward, Ralph—
who had gone in before me—saw that I was about to land.
My right leg was extended and was seconds from settling on
what appeared to be a rock.

As I descended, Ralph grabbed me and jerked my
arm. He yanked me sideways and pulled me to the surface.
I was bewildered, shocked, and angry.

"Don't grab me like that!"

"All right. Next time I'll let you get killed."

"I was fine."

"Ever hear of a stonefish?"

"What about it?"

"It's the most poisonous fish in the ocean. It's camou-
flaged with a crusty exterior and resembles a grayish brown
rock."

He went on to explain that a stonefish has spines on
top of it that contain lethal poison. The venom is present
along the dorsal spines, and when contacted, the spine will
enter the skin and inject the poison. There are two other
fish that do the same thing—the scorpion fish and the lion
fish, all from the same family. Contact causes severe pain,
swelling and redness, muscle weakness, cramps, and
finally heart and lung failure.

"And you were about to land on one."

Ralph had a flair for the dramatic, a tendency to
exaggerate for the sake of a good story, so I shrugged.

"You don't believe it? Come back down with me."

I followed him, very carefully this time, head first,
and he showed me the stonefish at close range. It was amazing how effective its rock-like camouflage was, but as I

stared very carefully, I could see the tiny, beady eyes moving.

When we returned to the boat, he kissed me and said, "Okay. You owe me your life."

He said it kiddingly, but I had a feeling he meant every word.

The treasure dive, which we eagerly awaited as the highlight of the trip, showed that predators are equally plentiful above the water line.

There were two different boats in our group with separate captains. Someone—we never learned who—had bribed Ramon, the captain of our boat, to take us to the exact spot where a legendary ship, the *Matancero* (nicknamed for its Point Matanceros location) had gone down filled with treasure. It was a 270-ton merchant ship, originally named *Nuestra Senora de los Milagros* (Our Lady of the Miracles) and wrecked in 1741 en route to America.

Treasure hunter Robert Marx located the wreck off Point Matanceros, where he had seen a large anchor and six coral-encrusted cannons twenty feet down. He found green glass bottles embedded in the reef, along with pewter belt buckles and a handful of cut stones which he took to be diamonds. They turned out to be paste, but Marx and his friend, journalist Clay Blair, organized an expedition in the winter of 1957-58. Blair nearly drowned when his air hose kinked, and Marx had a dramatic free escape when his air hose unscrewed itself because the surge had made him turn so many somersaults.

Eventually twelve thousand objects were recovered from the wreck, including hundreds of devotional medals, metal buttons, beads in metal settings, knife handles, and crucifixes.

In theory, no captain was supposed to reveal the whereabouts of the *Matancero* to the diving parties that hired him, even if he knew where it was, but someone had made it worth Ramon's while.

He was small but wiry, with a deep tan and long jet black hair that kept tumbling over his eyebrows. He wore a gold cross around his neck that looked as if it weighed more than he did. He deposited us right on the spot where the *Matancero* lay.

We soon found out why there were still remaining artifacts on this wreck that had been discovered by Marx. The water was shallow from five feet to thirty feet deep farther out. But many previous divers claimed it was the hardest site they had ever worked. There was a fierce surge that kept on pulling us out and returning us back in, and the cement-hard coral had swallowed up most of the artifacts. Our group used chisels and hammers to chop out big chunks of coral, in which dozens of artifacts were embedded.

Complete bedlam ensued from the beginning. Only three tanks were allotted to each person for the day's dives. As some divers returned to the boat, they found that others had grabbed their air cylinders, leaving them without the air bottles to make the dives they had planned on. Threats and fistfights exploded over the stolen tanks, with Ramon struggling to keep divers from injuring or killing each other.

Carl, a young blond German who spoke excellent English, pulled out his diving knife and held it to Ramon's throat. He pointed to a thirty-year-old American schoolteacher, Bill, and said, "You let him steal my tank and you didn't stop him. What the hell kind of captain are you?"

Ralph, who was skilled in defusing tense situations, stepped between Carl and Bill.

"Put the knife away," he said in a commanding but calm tone.

"This isn't your business," said Carl. "You want a knife in the heart, keep talking."

"Give it to me," Ralph insisted.

Ralph was fearless. Carl stood silent for an instant, then lashed out, almost stabbing Ralph's neck. Ralph was caught off guard; he was usually able to intimidate people with his height and tough attitude. I moved forward.

"Stay back," Ralph warned. Carl's hand whipped out again in another slashing motion, but this time Ralph caught hold of his arm and twisted it. Carl fought to break free, but Ralph had the strength of three men—in addition to being a former defense instructor—and he kept his hold until Carl screamed in pain and dropped the knife. Ramon strutted forward, acting as if he had personally disarmed Carl. He tied Carl's arms with rope, bound them at the wrists and took Carl to the pilothouse where he could keep an eye on him.

When treasure was brought up, people in our party continued to fight and threaten each other. There were cries of "This is mine, you took it—you're a goddamned thief," and I was sure that if I found something, I'd have to defend it within an inch of my life.

While underwater, I chipped away at the coral with a rock hammer, a hammer designed by archaeologists to dig beneath coral that encrusts objects after years in the ocean. It was a miracle, in view of the hostile, overcrowded thrusting and pushing of the other divers, that I discovered any of the sea treasure, but I seemed to have good instincts for undiscovered places and found two crosses and some other encrusted pieces of jewelry: women's earrings, beads, hat pins, ship's parts, and two crucifixes, one of which I gave to Ralph.

Content, feeling fortunate that on my first diving adventure I met with success, I rose to the surface and volunteered my air tank to some of the others still desperate to find gold, jewels, or any memento to take home. Cozumel was more than the high spot of my life up to that point. It taught me the meaning of treasure fever and the competitive lengths people would go to secure valuable artifacts for themselves.

However, when I returned, I realized I still had a lot to learn about scuba diving. My failure to recognize the stonefish made it clear that I needed to be thoroughly familiar with every form of marine life, whether it be sea snakes in Fiji or white sharks off Catalina, the island off the coast of southern California where many of my dives were made. My studies reinforced the fact that rule-breaking can be fatal; more than 50 percent of fatalities from scuba diving occur in less than forty feet of water, a depth considered extremely safe because you don't have to worry about decompression tables.

My wonderful children and my tedious but necessary job occupied most of my time, but at night when it was quiet I studied marine biology, diving diseases, all medical aspects of diving, decompression sickness, dive tables, and how to save a life at sea. On weekends, I brought Brent, Kevin, and Derek into my studies and taught them scuba diving in my mother's pool. They loved it. Once in the water, I couldn't get them out, just as my mother hadn't been able to tear me away from swimming when I was a child.

Diving emphasized the urgent need to be physically

fit, and so I stepped up my running, slowly extending my initial running schedule from two miles a day to five. Running was a release for me, providing joy and relief from stress. It gave me the strength to raise my three sons and maintain a career in which I was gaining some success if not fulfillment.

Running also gave me the physical strength to cope with Ralph's next step in our program—skydiving.

Skydiving was the final feature of Ralph's conquer-your-fear program. Before I met him, he had been a photographer for "ABC Wide World of Sports." I was impressed when he told me he was the first to use a small camera attached to his helmet in order to film people in the air as they jumped out of planes. He used this to film relative work—the joining up of skydivers in the air in circles—and to film competitions. At one time, Ralph had also filmed the United States Parachute Team.

Skydiving was second nature to Ralph. Years before, he had run his own skydiving school, and he wanted me to share his excitement for the sport.

My first jump was scheduled to take place in a tiny town not far from Bakersfield, California, called Taft. Taft is a farming community so far out in the middle of nowhere that it reminded me of the small dusty town in *The Last Picture Show*.

I had thought I was prepared, but upon arrival my heart leapt into my throat. I felt fear grip me, making my stomach churn and my palms sweat. No matter how I tried, I couldn't go through with it. I knew Ralph was disappointed and saw me as a "chicken." I was ashamed too, and I vowed to do better the next time.

My first actual jump was on static line, a regulation of the jump school in which your jumpmaster watches you to make sure you pull your dummy ripcord in the proper manner. After six more of these carefully regulated maneuvers, I was allowed to make my first free fall.

That morning, I woke up excited and anxious. I felt prepared, despite the butterflies in my stomach. Driving to the airfield, I had a moment when I wished I could postpone it. But I was also ready to embrace the experience.

Inside the plane, after checking my equipment, my terror escalated.

I geared up mentally for the moment when I would be jumping 2,500 feet off the ground. My palms were wet and my heart was pounding as the plane leveled off.

I felt the muscles of my forearms tighten over the wing, and my feet were precariously situated on the strut. Then I was outside of the plane, the wind rushing past me at 200 miles an hour. My hands pushed away from the wing and stretched outward in a flying position. My legs were at their full extension, spread-eagled, and, as I fell away, I could see the plane above me. I looked toward the ground. I was plunging down, wind whipping my uniform and my face. It was thrilling beyond belief. I was flying. The sensation was one of total freedom and ecstasy.

I pulled my ripcord. My parachute opened and I looked up, elated, to see a colorful, circular piece of red and black nylon flying above me. Then I heard my jumpmaster's instructions, "Pull on the right, pull on the right." He was trying to turn me so I would land straight into the wind and closer to the drop zone. Suddenly my dive ended and I was standing upright on the ground, an unusual feat for a beginner—reveling in Ralph's embrace, the hugs and kisses of my children, and a chorus of congratulations. A bottle of Korbel brut was opened and poured on my head—a good-old-boy testament to my success.

Four months and twenty-one jumps later, I wasn't so fortunate.

I was wearing Ralph's rig when I jumped from the Cessna at 4,500 feet. I was free-falling in excess of 170 feet per second. I had made a back loop and was tracking, which speeds up your descent enormously. Both arms are held close to your body, so that aerodynamically there's less wind resistance.

Then I looked at my altimeter—which read 2,300 feet—and decided to pull. My ripcord was stuck.

I jerked again and again. Nothing happened. These jerking motions threw me into a tailspin.

My rational mind was gone, which was why I didn't think to pull my reserve chute as I had been taught. Instead, I kept on trying to open the main chute—sheer insanity. All of this happened within five seconds, but it felt like forever.

I blacked out while plummeting 200 miles an hour.

With the last hard jerk of my ripcord, I thought, *This is it, I'm going to die*. And then blackness enfolded me. I was suddenly yanked out of unconsciousness when the chute opened, a jerk so brutally hard that it felt like my arms were being pulled out of their sockets. This violent motion sent unbearable shooting pains through my neck.

But I was awake and alive. I truly felt that some angel must have been looking over my shoulder. I couldn't imagine why I survived. The chute had opened 850 feet shy of the ground, which left me only four to five seconds before I crashed into the earth.

My jumpmaster, Art Armstrong, owner of the Taft Parachuting Drop Zone, was in a rage about the low opening, and ran over to chastise me for breaking the rules.

"What in the hell did you think you were doing?" he screamed.

Embarrassed as I was, I understood his anger. He had lost a son the year before, a son who had been reckless, playing chicken with a friend to see who could wait the longest to open. In this macho and potentially fatal game, divers in free fall drop, watching each other and waiting to see who's going to pull the ripcord first.

"No one's going to die in my school," he shouted as I fought to interrupt and explain the circumstances. I was crying because I couldn't believe I had been spared, and I was frustrated that I couldn't make him understand. I knew all his pent-up grief and rage were being showered on me, things he wished he could have said to his son to save the boy's life.

When he finally saw how badly the chute pin was bent and grasped what had happened, he mumbled an apology and walked off.

"I don't understand," I said to Ralph, after I had a chance to calm down. "How was my chute able to open with such a bent pin?"

"You must have pulled it just before you passed out. The automatic opener wasn't triggered."

"Well, that's it. I'm sticking to scuba diving from now on."

"No, you're not. You're going back up right now. If you don't, you'll never try again."

"Forget it," I told him.

"No marine would give up."

"When was I ever a marine?"

Ralph looked at me squarely. "And you wouldn't want me to think you were a coward."

He hit a nerve. It was true; I *didn't* want him to think I was afraid. The unspoken rule of our relationship was: Whatever I do, you have to do. Whatever chances I take, *you* have to take.

Half an hour later, we were up in the sky again, free falling from 7,500 feet and swooping together in a relative work move called a kiss pass—where you join up and kiss in mid-air. Then I backed off and made two somersaults. He thought I was daring, but in truth, I was grateful to be alive.

The last phase of my initiation into the world of close calls took place when Ralph suggested I join the Los Angeles Sheriff's Department. He had volunteered a year before.

This time I said no. I disliked guns, primarily because Kurt collected them and defined his power by flashing them around. I also distrusted the police. They represented authority, and I wanted nothing to do with controlling, overly macho authority figures. I was convinced that most of them looked down on women and felt them to be inferior officer material.

But I still had nightmares about my ex-husband hurting me or the children. Learning to deal with thieves, drug pushers, and gang members would reinforce my confidence that I could face Kurt in any situation and not feel fear. I learned karate. My confidence further increased. How could he hurt me? He didn't know karate, and I did. I laughed at the thought of striking a karate pose and causing him to back off. But the thought of him still made me shudder.

Despite my resolve, one aspect of the job that plunged me into despair was my exposure to gang members, some as young as eleven or twelve years old. Like most people, I had been force-fed the idea that love and tenderness could instantly cure the hardest criminal. It wasn't true. These kids had no conscience.

The greatest tragedy, I found, was that many of them had been forced into joining a gang at an early age, threatened with daily beatings unless they complied. After a while, murder became routine to them. For their gang they'd kill automatically and think nothing of the lives they had taken. None of them admitted to any fear of dying. None, in fact, counted on reaching adulthood, and they didn't care.

It scared me, as a parent of three sons, to see how peer pressure had ruined the lives of these boys and girls. With a scared-straight scenario in my mind, I decided to introduce Derek, Brent, and Kevin to one former gang member who had broken free of his group and kicked drugs. The story he told them of stabbing someone to death at the age of twelve made a deep and lasting impression. I trusted my sons to know right from wrong, but I also felt it was vital to underscore the harsh realities of life.

As veils of sentimentality dropped from my eyes, I found that another false perception disappeared. Police officers were not macho phonies, and they weren't crude control freaks. They were, instead—barring a few bad apples—a courageous, dedicated group of people who laid their lives on the line daily. They took risks that critical outsiders would never take. Often, they were all that stood between innocent men, women, and children and the monstrously evil forces operating in the street. As I watched them fight for public safety—and some close friends die in the process—my admiration grew.

Ralph and I gave as much of our time as we could to police work, making training films for the other officers. Constantly confronting all these life and death situations emphasized the need to live life as though every day was the last. During these years, though I worked hard during the week in our spare time, Ralph and I pursued every imaginable adventure: parasailing, ballooning, river rafting, hang gliding, skiing.

That was also the year we made an unexpected and enchanting trip to Drumnadrochit, Scotland. Ralph and I went there as working divers for Emory Kristof, Ralph's close friend and a famous staff photographer for *National Geographic*. Emory was on assignment for *Geographic* to find and film the Loch Ness monster.

It was in Scotland that we spoke to a man who shared our fascination with the *Titanic*. This world-renowned scientist had more on his mind than simply analyzing the reasons for her fate or reviewing her history.

The man's name was Bob Ballard.

Chapter 4

Search for the
Loch Ness Monster

Like many adventurers and explorers, Bob Ballard is ruled by overwhelming desires. He may appear to be an easygoing, amiable person, but his inner voice is constantly roaring, fueled by visions of conquering what others say is impossible.

His vision in 1976 was to locate and photograph the *Titanic*.

As Bob explained, "Submarines fascinate me. I was gripped by the challenge of actually exploring the hidden ocean depths. It seemed possible that humans would one day live and work beneath the sea, and I wanted to be in the vanguard of the wave of exploration that would make the dream reality."

His background had prepared him. Son of a test flight engineer, graduate student of oceanography at the University of Hawaii in Honolulu, then a dolphin trainer at Sea Life Park in Hawaii, Bob eventually landed, as he put it "one of the best jobs any aspiring ocean scientist could imagine. North American Aviation Ocean Systems Group offered me a full-time position."

This position required him to work in the group's research program, developing potential missions for *Beaver Mark IV*, their first manned deep submersible.

"My first assignment was helping to build a permanent undersea work facility, to be serviced by the *Beaver*. The concept was to actually build an underwater oil exploration and production base that was completely independent of the surface, an inner-space station."

He was as gripped as I by the challenge of exploring hidden ocean depths. When we met, he was already recognized as an accomplished oceanographer, a man who "did for oceanography what Carl Sagan did for astronomy." He had come to Scotland to spend some time with his friend, Emory Kristof, the brains behind the Loch Ness expedition.

Emory, a *National Geographic* staff photographer, had burning coal-black eyes, a thick dark beard, and crackling, inexhaustible energy. Ideas poured out of him like cascading water from a waterfall. After joining the staff of *Geographic*, Emory became known as the foremost expert on photographic equipment used in undersea scientific exploration. It was his insatiable interest in science and technology that drew him to cutting edge innovations in photography and film, encompassing such developments as the use of 3D cameras and high definition technology. He had received numerous awards from the White House News Photographers Association, and had won the Picture of the Year competition.

Emory's newest idea was to do an article on all the research and theories about the Loch Ness monster for *National Geographic*.

He had read Roy Mackal's book, *The Monsters of Loch Ness,* with fascination. Mackal had done research and taught science for twenty years in the biological science division of the University of Chicago. Emory believed, as Mackal did, that Nessie was a plesiosaur, trapped in Loch Ness when the lower and upper half of Scotland moved together in prehistoric times. He believed there was more than one Nessie. In order for the monster to have survived, there would have to have been many Nessies procreating through millions of years.

Emory's goal was to find, once and for all, if Nessie existed. He planned to use a specially rigged underwater still camera that had motion sensors and huge flashes attached. With any luck, if the monster passed in front or anywhere near it, the flashes and camera would trigger, capturing a photograph of the first living dinosaur.

Ralph and Emory were old friends. Emory had hired Ralph and some Scottish divers to dive down every day to change the film and offer assistance on the underwater reconnaissance of Loch Ness. When Ralph asked Emory if I could be part of the crew, Emory agreed.

The loch had its own distinctively different character. The hillsides are the edges of a volcanic and glaciated slit in the rock that extend above the water in cliffs 1,000 feet high and to the bottom of the gorge 850 feet below the water's surface.

Loch Ness was once filled with salt water, back when it was part of the sea. Rivers dumped miles and miles of silt into the loch in the years following the ice age, blocking the seaward ends and turning it into a self-contained lake. The original sea water slowly evolved into fresh water, but the change occurred so gradually that marine creatures which had been trapped by the silt dam had a great many generations to acclimate themselves.

Nessie, if she existed, was a likely descendant of one of these creatures, evolving from an oceangoing inhabitant to a more dormant landlocked fresh water denizen of the lake. Studying a map of Scotland, it's clear where the two areas of land had been completely separate at one time and through plate tectonic movements, eventually came together.

The sky was overcast, the loch a flat, calm black mirror when we began our dives. We were immediately plunged into total darkness. Normally, light extends through the water for a good fifty feet before it starts becoming dim. Here, it was pitch black three feet below the surface. Day or night, the intense blackness is always the same, because sediment from the peat moss, which grows on the hills around the Loch, runs off the sides of the mountains and leaves thick residues in the water, making it totally dark from the bottom depths of 800 feet all the way up to the surface.

In all my dives around the world I'd never seen such conditions. We were forced to dive without sight, with only the powerful rays of our diving lights to guide us. The most brilliant sun could never penetrate the sediment. How terrifying, I thought, if we really did encounter a sea monster in this pitch-black world.

Other scientists over the years had attempted to photograph the monster with camera and sound equipment less sophisticated than ours. In one picture, they actually captured a shot of what some people claimed was a plesiosaur's fin. This gave validity to the theory that Nessie was still alive.

The earliest sighting was of a "fearsome beastie" in Loch Ness, and it was found in *The Latin Life of the Great St. Columba,* written in the year 565 AD. The manuscript was saved in the library of Schaffhausen, Switzerland. According to St. Columba, the ferocious monster killed one of the local inhabitants of the loch area. It seemed to him that another man might be threatened in addition, and St. Columba, the Abbot of Iona, caused the "fearsome beastie" to stop his bloodthirsty ways by commanding it with these words: "Go thou no further nor touch the man; go back at once."

The account goes on to say that the beast, upon hearing the words, was terrified and fled away more quickly than if it had been dragged off by ropes, although it had come within ten feet of Lugne, the saint's companion, who had been swimming in the loch.

Since that sixth century sighting, there have been over 250 others, and Loch Ness has been the site of strange observations for over 1,400 years.

Some of the candidates for a possible Nessie included an elephant seal, a Steller's sea cow, eels, and last of all, a plesiosaur, the most popular theory. Features of the plesiosaur fit the sightings: it fed on fish, had a long neck and flippers front and back, a hump along its back which was approximately twenty feet in length, and it could give birth to its young live in the water, as well as swim at a fast speed. Though considered to be extinct for sixty-five million years, most scientists are aware that the coelacanth, a primitive fish also believed to be extinct for seventy million years, was found alive in 1957 off the coast of Africa.

Based on all observations made, our best estimate was that the animal was around twenty to twenty-five feet. Eels have been found to be eight to ten feet, and it seemed possible, because of its serpentine body shape and the ability of an eel to raise its head out of the water, that Nessie could have been a gigantic eel, although the plesiosaur theory was equally plausible.

Whatever form it took, we assumed that Nessie would respond to food, and food meant more than a few scraps of fish. I was sent to an Inverness slaughterhouse to collect the guts of just-slaughtered cattle and take these guts back to the loch.

Just before I climbed into the company truck and drove off, I saw Emory and Ralph smiling. Their smiles had a devilish quality—a look that said, *You won't be able to handle this.* Apparently, my ability to come through would be equivalent to a rite of passage into the "boys' club."

When I arrived at the slaughterhouse, an enormous man with broad shoulders and meaty hands asked me what I wanted. After I told him, he ordered me to wait outside.

"I'd rather come in." I gritted my teeth.

"They shoulda sent a man. Why, for Christ's sake, are they sending a wee lassie like you?"

"It's okay," I lied. "I grew up on a farm."

He laughed, a guttural, contemptuous sound.

"Well then, you asked for it."

I followed him in. As I entered, my nose was attacked by an overwhelming stench. What I saw as my stomach flip-flopped was even more horrifying.

The floors were awash with blood. Huge men the size of linebackers—men of 250 to 300 pounds and more—filled the area. They all wore rubber aprons that came down below their knees and high rubber boots. A few stood on the ramp, and, as the cattle came through the ramp, they were clubbed over the head, then dragged and hung up on hooks after they were killed. Finally they were skinned.

I watched another man with a huge knife, who cut open the bellies. All the entrails were pulled out, then dumped. It was my job to scoop up the entrails into the oversized buckets I had brought for the task, and carry them back to the truck.

I felt nauseous. I'd never seen so much blood in my life, and there were pitiful moans from dying animals if they weren't finished off properly. I shuddered staring at the clatter of metal hooks that they hung the animals from, to let the blood drop out of them. Hanging made it easier for the workers to strip the skin off.

The men were glaring at me, and I could hear their thoughts: *Is she going to be sick? Will she throw up or scream or run out?*

I avoided looking back at them and clenched my fists. Digging my nails into my skin, I tried to keep my face expressionless, acting as if I'd done this a thousand times before. When I arrived back at the loch, I worked hard not to show any emotion.

No one knew if Nessie was herbivorous or carnivorous, but Emory said, "What do we have to lose? If it's a meat eater and we spread out the guts all over the lake, we might entice this mother to the surface. And look, we've got a full moon. It'll make for a great photograph."

That night, with the moon blazing, we went out on a motorboat, Ralph, Emory and I, with one of our Scottish divers. By the time we were finished, the lake was flooded with food for Nessie to feast on. We waited long hours in the area of Urquhart, the deepest spot along the lake and the spot where most sightings had occurred. Urquhart was also the area where we placed our underwater cameras.

By three in the morning, frozen to the bone, we realized Nessie probably preferred sturgeons' caviar or salmon to the cattle guts we'd supplied for her, but we refused to give up. The next day we went back to try to lure her again.

As the days went on, we dove from one end of the loch to the other, changing our film every other morning and filling time in between with pictures and interviews of all the living people along the loch who had sighted Nessie. Their stories were so convincing that we believed, against all rational thinking, that the monster would finally show itself.

These people were not the type who were seeking fortune and fame. Many of them didn't even want to talk to us, because their stories had been ridiculed by skeptics. Once they did trust us, they offered so many details that the monster became dramatically alive in my mind.

We also attended a colorful celebration of the Highland games on July 4, which Emory filmed in vivid detail—the throwing of the caber, a huge piece of wood the size of a telephone pole, the discus, and the many kilts. They ate *haggis,* a Scottish dish made from sheep's hearts, lungs, and liver. After my experience with the slaughter-house, I turned this delicacy down.

I loved living in Drumnadrochit. Emory and his warm attractive wife, Diana, had rented a charming old stone house with a thatched roof, a Scottish country cottage in the hills with its own black and white sheep dog. I arose early every morning and played with him while setting a fire in the ancient wood-burning stove to heat the house, then ran six miles around the lake. There were no real conveniences but it didn't matter, any more than it would have if my father had taken me to his primitive log cabin years before.

I also talked to Ballard at every opportunity. We would often have drinks in the hotel bar—the only one in town. It had been built in the 1800s, and its hundred-year-old interior was dark and densely smoky, because the Scots had cigarettes dangling from their lips like permanent fixtures. There were little wooden tables and Scotch of every variety, as well as whiskey, gin and lager, the Scottish word for beer, which contains a smaller alcoholic content and has a less bitter taste.

Bob was energetic, positive, overflowing with enthusiasm, and wonderful company. A magnetic figure in turtleneck and cap, lanky and tall, hyperkinetic, he created his own charismatic atmosphere. It didn't matter that the bar was rowdy, bursting with noise, packed with drunks— I heard only what Bob said. Over fish and chips, he talked about his plans to find the *Titanic*.

"Think of it," he exulted. "To bring up the safe from the *Titanic*—to find the jewel-encrusted volume of the *Rubaiyat of Omar Khayam*."

He spun wonderful tales about all the great myths, such as the mummy from the British museum that people said was on board. He told in great detail about the different technological aspects of finding the ship; what ships might be leased to do the job, what countries might be interested in an expedition. He tried to find out from Emory if *Geographic* would be excited about getting involved, as well as the camera systems that would be required to film at that depth.

"If there's an expedition, let me come along," I said, trying to sound light.

Bob smiled, treating my comment as a joke.

"I'm serious," I said.

"It's a long way down," Bob answered.

"Hell, she's not afraid," Ralph said. "If she can go to a slaughterhouse every day and pick up buckets of bloody innards, she can do anything."

"I guess she bloody well can, then. A toast to Jennifer," Emory cheered, and they raised liter-sized glasses of ale and clinked them together.

The Loch Ness Monster, if it exists, was distressingly consistent about ignoring our cameras and our bizarre menu. We had no luck locating her. All we found were giant-sized sturgeon, almost six feet in length, over-sized salmon, and ordinary eels in great quantity.

But if the Loch Ness Monster wasn't deep beneath the water, I knew the *Titanic* would be. Bob Ballard had once again stirred up my old fascination. Once again, *Titanic* fever burned.

Those stricken with *Titanic* fever make rock groupies and celebrity worshippers seem detached and unemotional. Worshippers pore over Captain E.J. Smith's decision in 1912 to move full-speed ahead in ice-cluttered waters as though it had happened a week ago. Analyzing why the *Californian,* so close by, failed to rescue the *Titanic* is a topic as contemporary as the president's latest statement about the economy. How did a ship as high as an eleven-story building, nearly 900 feet long, weighing over 46,000 gross tons and equipped with everything from palm veran-das to Turkish baths, set out to sea with so few lifeboats? Was White Star owner Bruce J. Ismay simply careless, or an irresponsible, heartless monster?

If you have *Titanic* fever, your link with the ship becomes intensely personal. You feel as though you know her, as though she was, and still is, human. You have inner conversations with her. For the rest of your life, you never cast her aside. You feel, protectively, that if you had been there, you could have done *something* to alter her fate.

After we left Loch Ness and returned to California, I made up my mind to keep in touch with Bob Ballard and follow his progress in mounting a *Titanic* expedition. In the meantime, I was destined to spend the next several years on water. In fact, my feet rarely touched solid ground.

It started when Emory called to let me know he

had recommended Ralph and me for a job at the National Geographic Society. A key producer of the society's television specials, Nick Noxon, was putting together one of the company's documentaries, *The Great Whales,* and Nick was looking for information about whales and people who knew about filming them.

Emory arranged a meeting for Ralph and me to meet Nick. Ralph hoped to be hired as cinematographer, and the lunch seemed to go extremely well. I decided instantly that this was a man I could deeply admire and respect. A superb producer, writer and director, Nick had worked with David Wolper and had written and produced "Biography," "Men in Crisis," and "Hollywood and the Stars" series, as well as three of the first National Geographic specials aired on CBS. He was a gentleman— well mannered, sensitive, exceptionally intelligent—and he clearly had strong creative visions and complete mastery over all he did. His awards included two Peabodys, two Emmys and several other Emmy nominations.

The problem was, his unassuming, low-key nature clashed with Ralph's more flamboyant personality. Ralph spoke openly, and with pride, about all his accomplishments; Nick was brought up in a background where parents trained children to let their work speak for itself. When I was taken on as associate producer for the show, I did everything I could to point out Ralph's extensive background, but Nick was adamant. He already had his own cinematographer, Erik Daarstad, and the subject was closed.

Time after time, I tried to reopen it. I loved Ralph and felt immeasurably grateful to him for literally giving me back my life. However, sometimes I chafed under his Svengali-like guidance. Sometimes I was a rebellious Eliza Doolittle, fighting to solidify my own identity. Even so, he was still a hero to me, a mentor, and the one man who had lifted me from a pit of despair and showed me that dreams were possible.

We remained friends but we were growing apart. His work took him all over the world, and I was anxious to concentrate on my work and build a career that could give me stronger financial security to support and educate my three boys. My mother had given me much help taking care of them, but I didn't want to miss these years while they were growing up. On my vacations from work we went on skiing or diving trips as a family. My three sons had inherited my eagerness to experiment and try new things. They were ready to try new foods, listen to all kinds of music, tackle any sport. They were my best friends and my sole personal focus. I shared my thoughts and feelings with them more freely than with any of my contemporaries.

The Great Whales was a tremendous success. It garnered an Emmy for best documentary special. The show was a labor of love for all concerned - for Nick, for our superb editor Barry Nye, our gifted and dedicated head of post production Linda Reavely, and for me.

I relished every minute of working for *Geographic*. The show took me to Boston, Hawaii, Mexico, San Diego, Vancouver, and British Colombia. I thought of Grace, the Rumanian psychic, and how her predictions for world travel were coming true. During school breaks, I made sure my sons joined me on location.

My traveling days had begun.

Chapter 5

Swimming with Sharks

Sharks have struck terror in the hearts of untold millions throughout the centuries. My fear persisted, even though I knew they rarely attacked humans. Nevertheless, when an opportunity came along to work again with Nick on a show about the predators, I jumped at the chance. I wanted to meet these creatures face to face and examine the combination of myth and superstition surrounding them.

We were filming off the coast of southern California, and we wanted to get a scene of world-renowned diver Valerie Taylor being attacked by sharks. Ron Taylor, her husband, had designed a shark suit to protect her, and everyone on the film crew prayed devoutly that the suit would work.

Our plan was to do the sequence in slow motion, and I had hired Howard Hall. One of the industry's most brilliant underwater cinematographers, Howard was also a marvelous person to work with—creative, enthusiastic, adventurous.

We were also fortunate to have Dr. John E. McCosker work on "The Sharks." As Director of the California Museum of Sciences, Steinhart Aquarium, he was an authority on the behavior of great whites, as well as other species. His on-camera explanations of their feeding and migration habits made the viewer understand how the jaws of the shark work when feeding, how deep and far the great white travels for its food and which senses are most important in their feeding patterns.

We had chosen an area where sharks were in particularly heavy concentration, and once again it was necessary to obtain food lure. I went to a fish factory in San Diego and purchased 500 pounds of mackerel. Our idea was to litter the water with bait, attract a swarm of sharks, and provoke a feeding frenzy. We would then film the sharks fighting over the food and demonstrate how Valerie's suit protected her from the hungry predators. Valerie was fully prepared, but the gloves she wore made her a little nervous. The gloves were separate from the rest of the suit and fastened at the wrists by velcro.

Two and a half hours of tossing out small pieces of mackerel failed to bring them within range of our cameras. The crew was growing impatient when fins finally came into view.

Blue sharks, between four and six feet long, began circling the stern of our boat. We lowered two diving cages, which were to be used by Howard Hall and our other cinematographers, Marty Snyderman and Valerie's husband and partner, Ron Taylor. The spine-chilling tests began. A seven-foot blue approached her; Valerie offered mackerel and then withdrew it, a teasing tactic, offering her arm instead to the shark to entice him to bite the suit. The shark tried to attack all the vulnerable portions of her body; it bit at her bottom and especially around the back of her neck.

It tore at her elbow, chewed down her arm and finally bit so hard at her hand that it pulled off the steel glove that was fastened with Velcro around Valerie's wrist and swallowed it. In doing so, her hand was left unprotected and the shark bit again, this time putting a big gash in her hand.

She came to the surface, at the stern of the boat, climbed onto the dive platform, and kneeling there, held her hand up, showing us the damage.

"He wouldn't let go," Valerie said. "This naked hand was in his mouth. I put my other hand in so he wouldn't crunch down, but he got the thumb."

She told us she screamed until her throat was sore, hoping someone would get the shark off of her, but in the confusion and flailing, no one realized what was happening.

We attempted to pull her up further and treat the injury, but she refused saying calmly to Nick and me, "Don't you want to film the damage with the topside camera?"

Burt Van Munster, topside cameraman, shot Valerie's reaction and her explanation of what had happened, as Nick directed the sequence. It was a prime example of bravery and professionalism.

The sequence was an electrifying one, a classic true-life adventure on camera. Later, Valerie admitted to being startled at first because "It's a natural reaction to seeing a neat set of razor sharp teeth grinding into one's body with mindless fury."

With Valerie's scene cinematically preserved by three underwater cameras, Howard offered to accompany me down to watch this huge congregation of sharks underwater through a diving cage.

Everything went smoothly at first. The cages were

approximately thirty to forty feet beneath the surface and a considerable distance from our boats. A very dangerous part of this procedure was swimming with Howard, surrounded by sharks, until I reached the cage and swam inside.

Howard then demonstrated how to hand-feed the sharks, holding the mackerel by the tail with my gloved hand, extending the fish bait outside the cage's steel bars. Sure enough it worked. The sharks came in, ravenously hungry, and grabbed the mackerel. I hand-fed them at least five or six mackerels. Successful previous dives in shark-infested waters had given me some sense of security, a sense that sharks—unless provoked—were not the monstrous creatures depicted in novels and movies.

But these sharks had been provoked into a frenzy by the presence of unlimited fish. They were overly excited and primed to riot.

Then, accidentally, the trapdoor of my cage opened, and a large blue swam in, obviously tempted by my goody bag filled with mackerel.

How ironic. The cage was supposed to protect me against predators, and yet I was trapped inside with an insanely angry blue shark.

The characteristics of the blue shark raced through my brain. *Attacks are unlikely unless excited. Not very reassuring*, I thought as I watched it move frantically about the cage. *Feeds on squid but will also decimate a floating whale or porpoise.* I knew of eight unprovoked attacks on people by blues, and three unprovoked attacks on boats. Statistically, that was small, but still threatening.

I crouched against the bottom corner of the cage, struggling to roll myself into a tiny, invisible ball. But the scuba tank was huge and took up an enormous amount of room.

In an effort to calm myself, I began counting backwards. It didn't work; my heart continued to hammer against my chest, and I was sucking huge amounts of air. In fact, I was breathing air so quickly from my tank that I was sure I'd run out before any chance of rescue.

Trembling in my wetsuit, I shifted position as the shark lurched toward me, trying to find an exit. Sharks are predators who roam freely, and this shark's rage grew when he realized he was caught in a claustrophobic elevator-sized enclosure with steel bars. I remembered a sparrow which had once flown into my home, flying around madly and butting itself into walls as it fought to escape the prison of my living room. This much larger, more lethal creature was doing the same thing, and I couldn't open a window, as I'd done with the bird, and return him to freedom.

Through a haze of fear I watched him. His sides were bright blue, his belly white. He had huge eyes and a long, pointed snout and was well over six feet long.

Just keep moving when sharks are around, Howard had told me earlier. *Smoothly. Don't thrash and don't lie still. If you lie still, a shark will perceive you as dead meat. If you thrash, it excites his sensory system and causes him to attack.*

I also knew that water conducted sound five times as fast as air and a loud noise could provoke the shark. I had to try not to bang my air cylinder against the metal cage bars.

The shark spun past me, moving closer. His vacant black eye was staring. An eye that was, as Peter Mattheson expressed, "as impenetrable and empty as the eye of God."

I was terrified that he would chew my limbs into fragments and swallow them with one gulp. As we took each other's measure, our eyes locked in a primordial stare. I braced myself for jaws that would take my head between rows of razor teeth and crush it.

Only a few minutes earlier, I'd been hand-feeding the shark with mackerel from my bait bag. Hoping to divert his attention, and his appetite, I tossed the bait bag through the cage bars. He continued to circle furiously. Rather than maintain my crouched position, I tried to edge around him and open the cage door. Each effort was thwarted by his crazed and continuous spinning.

Howard came to my rescue, just as I was about to use my camera to butt the shark on the snout. He opened the small, four-foot-wide, two-foot-high cage door flap, hoping the shark would immediately exit. He didn't, because he was confused and frustrated, and then Howard conceived a clever idea. He circled around to the back of the cage, inserting his bang stick through the openings between the bars. The shark instinctively twisted around and away from Howard and swam through the opened door. As it fled from confinement into the open seas, I had the presence of mind to grab my camera and film the creature.

I thought no more of sharks until a year later, when a fisherman called National Geographic Television. He had seen the show and had, it turned out, found the glove that had been ripped off Valerie's hand; he discovered it while gutting a shark that had been caught off the coast of California.

"The Sharks" became the highest rated special in PBS history.

Chapter 6

Titanic Survivor

On the *Queen Mary*, at a party being held in her honor, I met *Titanic* survivor Edwina Troutt MacKenzie. Charles Sachs, head of ONRS (Oceanic Navigational Research Society) was the man who had planned the event.

I had been introduced to Charles at the performance of an opera in UCLA's Royce Hall. The opera was about the *Titanic*, and the size of the audience was extraordinary—nearly 2,000 people, almost exactly the amount of people on board the *Titanic*. We were all assigned sections—first class (orchestra), second class (rear of the theatre) and third class (balcony).

The magnificent voices of the Berlin Opera Company brought the tragedy alive, but they were overshadowed by the evening's theatrics. Everyone attending was issued life vests and during the show's most electrifying moment—when the *Titanic* crashed into an iceberg—the crowd became an integral part of the drama. We were commandeered by the actors portraying the ship's crew on stage.

First class passengers were immediately allowed access to the lifeboats and actually climbed up on stage, as if moving to the Promenade Deck; from there they were escorted to the lifeboat area. Once they pantomimed getting into the boats, they were permitted to come back down from the stage and return to their seats. The people in third class and the men were left on the sinking ship when the opera concluded.

Although we all knew it was a theatrical exercise, the horror was felt by every observer. The production gave us a frightening sense of what it must have been like, since we were able to see—and imagine—the feelings of the victims by watching members of the audience go down with the ship.

Charles knew that I shared his involvement with the *Titanic*, and when he planned the elaborate party on the *Queen Mary* for Edwina he invited me.

This was only the latest in a string of parties Charles had orchestrated, to commemorate the anniversary of the *Titanic* sinking. Some of them were held at the Biltmore Hotel, an Italianate Beaux-Arts structure which had the elegant and palatial setting so typical of the *Titanic*. The *Queen Mary* was equally impressive, a vessel epitomizing art deco luxury, and the Queen's Grand Salon was a perfect setting for the 70th anniversary of the sinking.

When I told my son Kevin where I was going, he begged me to take him. He was already as deeply involved in *Titanic* history as I was. A natural mimic, Kevin did his own impersonations of Captain Smith and Bruce Ismay. One of his favorite games, with Brent and Derek, was to act out the iceberg collision and do the voices of all the people on board. My reaction was so enthusiastic that they took the show to school and created a sensation performing it in the Rolling Hills High School auditorium.

Charles had promised me I would be seated at a table with Edwina Troutt MacKenzie, *Titanic* survivor and guest of honor, ninety-six years old and as spry and alert as any woman half her age. I trusted him, although most of the others in attendance wanted that same coveted position. He was as good as his word. I was placed right next to her. Edwina was tiny and fragile like my grandmother, but she had a strength of personality that commanded the entire room.

The *Queen Mary* was an appropriate setting for Edwina's charm and charisma. At 1,019 feet in length and 81,237 tons, the ship was 136 feet longer than the *Titanic*, and resided in Long Beach. It functioned as a floating museum. In her day, she was the fastest transatlantic ocean liner and her reign lasted for fifteen years. At one time, the *Queen Mary* attained thirty-three knots, but her normal speed was 28.5 knots, four to five knots faster than the *Titanic*.

She served as a troop ship during World War II, returning to the commercial Atlantic run in 1947, and made her last voyage in 1967. Now the Queen had one of her worthier assignments, as a celebratory frame for Edwina's tribute.

Kevin, Edwina and I thoroughly enjoyed the main course, an exact replica of the meal First Class *Titanic* passengers had been served on their final night before the ship sank. The menu included spring pea soup, lobster thermidor with duchess potatoes, tournedos with morels on a bed of braised cabbage, rose water and mint sorbet, spring asparagus hollandaise, fresh fruit salad and orange surprise.

White bordeaux, white sherry, Madeira, dry Rhine, red bordeaux, sweet dessert wines such as muscatel and

Tokay and champagne accompanied these delicious courses.

Afterward, guests were treated to Edwina's show-stopping song and dance—a sailor's jig. The songs were *Pull For The Shore, Boys* (which they all sang in her lifeboat, Collapsible D, Number 16), and *It Was Sad When the Great Ship Went Down,* which became popular after the sinking. Elderly as she was, her renditions proved her to be a born performer. For her speech, and her irresistible music show-stopper, Edwina elicited a standing ovation. She then told her story, mesmerizing the onlookers.

"I'm from Bath, England," she began. "I was a twenty-seven year old schoolteacher when I sailed on the *Titanic* from Southhampton to New York. My final desti-nation was Massachusetts. Being on this ship was a great adventure for Edwina Celia Troutt."

Edwina occupied Cabin E 101, adjacent to the bandsmen's cabin. Her ticket number was 34218, for which she paid ten pounds, ten shillings, and her traveling companions and roommates were two close friends, Miss Nora Keane and Miss Suzie Webber.

She recalled her table on the *Titanic*—Table 8—and how congenial she found her dinner companions. Edwina felt a particularly keen rapport with Jacob Milling, a busi-nessman from Copenhagen.

"I felt I had known him for years," Edwina said. "It was the same for him. He even wrote to his wife about me."

The weather was magnificent on April 11, 1912, and Edwina sent a letter to her sister Emmeline's daughter Gladys: "I only wish you were enjoying yourself aboard the *Titanic*." She called it a floating palace and concluded, "you cannot realize what it is like."

This euphoria changed to alarm after the ship's fatal collision with the iceberg, a collision that had appeared mild at first.

"Those in third class were more afraid," Edwina recalled. "They were further down—they knew more quickly than we did how serious it was. I threw on a robe over my nightgown and went to investigate. A crewman said, it's *only an iceberg,* as if that was a minor disruption."

Back in her cabin, Edwina told Suzie and Nora about the crewman's optimistic estimate, but she felt the need to look into "further particulars." She remembered that passengers were joking, making light of the events. But she had talked to one of the men in third class, who told her that the water had already reached the bottom steps of the staircase near his room. She knew then that the ship was going to sink.

Returning to her stateroom, she replaced her dressing gown with a warm coat. One roommate was gone; the other wanted to waste precious time putting on her corset. Edwina flung it aside, irritated at such foolishness in a time of disaster.

"I didn't expect to be saved," she told us. "It would have been wicked to save single girls like myself when there were so many wives and husbands on board. I intended to stay aboard the ship to the very end."

Fate intervened, when a man holding a baby approached her.

"I don't want to be saved," he said. "But who will save this baby?"

The compassionate twenty-seven year old Edwina took the child in her arms. She felt she was meant to be rescued, so she could care for the helpless infant. Another woman ridiculed her for accepting such a responsibility under the calamitous circumstances.

Edwina showed her contempt for the woman's selfishness, called her a "nasty thing" and took the child with her onto Collapsible D. She remembered being assured by a crewman that the White Star Line would take care of them all. Along with Edwina, her friends Nora and Suzie survived.

One of her most vivid recollections, as the lifeboat pushed off, was the sight of two men attempting to jump into the boat after it had begun to be lowered. One landed in the bow and the other missed altogether, grabbing for it with his fingers as his legs dropped into the sea. As the drowning man's grip weakened, his friend made a powerful lunge and pulled him on board, saving his life.

Sitting with Edwina, after hearing her story, I monopolized her. I wanted to learn about any things she had left out.

She had a couple of glasses of sherry and asked Charles if he'd like one.

"No, thanks," said Charles. "I've already had two."

Ninety-six year old Edwina leaned over, eyes twinkling and said, "I hear *odd* is very lucky."

She told me about her background. Her home was in Hermosa Beach and she had outlived three husbands.

Our conversation was interrupted by the evening's culinary climax—an enormous cake, three feet long and made in the shape of the legendary ship, with funnels of marzipan. When it was brought into the dining room, all the lights were turned down, and as the cake made its arrival, we were treated to the sight of sparklers which had been lit to signify the rockets the *Titanic* sent up in its plea for rescue.

While sampling the delicious cake, Edwina said, "I'm fascinated by your interest in the sea." I talked to her about how since childhood I had been obsessed with the *Titanic*, about meeting Bob Ballard at Loch Ness and told her he was driven to find the *Titanic*. We discussed Jack Grimm's efforts—by then he had made two unsuccessful trips, and was to make one more.

"I've dreamed of being there when they find the *Titanic*," I went on.

"Oh, how I'd love to see the *Titanic* again," she said wistfully. "When it was proud and beautiful—before such terrible things happened. I wish you could have seen the Grand staircase. I still remember the men and women coming down in their beautiful evening clothes. What a sight they were."

Her memory made the staircase come alive for me too. From that touchingly melancholy note, her conversation suddenly veered to the stark horror of drowning people screaming in the water—chilling, deafening, piercing.

"I never forgot them," she recalled. "I have had nightmares all my life, waking up to those screams."

"Was it true," I asked her, "that Molly Brown really did row?"

"Absolutely true," she said. "She was in Lifeboat number 6 and I saw her rowing as they brought their lifeboat right up against ours. One of the passengers from our boat, the man who had fallen in the water, was transferred into theirs, and she took off her fur coat and put it around him. Yes, she was more concerned about that man and those in her boat than herself. I can still see it all."

Then Edwina gazed deeply into my eyes and said, "So long ago, but it feels like yesterday." She paused and then said softly but distinctly, "I don't know why, but I feel this—I *know* you'll see it. I feel it in my bones."

I told her about Grace, the psychic, and Edwina nodded, as though her wisdom had been confirmed by a powerful and reliable source. "I don't know if I'll be alive to see it. I pray I am. When you go—and I know you will—I want to see the pictures. If I'm alive, will you bring them to me?"

I promised I would.

Chapter 7

Peril on the *Majestic Explorer*

When I boarded the *Majestic Explorer* in September of 1982, I couldn't help comparing it to the *Titanic*.

On the surface, they are very different. The *Titanic* was 882 feet long, carrying over 2,200 passengers. The *Majestic Explorer* is slightly over 152 feet long and carries over 100. The *Titanic* was the phenomenon of its age, the largest moving mode of transportation created during the early twentieth century. The *Explorer* is a cruise ship, one of many, that traverses the Inside Passage, an area between Seattle and Alaska, including numerous islands and inlets along the Canadian coast. The *Titanic* made headlines around the world; the *Explorer* goes about its daily business without fuss or fanfare.

However, my mind kept forming peculiar parallels between the two ships. The women on board The *Explorer* were also wealthy, wearing expensive jewels and furs, and although the specific styles of their clothes were different, they reminded me of the first class *Titanic* passengers I had seen in photographs.

An elegant beaded gown in 1912 from Paris, with matching hat, gloves and shoes, had its modern counterpart on the *Majestic Explorer* in the most expensive brand of parka, whether Gore-tex or Patagonia. Such designs always cost between a thousand and two thousand dollars, and everything else the *Explorer* passengers owned—from two-hundred-dollar designer sneakers such as Mephistos, or Ralph Lauren jeans—testified to their wealth and privilege.

I saw women dressing down in Levi jeans and wool sweaters, but the giveaway was the diamond ring, the solid gold watch they wore, or the photographic equipment they carried that cost at least six or seven thousand dollars.

All the passengers on board were people who had been leaders in their fields of endeavor. The majority of them were now retired.

Lindblad cruise line was known for its efficient and capable management. Sven Lindblad, son of the originator of the Lindblad line, was in personal charge of my particular cruise, and he dedicated himself to keeping passengers contented.

This cruise meant a lot to me. I had worked nonstop for six years, devoting my life to *National Geographic*. Not that I minded; I loved the work and all my colleagues. But other than school and leisure time pursuits with my children, my personal life had become nonexistent. Ralph and I remained friends, although the romance had gone out of our relationship. I wanted so badly to prove myself to my *Geographic* co-workers and superiors that I had made my work the center of my existence.

This was the first really adult vacation I had taken in years, no less one that included someone else—a man I had met named Richard Ellis, whose life also revolved around the sea. Richard was one of the America's most celebrated marine artists, nationally renowned lecturer, and author of such critically acclaimed books as *The Book of Sharks* and *Dolphins and Porpoises.*

Richard was handsome and athletic, with a poet's eyes and the body of a long distance runner. What attracted me to him was his talent and his vast nautical knowledge. He had an extravagantly romantic nature and showered me with flowers, books, gifts, and cards that made me feel attractive and feminine, at a time when I was doing the work of ten men. It was time, I felt, to have a romantic holiday and shut out such realities as budgets, camera equipment, and the headaches of dealing with crew problems.

Along with writing and painting, Richard made money as a lecturer. He had written a bestseller called *The Book of Whales,* and was scheduled to speak about it on the *Majestic Explorer.* Sven told me he was going to show "The Great Whales," and asked me to give a speech for the ship's passengers, most of whom were well traveled, well educated and enthusiastic nature buffs, interested in everything they could learn about the whales, birds, animals, and fish of the Inside Passage.

My speech was a success, and a large number of people approached me afterward, asking me questions about the sea. Richard and I answered them all, feeling warm from the champagne and fully united by our shared interests. Sven Lindblad, the owner of the ship, invited us back to do a series of lectures on another cruise, and his show of approval—as well as the strong touch of Richard's hand in mine—made our first lap of the cruise perfect.

There was only one discordant note—a woman named Gloria Mane, whose attitude and bearing brought back images of the *Titanic.* Gloria had the arrogant, spoiled manner of an heiress who expected everyone to cater to her every whim. She was mildly complimentary about my speech, but she kept complaining to her husband, Myron, a short, narrow-shouldered man of sixty-three, with a salt and pepper mustache.

"I don't like the captain's attitude," she said.

"He invited us to be at his table, didn't he?"

"Only because he had to. He knows you own Emerald Manufacturing and the company's on the New York Stock Exchange."

Gloria then went on to say the drinks tasted bitter, the food was overdone, and the weather foul.

"I'm already seasick," she concluded, as though the weather had been personally arranged to inconvenience her.

I wasn't about to let Gloria's negative attitude affect me. Some of the other passengers were bothered by the rainy weather and choppy seas, but most of them were eagerly looking forward to their first sightings of humpbacks and killer whales. The area was known to be highly populated with whales and dolphins.

Gloria's exact opposite appeared in the form of an elderly naturalist named Anne. Anne was in her mid seventies, yet she had a sunny, grateful approach to everything. She complimented our waiter on the delicious salmon, our first mate on the ship's beautiful decor. No cynicism or bitterness invaded her clear green eyes, and she was insatiably curious—a quality often lost with age.

Anne took a motherly interest in me. She gasped when I told her I had been trapped in a cage with a shark. Her eyes widened when I told her I had done one hundred skydiving jumps.

"I wish I'd done all that," Anne said wistfully. "Now it's too late. But I can live vicariously through people like you."

"I've met skydivers in their seventies."

"Then who knows," she said, finishing her drink. "You might see me one day soaring through the sky like a bird. Or riding a dolphin. How's that for a picture? A seventy-six-year-old lady riding a dolphin."

Richard scribbled a quick sketch of Anne's imaginary ride on a napkin.

"Oh, that's wonderful," she exclaimed. "Can I keep it to show my granddaughter?"

"Of course," Richard said.

Shortly afterward everyone said their goodnights and went to their cabins. Richard and I stayed for a last, private drink.

Sven Lindblad joined us and we decided to play scrabble.

"How're you holding up?" he asked, referring to the swaying motion of the boat. "It's a bit rough out there."

"I'm fine," I said. Richard was holding up well too.

It was a little after nine o'clock the next morning, on September 10, when I heard the crash. Sven and I were on the bottom level, where my cabin was located. He had come along with me to borrow a book on the art of the Northwest Indians.

We were in the passageway when the shattering, cracking noise began. The boat shook so hard from the impact that we were both knocked to the floor of the passageway and had to steady ourselves against the walls. It was thunderous, deafening; not at all the muted sound that

Titanic passengers had heard. The jolt shook us so violently that we had to grab onto the railings in the passageway to steady ourselves.

The *Majestic Explorer* came to a sudden, violent stop.

I could tell by the look on Sven's face, and he could tell by the look on mine, that we both knew this was extremely serious.

"What the hell's going on?" he cried.

Before racing to the bridge to find out the status of the ship, he gave me a last word of advice: "Jennifer, quick, get your life vest and Richard's out of the cabin. Then come back to the lounge area. We may need your help getting passengers off the ship. And hurry."

The *Explorer* began to list, slanting perilously to the port side. People were rushing down, totally panicked, demanding to know what had happened.

Our cruise ship had struck a huge rock outcropping.

Minutes later, after investigating, Lindblad announced through the loudspeaker that we had to evacuate immediately.

"Go to the stern. And be calm. Don't take any luggage, any possessions. There's no room in the lifeboats. Take only what you can carry on your back."

Everyone responded in an orderly manner. Only the high-pitched voice of Gloria Mane could be heard, complaining loudly. "Will you please stop it," said Anne. "I'm sick of your whining. It's not the captain's fault."

"Then whose fault is it?"

The ship, it turned out, was in a precarious position. The chop in the water was too great to safely unload people from the stern. It was decided that we would evacuate the people from the side closest to the water, the port side where it was listing.

It had begun to rain, and the air was like ice. These adverse conditions made the problem of evacuation worse. Water made the inflatable boats slippery, and stepping into them was excruciatingly difficult for the elderly. Many had to be lifted.

As always in a crisis, the best and worst of human nature sprang up simultaneously. Some of the wealthy passengers wouldn't get off without their jewels, furs, and other possessions. They refused to leave anything behind, even though carrying extra weight endangered the lives of all aboard.

Gloria wore *two* fur coats, one on top of the other so that both could be saved. Three cameras were strung around her neck, and her purses were bulging. She could hardly walk, so burdened down was her body by objects.

"I spent a fortune for all these things," she protested, "and I'm not leaving them behind."

By now Richard and I suspected that the *Majestic Explorer* was destined to sink. As we began to evacuate people, the tilting of the ship got so bad that no one could stand without clutching onto something. All the chairs and tables in the lounge were sliding from the starboard side to the port side, where we were placing people onto the boats. Everyone tried to dodge them as they slid. Then they had to be moved so they didn't block the exit. I was assisting with that, as well as trying to keep passengers from panicking, talking to them calmly, urging them not to worry.

Richard and I pitched in together, stayed on board, and helped evacuate the oldest people first. Anne was a trouper, striding youthfully ahead and smiling at me. But the other seniors reacted unexpectedly. They displayed much more fear than the young passengers. Those in their seventies and eighties, who had lived most of their lives, were the most hysterical, the most anxious to cling to living, and they pushed and shoved because of their terror of going down with the ship.

I myself had come to terms with the fact that the *Explorer* would go under, and I began to think about what I'd do if Richard and I weren't able to get off in a life raft ourselves. I knew the water was freezing, and I knew I'd have to get to the top of the ship, where I could stay out of the sea for the longest possible time.

It was then, almost chillingly, the subject of my childhood obsession came catapulting back again. I thought about the *Titanic*, and how long it had taken before the ship went down. Images of the legendary sinking flooded my mind as I coped with the emergency taking place.

The *Explorer* was now listing almost sixty degrees from its upright position, but was so stuck on the rock outcropping that it managed not to tip over.

Then the accident happened.

We had evacuated some seven or eight boatloads. One of the crew members on top of the ship was given an order by the Captain to deploy the lifeboat canisters, enormous metal containers which hold inflatable boats that weigh three hundred pounds and sit on the very top of the cruise ship, on both the port and starboard sides. When they're deployed, they fall into the ocean and upon hitting the water's surface metal canisters open, and rubber boats automatically inflate.

The listing of the ship was so dramatic that the crew member couldn't see anything beneath him. He followed instructions and deployed the canister on the port side.

Directly below was an inflatable zodiac lifeboat holding eight to ten people. The zodiac was pushing off just at the time the lifeboat canister fell towards the ocean. It hit two of the passengers directly, a 300-pound canister, knocking them into the freezing water. It also hit James, a heavyset, bearded naturalist who was guiding the boat.

Anne's husband was knocked unconscious and seriously injured. Anne was killed instantly.

Complete chaos and screaming followed.

"Get it off, get it off!" shouted the passengers, smothered by the huge inflatable life raft which had opened upon impact. The inflatable covered everyone in the zodiac; they couldn't see, they couldn't hear and they were fighting to breathe. James, still in the freezing water, struggled with those in the zodiac to remove the inflatable. At first no one knew which way to push, and they were working in opposite directions, blindly, desperate to coordinate their efforts. Meanwhile, James would begin to suffer hypothermia soon if it had not begun to set in already. I knew that in icy currents, you could die within minutes. The only exception I'd heard of was the *Titanic's* chief baker, Charles Joughin, who had survived in the icy sea for two hours. He had imbibed a great deal of whiskey, which warmed his body sufficiently to keep him alive until the rescue came.

Finally, working together, the frantic passengers in the zodiac managed to flip the inflatable into the ocean and began rescuing those in the water. This was an extremely difficult feat because the weight of soaking wet clothes and bodies was enormous. James remained in the water and helped to get everyone into the zodiac, before he was pulled in by the others.

Once panic starts, it takes on a life of its own. Still

on the ship, I had to fight my own anxieties when I heard the wave of hysterical cries below. It was evident that the others on the ship with me were affected by the accident too, their own fears intensifying. People began pushing and shoving, fighting to get to the front of the line so they could get off the ship before it fell into the sea. Screams of "we're all going to die" and "it's sinking" filled the air.

Somehow I was able to maintain a calm exterior despite my conviction that we wouldn't all make it before the *Explorer* sank. I did my best to calm others and prayed for courage. If this was the end, if this was God's will, then I vowed to face it squarely. All my experiences in the last ten years had given me the strength to confront crisis, conquer my fears and face whatever fate dealt. To Richard's credit, he also stayed assisting passengers until we left on the last boat.

Fortunately, there were three fishing boats in the area, *The Maryann*, *The Commander* and *The Blackfish* that we were able to temporarily board, until hydrofoils were sent from Juneau to rescue us. I barely heard Gloria's hysterical sobs. All I could think of was that wonderful old lady, Anne, who would now never get to skydive or ride a dolphin.

Chapter 8

Death, Love, and
the Legendary Ship

Anne's death continued to haunt me. Her tragic end, and the near-fatal injuries her husband sustained, had been needless, caused less by nature than by careless captain-caused error.

The physical facts were made clear immediately. *Majestic Explorer* had crashed into a rock, but not accidentally. Part of the problem was the area, an area of rapidly changing tides. When the tides were in, rocks like these were covered over by water, but when the tides changed and water rushed out of the strait, the rocks were left exposed.

The captain had misread the tides and thought they had come in, but in reality, they were going out. A Board of Inquiry later charged him with negligence following the Friday morning incident.

"We found that he failed to navigate in an area of charted shoals with due caution," was the verdict rendered.

I couldn't help drawing a parallel between this

captain and Captain E.J. Smith of the *Titanic*. Captain
Smith had ignored countless iceberg warnings, placing his
passengers in mortal danger. It was spine-chilling to think
that thoroughly preventable mistakes had been made by
both captains, causing the destruction and sinking of their
ships.

Months later, I was still having nightmares about
the *Majestic Explorer*. The sound of Anne's last, sharp,
earsplitting scream had not subsided in my mind. The sight
of petrified passengers clustered together in the rain filled
my thoughts and my dreams.

Gradually, that traumatic Alaskan night began to
fade, but bits and pieces of it flashed back into my consciousness during odd times—crossing a street, paying a
bill, helping my sons with their homework.

My sons were growing into teenagers. Kevin, the
youngest and most outgoing, was an honor student, a
skilled guitarist and singer, and was developing quite a
flair for acting. Brent was always reading books on psy-
chology and philosophy, already projecting way ahead to a
possible career as a psychologist. Derek loved music,
although his obsession with Pink Floyd and "The Wall"
often made my head ache.

During these adolescent years, I often wished I had
a husband to complete the family unit. Ralph came and
went, offering the boys occasional male companionship.
Richard never got to know them well. My relationship with
Richard was a romantic and beautiful one, but not destined
for permanence. I had a wonderful friendship with John
Weisman, author of *Guerrilla Theater: Scenarios for
Revolution* and the bestselling Richard Marcinko story
Rogue Warrior. He introduced me to a diverse group of people, from foreign correspondents to daring test pilots. I made
some great friends, yet I did not meet that special someone.

Oddly enough, just as I was despairing of ever finding the right person, permanence came in the form of an individual who was, on the surface, very different from me in every way. His name was Joel Hirschhorn and he was a songwriter. Skydiving, scuba diving and river rafting were not high priorities in the Bronx, where he grew up. Most residents of the Grand Concourse never swam with sharks or dove in Cozumel for buried treasure.

We met on a blind date, arranged by Jack Tillar, a close friend and music editor at *National Geographic*. Jack had just worked with Joel on a movie called *The Dream Chasers*, and Joel, recently divorced, had expressed an interest in meeting "the right woman."

Jack was convinced I was this right woman and gave Joel my phone number. He called and invited me to a party at Rosemary Clooney's house. When he showed up at my Santa Monica apartment, I was pleasantly surprised that a blind date, for once, was not a cause for mourning. Joel was tall and good-looking, with a warmly infectious grin and a fantastically witty sense of humor.

Sure enough, we hit it off incredibly well. Never once did we stumble into those awkward gaps or nervous silences. In fact, we couldn't stop talking. It was as if we'd known each other all our lives. We found a mutual passion for books, although he leaned toward fiction and I preferred non-fiction. But we compared notes and discovered we could live in a bookstore all day and never get bored.

Our musical tastes were almost identical. I loved Broadway shows, Tchaikovsky and Beethoven, Paul Simon and Bob Dylan; so did he. As for books and authors, my favorites were Clive Cussler, Michael Crichton, Sylvia Earle's *Exploring the Deep Frontier* and William Beebe's *Half Mile Down*. Joel's literary idol was Pat Conroy, and we both had a special admiration for Anne Morrow

Lindbergh's *Gift From the Sea* and Maya Angelou's auto-biographies. It's a good thing I had eclectic taste, because Joel's career as a solid gold songwriter spanned everyone from Elvis Presley to Aretha Franklin, Maureen McGovern to Taj Mahal. He was an extraordinary pianist, who could play Rachmaninoff's Second just as skillfully as the blues.

The signposts were particularly favorable, because that night just happened, by coincidence, to be Valentine's day.

The party was a wonderful setting for our first date. Rosemary Clooney sang for hours, accompanied by a remarkably gifted but then unknown musician named Michael Feinstein. Rosemary and Michael ran the gamut from Gershwin to Rodgers and Hart, and then Joel sat down and played his Oscar-winning song "The Morning After," from *The Poseidon Adventure*.

"There's got to be a morning after

"If we can hold on through the night..."

Of all things, those words referred to an imminent sea disaster! Joel didn't scuba dive, but his reputation largely rested on a hit song about the sea.

"Have you ever wanted to scuba dive?" I asked him.

"Honestly? Never."

"Well...do you love to swim?"

"I don't know how."

"How about books? Do you like *Moby Dick*?"

"I prefer *The Great Gatsby*."

"All right then—how do you feel about the *Titanic*?"

"I'm glad I wasn't on it," he quipped.

Even though Joel had no particular emotional involvement with the *Titanic*, he was—amusingly enough—referred to by newspapers as "the master of dis-aster," because his material so often centered on natural catastrophes. Joel's other Oscar-winning tune was "We May Never Love Like This Again," from *The Towering Inferno*—a romantic ode to a burning building—and a third song, Oscar-nominated, was "Candle on the Water," detailing the heroine's dream of being reunited with her boyfriend, considered lost in a shipwreck.

We laughed when I talked about being confronted by sharks.

"Mine are on land," Joel said in his dry way. "Publishers, record producers, stars. I know they wear suits, but believe me, they're as lethal as any undersea predator you'll meet."

Most crucially, Joel let me be who I was. He had no interest in molding me, but he wanted to make sure I had no interest in remaking him.

"I'll never jump from a plane," he told me, on our second date. "You won't see me in a scuba suit, unless I'm going to a costume party, and I won't go near a shark unless *Jaws* is on television."

Somehow it didn't matter. We had fun, and we shared our deepest feelings. Joel had never had children of his own, and he welcomed a chance to be a father to my sons. His relationship to Kevin, Brent, and Derek was affectionate and close from the start.

Within a year, we knew we wanted to be married. Joel moved into my apartment on Third Street in Santa Monica, two blocks from the ocean. Although he claimed to be constitutionally against exercise, he came along with me in the early morning and ran alongside me on the sand. Usually we ran at six-thirty, when the sky was always a mass of reds, yellows and purples. Sometimes I wore my

running shoes; other times I was barefoot, because I loved
to feel the water lapping up against my toes. We made a
habit of picking up seashells and bringing them home to
put on top of the piano. Often he'd place a conch shell to
his ear and exclaim, "I hear a hit!" then put his hands on
the keyboard and produce a beautiful melody.

In June of 1985 we said our vows. I had found a
safe harbor at last.

Three months later, on September 1, Bob Ballard
found the *Titanic*. I could feel Joel watching me when I
spread the paper on our breakfast table and reread the
story a dozen times.

"It was like landing on the moon," Bob told the
New York Times.

The 245-foot U.S. Navy oceanographic vessel
Knorr had been in a search pattern for sixteen days, while
scientists watched images transmitted from the ocean
floor. The first thing Ballard and partner Jean-Louis
Michel of Ifremer saw was a giant boiler on the ocean
floor, followed by a full view of the *Titanic*, almost perfectly preserved.

"Our first thoughts were naturally excitement,"
Bob said in the paper. "It was early Sunday morning when
we first spotted the wreckage, about an hour before the
time the *Titanic* sank. Then I was hit with remorse and
sadness. I hadn't expected it to hit me as hard as it did."

His discovery came twenty-two days after the
French research ship, *Le Suroit,* had roamed over a 150-
square-mile target area using side-scanning sonar. *Le
Suroit* scanned over eighty percent of the expanse without
finding any trace of the *Titanic*. Following that, Ballard's
team, including three French scientists on the *Knorr*

research vessel, started to comb the other twenty percent with a computerized sled named *Argo,* which carries powerful strobe lights, sonar, and video equipment.

"We designed and built *Argo,*" Bob recalled. "The four-thousand-ton *Argo* can operate at depths of twenty thousand feet. It's towed by a cable that carries videos and other signals back to the surface ship."

On the morning of August 1, Ballard and Jean-Louis Michel discovered the video image of the boiler on the ocean floor. Wildly excited, they were able to locate the main section of the *Titanic*, after which they determined the great ship's latitude and longitude.

I remembered Bob's projections in Loch Ness. I felt tremendous admiration for him, because he had persevered for so many years despite all opposition. Unwaveringly, he had kept to what he called, "a goal of mine for over a decade."

"Well, they found it and I wasn't there," I said disappointedly to Joel.

"Then don't read about it. It'll only torture you."

That was like saying to a cocaine user at the height of his addiction that he should quit cold turkey. Through the years I had been in the grip of *Titanic* fever and it still consumed me.

I turned back to Bob Ballard's account in the *Times*, once again enthralled.

"On *Argo*'s monitors, we watched a procession of bronze portholes, twisted sections of railing, hull plating, and small deck equipment stream by on the rolling gray mud of the bottom.

"Most of us had forgotten how huge a ship *Titanic* had been, that she had been assembled from hundreds and thousands of these individual bits and pieces, now revealed in the glare of *Argo*'s footlights for the first time in seventy-three years.

"*Titanic* had been an abstraction to us, a dream; we were not prepared for the mundane reality of the deck-lamp stanchion, bent like a shepherd's crook, the fragile old light bulb still in place, or the clustered sprouts of the ship's steam whistle, now forever mute."

The event made front page headlines around the world. Ralph and Emory were both participants in the expedition, Ralph as topside cinematographer and Emory representing *National Geographic* as still photographer.

I knew I would hear the details of the discovery millions of times over, and my reaction was complex. I was torn between wanting to learn every single detail and not wanting to read anything at all because I hadn't been part of it.

After finding the *Titanic*, according to Ralph, "Ballard attempted to keep its location a secret by seizing the navigation charts. But thanks to my Marine Corps reconnaissance training, I memorized the chart upside down across the table."

Through all the accounts, I recognized a "macho" approach taken by Bob in his interviews. As he put it, "It's sort of like, 'I just married someone and is this something I want to be married to?' It seemed nice at the time—you know, she was cute, she was nice and all that sort of thing—but now I'm married to her and wondering if I made a mistake. And I just can't walk away from this one. She won't let me."

Later on, he embellished on his theme.

"There is no divorcing the *Titanic*. Ever."

Others on the Ballard expedition also spoke of their adventure as an experience "that tests all men to the limits and makes their wives and girlfriends proud back home."

Only later did I console myself that although the legendary ship had been discovered, photographed, and written about, no one had actually gone down there, found the long lost artifacts, and brought them to the surface. And, of course, I fantasized that the person who would accomplish that incredible feat would be me.

Jennifer's first sky-diving experience and the forerunner of 100 other jumps.

Photo: Ralph White

Silhouette shot of Jennifer and her two sons Brent and Kevin snorkeling, surrounded by a school of tropical fish in Hawaii.

Photo: Ed Robinson

It was quite an experience for Jennifer Carter hand-feeding a massive twelve foot tiger shark in Sydney, Australia.

Photo: Jennifer Carter

The *Majestic Explorer*, listing dramatically after crashing on a rock. During the rescue, one person was killed, and two others injured.

Chapter 9

Opportunity of a Lifetime

"There's a French-American expedition to the ruins of the *Titanic* planned for August, and Westgate International is making a documentary of it," said Ralph, telephoning me. "I said you were a great coordinator and had a sea background, so they want to meet you."

A bell rang in my head. Could this be the opportunity I'd been waiting a lifetime for? I recalled the psychic, Grace, pointing to a spot in the North Atlantic and telling me I would go there several times.

Within days I was slated for an interview with the respected producer, Michael Seligman.

Seligman, a dynamic man of medium height who smoked cigars incessantly, was the producer of all the Oscar specials and sparked visibly when I mentioned that Joel was a two-time Oscar winner and had been nominated twice beyond that.

Luck was with me. Seligman had been asked to produce another special concurrently with this one, and he had to spend a lot of time in Philadelphia, as well as fly back and forth to different locations.

"I need someone who can handle everything," he said. Everything was a tall order, but I obeyed the first commandment of show business: always say yes. I told myself everything I had done in the intervening years since I'd gotten my job at Geographic had prepared me for a mission like this: planning ocean expeditions to the Red Sea, Greece, Egypt and Israel; expeditions to San Ignacio and Magdalena Bay for "The Great Whales"; and working as assistant producer to Al Giddings and Jim Lipscomb on a Peter Guber special titled "Mysteries of the Sea." All of these seemed to be the right background for knowing what kind of people and equipment were needed for a responsibility this complicated, and with such potential for difficult conditions. Nonetheless, I was nervous at boasting about my own accomplishments and worried how they might be judged by someone like Seligman.

Nevertheless, he seemed very pleased at my experience, and with Seligman's endorsement, I got to meet the next two executive producers who had to approve his decision, John Joslyn and Doug Llewelyn.

"We need someone to act as liaison," said Doug, brushing his hand through his blond hair.

I understood what he meant, having studied the prospectus. This expedition had three separate organizations that were involved in the funding: Oceanic Research Explorations, Ltd., headed by George Tulloch; Taurus International, owned by Robert Chappaz and Yves Cornet; and Ifremer, part of the French Government. A fourth entity to complete the circle was Westgate Productions, headed by John and Doug, who were producing the film and had put together all the partners.

"It will be chaos," said Doug, "especially if we don't have someone to interface all the organizations involved and to work with them and get them to coexist peacefully. Jennifer, how would you like to be expedition leader?"

Knowing that the *Titanic* was at the center of it all, it took me about half a second to say yes.

Finally, I was told I had to be somewhat of a journalist, chronicling day to day activities in a log, faxing information about the dives, preparing film reports, weather reports, safety reports, and listing what artifacts we planned to recover.

It was July of 1987. *Could it really be true,* I asked myself, *that in a few more weeks my dream would become a reality?* I would be on a ship, floating squarely on top of the *Titanic*.

Joel was excited for me, but he had trepidations.

"If they let you dive..."

"Not *if,*" I answered. "When!"

"But no one's said you could go down, did they?"

"I'll find a way."

"Okay. Let's say you *do* go down. Can you be rescued if something goes wrong?"

I had to be honest. "No."

"That's not a very comforting answer."

Brent and Kevin looked just as concerned as Joel did.

"Mom, maybe you'd better think twice."

I looked Kevin and Brent directly in the eye, trying to convey my own excitement.

"One question. If either of you had a chance to go down to the *Titanic* in a submersible, and there was danger—even a chance you might not come back—would you take that chance or not?"

Kevin grinned.

"In a minute."

"Me too," said Brent.

"We don't have to ask what you'd do," I said to Joel.

"No. I'd tell everybody I had a song to write and to count me out. I'd be like General Custer in that old joke— telling his men about the suicidal confrontation laying in wait for them. And after he explains all the gory possibilities, he says, 'I only *wish* I could join you.'"

Everyone laughed.

"Seriously, I love you and I'm worried," Joel said, putting his arms around me.

"I promise to be careful."

"All right, I'll have to be content with that. But I'll miss you."

That night, as we lay in bed holding each other, Joel said, "Some husbands have to face the rivalry of other men. Whoever thought I'd be competing with a ship?"

My next step was to choose a crew. The timing was right, and some outstanding people were available.

I chose Peter Pilafian as our cinematographer. Peter was dark and wiry, with a mountain climber's build and a firm handshake. He had suggested Randy Wimberg as his assistant and sound man. Randy was six-feet-six, with brown hair and a winning smile. He was twenty-eight, also a mountain climber, river runner, and a man who ran nature and river tours. He radiated positiveness and I liked him at once.

"Call me Stretch," Randy said, shaking my hand. "Or King Kong. Either one."

I decided to stick with Randy.

The still photographer Doug Llewelyn chose was Adam Jahiel. Tall, dark, with a mustache and thick hair, Adam was in his late twenties and spoke fluent French.

Mark Burnett was a video technician who had been referred to me by Berc, our rental house. I needed someone who was technically able to take apart and put together video equipment in the field in the event of breakdowns, and Mark had vast experience in that area. I called him, and he immediately agreed to come.

Ralph's presence was a great asset, since he had been on the 1985 *Titanic* expedition with Emory and Bob. Westgate engaged him as director of submersible photography. I was grateful to him for involving me.

All of my crew, with the exception of Mark, were scuba divers and had handled wilderness experiences frequently. I needed to have people who were strong in the field, rather than those accustomed only to working on a set. All these men were in superb physical condition, particularly Peter, who had already participated in some of the most taxing climbs in the world, climbs that were frequently designed for filming. If you can hang off the side of a cliff and change film in the camera, under heavy winds and impossible photographic conditions, you can handle anything.

I hoped all of them would get along well, once the hardships of a two-month expedition began to mount.

Only three operational submersibles in the world were capable of making dives deep enough (13,000 feet) to visit the *Titanic* in 1987. The pressure at the wreck's depth is an astounding 6,800 pounds per square inch. Both Woods Hole Oceanographic Institute's *Alvin* and the *Sea Cliff,* owned by the United States Navy, were unavailable, and not our first choices in any case. We decided to lease the French submersible *Nautile,* from Ifremer (The French Institute of Research and Exploration of the Sea), along with its support vessel *Nadir* and an experienced French crew.

Nadir was called the mother ship, because it car-ried *Nautile*, a twenty-million-dollar, three-man subma-rine, with the ability to dive to a depth of 6,000 meters. Equipped with the most advanced instrumentation avail-able in the world, as well as a titanium alloy hull, *Nautile* had a pair of articulated arms that were vastly superior to the arms on the other two submersibles, arms which enabled it to retrieve objects on the ocean floor.

Another ship, the *Abeille Supporter,* was slated to be used for storing the artifacts recovered. Over fifty peo-ple would take part in the expedition, and plans were made to film all dives and edit them into a television special and videotape. Fifteen years of film and oceanic background gave me the necessary credentials to participate as expedi-tion leader.

The building excitement was palpable. Unfortu-nately, Bob Ballard's fight to stop salvage of the artifacts burst onto the scene.

"Grave robbers," he cried out to the world. "There is no light at that depth and little life can be found. It's a quiet peaceful place and a fitting place for the remains of this greatest of sea tragedies to rest. Forever may it remain that way."

The groundswell of disastrous publicity had been building for more than a year prior to our expedition. Congress, even though it had no jurisdiction over interna-tional waters, had passed a bill stating that the *Titanic* was a memorial and prohibiting its desecration. President Reagan, influenced by intense pressure, signed the bill into law in October 1986.

In August of 1987, the voices grew stormier. Senator Lowell Weicker pushed through a bill banning the importation of objects from the *Titanic* "for the purpose of commercial gain." That same month, Eva Hart, a *Titanic* survivor whose father was among the 1,513 passengers who died when the liner sank, cried out, "Fortune hunters, vultures, pirates!"

Every negative newspaper article, every vicious editorial, made me angrier. I knew that the men who wanted to launch *Titanic 87*—American and French— were not in it as fortune hunters or vultures. They were idealists who believed they were rescuing pieces of history. They had every intention of collecting the artifacts and placing them in museums. But nothing could minimize the misleading and hysterical attacks, and I was genuinely worried that this massive propaganda would stop the expedition dead in its tracks.

When I showed the articles to Joel, I waited for his words of indignation. Always his belief in me and the honor of my intentions reassured me. He didn't disappoint me.

But then, one dark, foggy morning, unusual for Los Angeles in July, there was a particularly intense attack on our upcoming expedition in the newspaper which I found on the kitchen table. I shivered and brought the newspaper over to Joel, who was awake, but still in bed.

He scanned the new article for a few moments. Then he said casually, "Maybe you shouldn't go."

"Are you kidding?"

"No. Maybe Ballard's right. Maybe all these guys are right. Maybe everybody should leave the wreck alone."

Joel watched me intensely.

"I can't believe you're saying this."

Joel got out of bed. "Forget it. Pack your gear and leave. The ship's waiting."

"Wait. Are you saying you agree with Ballard and Weicker and the others, or that you agree with me?"

He looked pained. "I think these salvaging opportunists are going to dive down there, yank all these belongings from their rightful resting place and sell them for commercial gain. I don't believe any of that bullshit about museums and putting them on display, or all that high-minded talk about preserving the artifacts for the sake of history. There won't be a goddamn artifact left three weeks after the dives are finished."

"And that makes me an opportunist too?"

"I didn't say that."

"You might as well have. No one will sell off these artifacts, and they *will* be put in museums. Joslyn and Llewelyn and all the rest want to do something important for history."

"Give me a break."

"Now I find out that Mr. Positive is really a cynic."

"Not a cynic, a realist. Just because I'm an optimist doesn't mean I don't know human nature. Sure, they talk about bringing artifacts up and putting them in museums around the world so that people will remember and a tragedy like that won't happen again. It sounds good. But when they find priceless jewels —when they're *staring, inches away,* at glittering gold coins and bank notes and other mementos that belonged to millionaires like John Jacob Astor and Benjamin Guggenheim—once that stuff is in their hot little hands—it'll be hard to drop them in some glass case and forget about all that lovely *money* they could have made. I'm with Eva Hart. Let the dead rest in peace, along with the things that belonged to them."

He stopped. His sudden silence made the distant swell of the ocean sound unusually loud and harsh.

"I'll make you a bet right now. No one will steal artifacts and no one will sell them on the open market. I'll bet our marriage on it." My voice was cryptic.

"I see a divorce looming."

"That's how sure I am." I started to laugh at his stricken look. "No, I won't bet our marriage on it. If it was a contest between you and the *Titanic*, you would win."

"That's a relief."

Joel put his arms around me.

"Maybe I overstated just a little. Maybe I'm just unhappy that you have to leave for eight weeks, and I dread the thought of being without you all that time. I love you, you know. I love you more than anything in the world."

"I love you too. And I'll write every day."

"I can't make love to a letter."

"Well, I'm here now." He held me tighter.

On July 30, 1987, I left for St. John's, Newfoundland, to start the first leg of my *Titanic* journey. Joel was originally going to fly with me to St. John's, until I spoke to my mother.

"It's bad luck for a lover to see you off when you go to sea," she warned me. "No sailor ever lets his sweetheart watch him when he gets on board a ship."

Joel laughed.

"I'm not superstitious," he said.

"Well, I am. And since this is such a strange, unusual kind of expedition, maybe you'd better just come with me to the airport."

He came with me to the Air Canada entrance, shook hands with Peter, Ralph, Doug, and the others joining the expedition.

"I'd better make it a good one," he said, kissing me. "It has to last for eight weeks. Besides, you'll be the only woman on a ship with fifty men. And Ralph!"

"Don't worry," I told him. "I'm true blue."

"I'm not worried about you," Joel said. "It's the fifty men I'm worried about."

Suddenly I realized how much it hurt to leave Joel. We were so happy we still felt like newlyweds, and I was off to the high seas without him. At that moment, I was so torn I began to wonder if I'd made the right decision.

"Come on," called Ralph. "We'll miss the plane."

The lure of the Great Ship was too strong. I kissed Joel one last time and hurried to the ramp, on the way to my long-dreamed-of rendezvous with the *Titanic*.

Chapter 10

Buried Treasures

The *Abeille Supporter*, the large yellow ship my crew and I would live on throughout the expedition, was built in 1975 and converted a year later into a diving support ship. When it wasn't underway and there were heavy swells, the *Abeille* made a weirdly chilling, groaning sound—a cross between the eerie songs of humpback whales and ghostly cries. Every time I heard it, I would imagine the screams of 1,500 people in freezing water, thrashing helplessly and doomed to drown because of the lifeboat shortage. The sounds were particularly harsh when there were heavy seas, because the *Abeille* drew air underneath the stern and, as it tipped back and forth and expelled the same air it pulled in, the bizarre mechanical screams automatically appeared. The nightmarish noises erupted when the ship was stationary, and before long, I welcomed any movement that would obliterate them.

Two hundred and nine feet long and forty-four feet wide, the *Abeille* was leased to hold our divers and all the huge square containers that held the artifacts. It also furnished housing for the crew and the divers, as well as supplies for the expedition. Most important, the *Abeille*'s crew would handle the taxing and dangerous job of launching and recovering retrieval baskets which carried the *Titanic*'s treasures.

This procedure is especially dangerous in bad weather, when the baskets are packed with priceless artifacts that often weigh close to five hundred pounds. Swinging back and forth with such a heavy cargo in heavy winds, unable to be controlled, it's easy to imagine what catastrophes are possible if individuals are hampered with this extreme weight. Besides possible damage to human life, there could be the loss of the priceless artifacts we all hoped to bring to the surface.

The *Abeille* had three lifeboats on board, five rescue inflatable dinghies, and one work boat with an eighty horsepower engine. It also had two zodiacs—inflatable rubber boats with engines. One zodiac's engine was forty horsepower and the other's twenty-five horsepower. Our ship could travel at a top speed of fourteen knots, ten less than the *Titanic*'s top speed. It had hydraulic winches and a hydraulic "A" frame of thirty tons lifting capacity.

"Yeah, this ship has everything but living space," remarked a member of the crew.

I was surprised to hear that kind of complaint, so early in the game. Nobody was on the *Abeille* to take a luxury cruise; no one was going to wear tuxedos and mingle with multimillionaires.

My accommodations, in fact, were fairly tolerable. True, the room was small, ten feet long and eight feet wide. That width included the bunk beds and the desk, which were built in. I also had a closet—to stretch the term to its limit—with enough space to sandwich in my foul weather gear, a pair of large rubber boots, and my survival suit. Unfortunately, between bed, desk, bathroom, and closet, I could barely move.

The duffel bags with my clothes had to be stored in two drawers beneath the bunk bed. The bunk bed was said to be six feet long, although a tape measure would have revealed that estimate to be a gross exaggeration. It had a plywood board supporting a foam mattress. The difference between my accommodations and most of the other members of my crew was that I was above board instead of below, which allowed me to open my door and get fresh air.

My quarters—as Captain Rowarch extravagantly referred to them—also allowed me access to the technical room where we stored our video equipment and where we could view our tapes from day to day. My built-in desk was tiny but adequate enough for me to do my dive plans, prepare the text for telexes, and devise a daily list naming the artifacts which were to be brought up, as well as choosing which members of my crew would go down in the submarine from day to day.

Least satisfactory was my bathroom, which was exceedingly narrow. The toilet facilities and shower facilities coexisted uneasily, shower head squeezed between toilet and sink. All these items together couldn't have been more than four by four.

Unlike my tiny accommodations, however, the *Abeille*'s meals were worthy of a luxury liner—perhaps even the *Titanic* in her heyday. Camille Stephan, our chef, at only thirty-three years old already had seventeen years of experience. He had been chef for the Jules Verne Restaurant on the Eiffel Tower and was a perfectionist. Slight of build and with a friendly smile, he nevertheless conveyed a strong warning: *Be on time for meals, no matter what else is happening. I will accept no excuse!*

No one would have dared to give one. I sensed that, even in a hurricane, we would be expected to ignore the raging winds and rocking waves and show proper respect for Camille's culinary masterpieces—delicacies such as quiche appetizers, prosciutto with honeydew melon, courses of fruit and cheese, and varieties of pâtés and sausages with French bread. The main courses were veal chops, pork chops, roast beef, chicken, and fish, with a variety of sauces, a new one every day. Camille had been a sous chef and his sauces were extraordinary. Desserts included chocolate cake, fruit tarts of all varieties, chocolate fudge sundaes, Napoleons, eclairs, and other French pastries filled with custard.

A friendly rivalry existed on the *Abeille* and the *Nadir* as to who had the best chef. We felt that Camille won hands down. I thought of Joel, who loved sweets, and Kevin and Brent, who loved them even more than Joel did. How they would have relished Camille's fudge sundaes!

If the old cliché, "A captain is only as good as his chef" was true, then Captain Rowarch was one of the best captains in history.

The dining room was simple and unadorned—six long oblong tables with benches, structured to accommodate six people on either side of an individual table. There were ashtrays everywhere; as I staggered through a dark gray curtain of tobacco-induced fog, it became evident quickly that I was the only non-smoker on board. A huge wall clock served as reminder that everyone was to be on time, and a television set and VCR hung from the wall in the far corner, enabling crew members to watch videotapes after dinner. One problem: it was made to European standard, not American, which meant that you couldn't play United States tapes on it. Therefore, the Americans were shut out of all television entertainment.

I was basically told that television was off limits at night anyway, and I knew that some wild X-rated videos were played for male entertainment. The night *Deep Throat* made its debut on the *Abeille*, I had no desire to be included in a man's world.

Ultramodern equipment filled the galley, including massive refrigerators and freezers. In order to cook enough food for a crew of this size, we needed huge commercial ranges, two or three of them, to supply Camille with enough burners.

As an American, I confess to loving another morning ritual—being kissed by all the crew before I sat down to eat. I knew this was a French custom, probably no more than ordinary Gallic politeness, but it made me feel admired and special.

It took thirty-six hours for the *Abeille* to reach the *Titanic* site, and I could feel the excitement on board building. Everyone involved—our American film crew of six and the eighteen additional crew members of the *Abeille*—had a sense of being part of history, and they were anxious to begin.

"Hope you get to dive," Ralph said to me, as we were standing on deck, looking at a spectacular sunset of vibrant blues, oranges, and pinks—the kind of sunset that had once meant so much to us, back in Cozumel.

"I think I will."

"Don't count on it," he said, shaking his head. "I know you're expedition leader, but there are only a limited amount of dives, and we'll need them for those who are supposed to bring up the relics. Not only that, the owners and investors will be coming out, and *they'll* want to dive. So don't get your hopes up."

I could see that Ralph had dozens of dives planned for himself. Even though my role was to coordinate, and no one had guaranteed me a dive, I secretly vowed I'd have one. Ralph had to know my intense feeling. I surveyed him and thought he was probably testing me.

Joel, the ultimate diplomat, had warned me not to react when Ralph teased me. Ralph knew my buttons; he always knew how to make me react strongly. It was a game, and he had always relished seeing me flare up, eyes flashing fire, like someone who had just been prodded with a branding iron. Only Ralph could provoke that kind of response.

"Well," I answered, more calmly than I felt, "I'll dive or I won't. We'll see."

"I just don't want you to be too disappointed."

Accompanying the *Abeille,* the *Nadir* was the other ship instrumental to the success of our expedition, a support vessel for underwater research. Called the mother ship, the *Nadir* was 183 feet long and had four engines with a total output of 2,400 horsepower. Most important, it possessed a satellite navigation system telephone/fax, which the *Abeille* lacked.

Nadir served the most crucially valuable function of all. It carried our expedition's lifeblood, the submersible *Nautile*. *Nadir* had a special A-frame stern gantry weighing twenty tons which, when operated hydraulically, could lift the *Nautile* up and out over the ocean and back upon returning. The *Nadir* also offered a rolling platform sometimes referred to as the "wagon" by the crew, which could transfer the submersible to and from the workshop. The workshop was an area about thirty feet aft the stern, where maintenance was carried out after each dive.

The *Nadir*'s cabins held twenty-six crew members. It also had twenty-foot laboratory containers and one main crane that weighed three tons and was forty-eight feet high. Its long narrow containers functioned as tool shops, workrooms, projection rooms, and photo lab.

The *Nautile* was everybody's pride—a bright yellow, manned submersible that had a depth rating of 20,000 feet. It possessed two manipulator arms, which resembled the arms of a giant crab, and a retractable sample basket. These arms could lift heavy objects, transport them, and fill a basket that was positioned in front of the submarine. The retrieval basket was capable of containing up to 200 kilos. *Nautile*'s arms had amazing flexibility. They were so advanced they could make unfathomably small knots, and Captain Nargeolet claimed the submersible's arms were so precise that they could even hold an egg without breaking it.

The pincer part of the left arm could be disengaged and a vacuum device made of rubber substituted. When that was completed, it allowed the pilot to pick up extremely fragile items with no threat of damage.

All this remarkable equipment was indispensable, but even more crucial, the weather had to be perfect for diving. John Joslyn and Doug Llewelyn were astute enough to lease the *Nadir* and *Nautile* during the prime season, the *only* season one could visit the *Titanic* site to do work safely in the North Atlantic. That period ranges from mid-July through mid-September, and as people who know the North Atlantic are aware, even during this supposedly safe time you can encounter violent storms and occasionally, hurricanes.

We were a day from the *Titanic* site 453 miles southeast of St. John's, Newfoundland, approximately 963 miles east of the coast of New York. The stern section and boilers are at forty-nine degrees 56' 54" west, forty-one

degrees 43' 32" north. The bow section of the *Titanic* rests
approximately 1,970 feet from the stern at forty-nine
degrees 56' 49" west, forty-one degrees 43' 32" north, pointing in the opposite direction.

We knew the position of the *Titanic*, although Bob
Ballard who discovered it didn't publish the exact location.
Most people don't realize that Ballard's co-leader, Jean-
Louis Michel of Ifremer, was the person on duty the time
the *Titanic* was found. Ballard's expedition was actually a
joint American and French one, utilizing a French ship, *Le
Suroit*, for the first half and an American ship, the *Knorr*,
for the second. Since our expedition was *also* American and
French, using Ifremer's *Nautile* and *Nadir*, this French
connection gave us access to the exact location as well.

Before arriving at the site, we were legally required
to undergo lifeboat training. This mandatory training came
about as a result of the *Titanic* tragedy. Three safety procedures were instituted, procedures that are rigorously followed today. There must be enough lifeboats for every single person on board; ships carrying more than fifty people
are required to have lifeboat drills within twelve hours of
departure; and ship radios can never be turned off.
Another important regulation calls for a twenty-four-hour,
round-the-clock radio watch.

In 1913, a year after the sinking, the International
Ice Patrol was formed to warn ships of icebergs in the
North Atlantic. Today, there are special patrol airplanes
that keep track of exactly where every iceberg is located,
and they warn ships in the area so that no one is taken by
surprise.

First mate Christian Quillivic (known by his com-
patriots as Giscard but to me as "Mr. Christian," hero of

Mutiny on the Bounty) conducted the lifeboat drill. At thirty-four years old, with dark hair and a firm jaw, he was a fifteen-year veteran at sea. Christian resembled a young Humphrey Bogart and treated the whole drill with morbid, somber seriousness. He taught us the proper way to jump into the water in an emergency and described the proper method of climbing into the lifeboats.

"You will not be using the wooden lifeboats on board," he said. "It is extremely dangerous to lower them with crew members inside if we are being tossed around by heavy seas." Instead, he explained, metal lifeboat canisters would be deployed from the top of the ship and as they collided with the water, the rubber life rafts inside would open up and inflate. Those were the lifeboats we would utilize if disaster struck.

Hearing the canisters mentioned brought back horrifying memories of Anne dying on the *Majestic Explorer* when a falling canister weighing 300 pounds fell. I thought to myself, *Next time I have to evacuate ship I'm going to know where every single lifeboat canister is so I don't get hit.*

A more comical, yet equally necessary aspect of our training related to the thick survival suit we had to don, which looked as though it could double for a rubber Santa Claus costume. The drysuits are the only means of surviving in icy waters. Should there be a savage storm that either tips over the lifeboats or inflatable boats, no one could stay alive until rescue without the protection of these suits. My own sense was that the suits only afforded protection for a limited amount of time, but they at least offered people a fighting chance.

What made it so difficult as I struggled to get into my drysuit was that it was all one piece, including the hands and the feet—unlike a wetsuit, where you'll squeeze into the pants first and the jacket separately, then slip on gloves and booties. Since it's all one piece, I first had to lie down on the floor and wriggle like a worm, trying to squirm my way until my feet reached the soles of the suit. Then, I concentrated on getting my hands all the way down to the fingers of the suit. You wear your clothes underneath this drysuit, except for your shoes. Clothes unfortunately impede the whole process, and the sticky rubber doesn't slide easily. They gave me talcum powder to douse my hands with, but it was still a formidable task.

The suits are one size, enormous—big enough for a person weighing 250 pounds. Since I was small, I knew I looked particularly ludicrous—like a clown or a life-size Macy's Thanksgiving Day parade balloon. Once I forced my legs in, I fought to pull myself to a standing position and jumped. I jumped up and down, because I still had not really positioned my feet properly in the suit. At that point, I started working on the arms. And that wasn't all; once I'd completed everything and gotten my hands into the fingers of the suit, I had to reach over my back and grab the zipper. This was a feat in itself because the zipper came down past the middle of my back, and I was required to pull it up all the way or I wouldn't have a tight seal on the drysuit.

"It's not so hard, is it?" Christian said, as we all silently cursed him. It was time to lift the hood over our heads and chins, so that at the end, our chins were completely covered and our foreheads down to our eyebrows concealed as well. The only thing left was a small hole showing our eyes, nose, and mouth.

"Once you're in the ocean," Christian concluded, "there is a little beacon attached that you can disarm, which sends a signal that will—*hopefully*—help the Coast

Guard to find you. And attached to the front is a large, red, envelope-shaped life vest covering you from chest to knees. When you trigger this vest, it inflates, protecting you if you get tossed into the ocean."

"This damn thing'll keep you so busy, you won't have time to think about dying," said Ralph. In a genuine emergency, how could anybody get into such a cumbersome outfit, unless he was David Copperfield? It was hard enough to squeeze into such a monstrosity under calm conditions.

Christian called out, "No matter how severe the circumstances, statistics show you'll have two minutes time to put your survival suit on." The time span held no comfort.

Out came his stop watch. We were now going to be timed.

"You think this is funny," Christian said. "I can see this is a real ship of fools."

His analogy seemed accurate when Randy and Ralph, six-feet-six and six-feet-four respectively, went through a series of ludicrous contortions to slip their suits on. Occasionally Christian permitted himself a sly half-smile while he watched us make fools of ourselves. I don't think anyone achieved the two-minute deadline, and some of us had to perform the grotesque ritual twice. There was a cassette player in the wheelhouse and it was brought down. Randy selected a cassette with an assortment of seventies disco classics, songs that suited the comic mood of the occasion—"YMCA", "Jump for Your Love" by the Pointer Sisters, and Donna Summer's "Hot Stuff" and "She Works Hard for the Money."

As time began to run out on the stop watch, Christian barked out a countdown. "One minute...forty five seconds...thirty seconds...fifteen...." The action became faster, the wriggling more hysterical, the uncoordinated movements more frantic.

Through all our comical maneuvering, as the one woman in a ship of only men, there were sexist remarks and jokes that called attention to the fact that I was not only a woman, but a woman in a leadership position. I ignored them all. I had always been the kind of woman that men confided in and told their troubles to. Rough language didn't bother me, and I could take the kidding. All that mattered was pulling my own weight, and not insisting on extra courtesies because of my sex.

Arriving on the site of the *Titanic* is akin to a religious experience.

As soon as the *Abeille Supporter* reached our destination point and turned off its engines, I immediately envisioned the wreck directly beneath us. I had a sense of ghostlike people pulling on our ship, grasping with every bit of strength, as though the *Abeille* could lift them from their prison of permanent darkness.

At the same time, I was feverishly anticipating the work ahead. I only knew the *Titanic* cast of characters from books—Captain E.J. Smith, Bruce Ismay, John Jacob Astor, Benjamin Guggenheim—but discovering artifacts would be a way of knowing them more intimately, relating to them in a mystical way that superseded motion pictures and books. In a symbolic way, it would restore the victims to life, by giving them a fresh and powerful significance to the world.

The first dive of our mission to the deepest shipwreck of our century would be forever engraved in my memory. Ralph, our underwater cinematographer, became the first crew member of our expedition to descend to the ocean floor. "It's one thing to see the *Titanic* on a tiny video monitor," Ralph said. "But to actually see it from the ocean floor and bring up artifacts—*well, it just doesn't get much better than that.*" He was a veteran of many expeditions, a seasoned adventurer. But today his face was flushed, his body tense with anticipation. Most of the time he presented a picture of I've-been-there-done-that. Today, his joy was almost virginal, and I couldn't blame him.

Nobody admitted it, but I knew my whole crew would have leaped at the chance to trade places with Ralph. They envied him and had to hide it. Patience is hard to come by when every cell inside you screams to dive.

It wasn't ideal weather. Swells were running six to ten feet, which made boarding the *Nadir* precarious. Many of the men were suffering from seasickness, and two were so immobilized by nausea that they couldn't eat at all. But none of this seemed to bother Ralph.

"Maybe I'll be the first one to find the hole," Ralph said, referring to the oft rumored huge gash on the side of the *Titanic* which many denied existed.

As he climbed into the bright yellow *Nautile* and disappeared underwater, I knew I wouldn't be able to rest until he returned, until I heard every detail of his reactions. As the first dive of our expedition, this one would certify officially that the journey was safe, that one of our crew had gone to the bottom and come back unharmed.

Seven hours later, Ralph emerged from the submersible with pilots P.H. Nargeolet and Pierre-Yves Le Bigot, bringing back with him the first artifacts in history to be secured from the *Titanic*.

Mesmerized, we watched the crew retrieve the bell, the same bell that *Titanic* lookouts Frederick Fleet and Reginald Lee had tolled in the crow's nest before reporting by ship's telephone of approaching collision. They had come on duty at 10:00 P.M. At eleven-thirty, just half an hour before they were due to be relieved, a fog had appeared. Fifty feet above the fo'c's'le deck, high in the crow's nest, Fleet cried, "Iceberg right ahead" and gave the bell three piercing rings.

Aside from the bell, the retrieval basket also carried breathtaking dinner plates—lapis lazuli blue, a rich royal blue enameled on the outside border with a gold scalloped trim. They resembled French Limoges china, but were actually English, made by Royal Crown Derby, supplier of china to the Royal Family.

"May I pick up one of the plates?" I asked.

"Yes," said P.H. Nargeolet. "But be very careful."

I lay my fingers on one of the plates. It was so delicate, yet it had survived seventy-five years at 12,500 feet. I couldn't help but wonder if this was John Jacob Astor's set of china, which he had brought on board to please his new wife Madeleine, the eighteen year old whose pregnancy had created such a scandal.

"Here is third class china," said Pierre-Yves. The stoneware was plain white with a white star in the center of a red flag, that appeared in the center of the plate—symbol of the White Star Line. I had read that there were nine different types of china on board, and a few of the millionaires had their own sets.

"Look," I shouted. "It's the megaphone—the one that belonged to E. J. Smith."

The megaphone, unlike the china, was too fragile to touch. It was instantly placed into water tanks; exposure to air would have completely destroyed it. Patrice Lardeau, the historian on board, suspected that the megaphone was made of aluminum, and aluminum is one of the most difficult items to restore.

There were more unexpected treasures—a sterling silver table bell, evidently from the first class dining room. Perhaps Molly (Margaret Tobin) Brown had used it to call the waiter for another order of wine. Or Isador and Ida Straus. We saw a silver chocolate pot, another silver tray, a bed lamp, a rubber linoleum tile which came from the third class smoking lounge. A bottle with a blue stopper, an egg plate, a ceramic floor tile, an oblong silver tray, a bottle of beer—there were 20,000 bottles of beer aboard the *Titanic*—and a bottle of wine, one of 1,500 bottles.

It wasn't only the artifacts; it was the ship itself, waiting to be seen and photographed on the bottom. All of us huddled together over the monitor in our little video room and studied the distinguishing characteristics of the legendary *Titanic*.

We were electrified by images of the bow, partially covered by sediment but still triumphantly visible. As the *Nautile* passed over the top of the bow, we could see the bower anchor. Known also as the central anchor, it was the next thing on the top of the deck. I knew from research that it weighed fifteen and a half tons and was so heavy it required twenty horses to pull it on its cart, from its original location to the ship.

The bower anchor was installed on the fo'c's'le deck, along with 1,050 feet of massive anchor chain. We saw the windlasses, huge vertical drums which rotate horizontally and function to wind in the enormous chains of the *Titanic's* anchors. We could also clearly see the bronze capstans and bollards, which were used for securing docking lines.

Even on a tiny video monitor, the colors were unforgettable. The rusticles weren't gray or dark black, but vividly red, gold and orange rust, hanging off the prow—just like icing falling over the side of a cake. We continued aft in a straight line and next saw the fallen foremast. The railings along the port and starboard side were basically unaltered; only a few places had collapsed. We saw the foremast holding the crow's nest which had fallen backwards during the sinking. This was where Frederick Fleet and Reginald Lee had originally sighted the iceberg.

Also clear were the cranes on the well deck that had been used to load cargo into the number one hatch, then hatch number two and number three. These cranes had lifted William Carter's red Renault so it could be shipped to America.

Then the bridge came into view, with the Officer's Quarters. The pilothouse itself was gone, but I could see the bronze telemotor, a stanchion which had originally held the ship's wheel that Captain Smith had commanded.

Just to either side, port and starboard, were the davits—on the starboard side for lifeboat Number One and on the port side for lifeboat Number Two.

We were fascinated by the sight of the empty hole for the number one funnel opening. All the funnels had been knocked off during the sinking. As soon as we passed over the funnel opening, we saw the square hole that was the skylight for the Marconi office, where Bride and Philips had tried in vain to reach the *Californian*. Immediately after that, the opening for the first class forward staircase presented itself. The skylight glass dome was no longer visible.

On the starboard side, a bit further in the distance, I could tell that the gymnasium roof had collapsed, and adjacent to that was the number two funnel opening, completely ripped open.

Soon after we passed over this funnel hole, the ship

collapsed downward, and it was clear where it had ripped apart at the surface; almost exactly at the third funnel.

With the first glimpse of artifacts, photographs and video, I felt myself catapulted back into another time and place. The sight of cups that had once touched the lips of deceased *Titanic* passengers brought their pain into sharp focus. I identified with their slowly heightening terror, as the truth of the damage became known, as so many of them began to grapple with the prospect of certain death in ice cold waters.

The mood of the crew reflected this realization. Immediately after seeing the artifacts and video, their normally ebullient, outgoing behavior turned quiet, pensive. The adventure of finding and filming such items as the bell and the megaphone acquired a new significance. One of them had tears in his eyes as he watched the bell being lifted in the retrieval basket, although he would have denied the tears if I had made the mistake of mentioning them.

Chapter 11

Mutiny

On August 2 I learned that Captain Nargeolet had lassoed the safe; he now expected his men to be paid a promised bonus. Shots of the safe on video whetted everyone's appetite. Photographed on video, it looked like a beautiful birthday present, with rope tied just the way one would wrap ribbon around a big box, surrounding it on all sides to make sure it didn't slip out when placed in the artifact basket.

There was only one major problem: the pilots had left the artifact basket, and the safe inside it, on the ocean floor.

"We're not bringing it up," they said, "until our bonus comes."

All the other artifacts scheduled for that day had been lifted, but the safe rested two and a half miles down.

No one knew what this safe contained, but for years stories had abounded of jewels and booty. When our television show was aired, we were going to open it, and its hoped-for secret treasures—diamonds, emeralds, currency—were to be revealed before a breathless world.

The promised bonus was a particular sore point.

"All this talk about a bonus," said Pierre-Yves Le Bigot. "They were weeks late on basic salary. Why should we believe they'll ever pay us this bonus?"

"Because they want this mission to go smoothly," I said. "They've spent years putting it together."

Tension had been palpable but relatively mild since our arrival. But when the plan became clear—when the Americans realized the French were holding their coveted prize for ransom—they exploded.

"You can't do that. It's blackmail," cried our investors. "We want the safe and we want it now."

But the French had the technology, they had the pilots, they had special expertise. And their attitude was explosively clear: Never.

On August 4, four days after our initial crisis in St. John's, Rowarch ordered all work to be stopped.

I had images of that safe, floating beneath the sea. Video we had seen made it a startling reality. It was like being sadistically teased: See, here it is. You can look at it, you can imagine its priceless treasures, but you can't go near it.

"Those Americans," said the French, and the words sounded like curses.

"Those goddamn French," said the Americans.

Every day without dives would cost $50,000.

The dining room, center of friendly talk, became as silent as a tomb. The French clustered together in their own corner, the Americans in theirs. Poisonous expressions were exchanged across the table.

"Maybe we'll untie the safe and let it float away," said one particularly hostile French crewman. "Goodbye jewels—goodbye millions."

I spoke to Captain Nargeolet, who I respected—who I knew was a fair man.

"What will happen if you don't get your pay and your bonus? Some people are so mad they're saying the French will destroy the safe."

He smiled. "Jennifer, we have too much respect for the *Titanic* and its history to ever destroy any part of it."

"If you leave it there, someone later on will bring it up," I said.

"We won't leave it there. We'll bring it up and keep it—and we'll make sure it never falls into the hands of the Americans."

"I'm American," I said, to another French crew member who kept expressing anti-American sentiment. "It's not the *Americans* who are doing this."

"They're only out for *dollars*. They're thinking about their television show, about their publicity."

I realized that the resentments went much deeper than financial compensation, and each day of silence and non-communication only fed the escalating rage. It was imperative to keep the lines open and after speaking to Ralph and the *Abeille* crew, we knew there was only one course—to be friendly and ignore the hostilities as much as possible. It wasn't easy; anger was thicker than a North Atlantic fog. The only thing that could have dissipated it—activity—was a closed option.

"I just want to dive," Randy said. "I don't care if we get the goddamn safe, or an egg plate or just a door knob."

Being on a ship is confining enough; there's no room to stretch out, run, break loose, especially for a self-named "King Kong" of 6'6". To live with enforced immobility is unbearable for a sailor, or for those on board any length of time. Arguments were always on the verge of erupting, because each side blamed the other.

The safe became alive to all of us on the *Nadir* and the *Abeille*, more than any other artifact. It became almost human. The situation was a perfect example of the power men held when they were in possession of the right technology. He who had the gold made the rules. We were impotent—video technicians, still photographers, cinematographers—whose function was to immortalize artifacts after their recovery. Without them, we had nothing to film, nothing to catalogue, nothing to organize.

Heavy swells added to the tension. A storm was brewing, thousands of miles away, just beginning to announce itself with rough waves and wind.

"It could be worse," said Ralph. "Remember that lunatic in Cozumel, coming at me with a knife. At least no one here is putting a knife in my back."

"Wait. If they don't send money soon, someone might."

The situation reached its height when the French announced they would be turning around and leaving the site.

I went to Rowarch with a plan, and found him pleasant and agreeable. He and I had gotten along well from the beginning, and he always listened to my suggestions.

"What I'm proposing," I began, "is that we continue work and bring up everything *except* the safe. Leave it there until you get your bonus. And when you're paid, you can hand it over."

He didn't like that phrase, I could tell. Emotionally, he resisted the idea of ever handing it over.

He shook his head emphatically. "No, either the bonus or nothing."

A few hours later I saw him again, and this time he promised to think it through and consult with Captain Deshommes, Captain Nargeolet and the others from the *Nadir*.

After the meeting I boarded the zodiac and went to the *Nadir*. They welcomed me and treated me warmly; no one, they explained, had any personal quarrel with me, and they didn't want to lose any more days.

"We believe you," said Captain Deshommes, when I guaranteed that the bonus money was on its way. The dives resumed. My first endeavor as liaison between French and Americans was a success.

But the safe remained on the ocean floor.

Chapter 12

Clash at Sea

Oddly enough, some of the Americans referred to me as "The Queen Bee", since the word Abeille meant 'bee' in English—implying that I was the one female supervising while they did the hard work. The French, however, considered chauvinistic by so many women, gave me all the respect I could possibly ask for. Captain Nargeolet, Captain of the *Nautile*, treated me as a complete equal.

Still, there was behavior that seemed harmless and well meant, but subtly emphasized differences. One obvious example was the zodiac incident which took place two days after we arrived at the site.

Zodiacs are gray rubber boats that can hold six people fully loaded. When zodiacs are inflated, the huge round tubes of rubber on the sides are a good two-and-one-half feet in diameter. On our zodiac, there was a forty horsepower outboard motor, and we had a second zodiac for backup.

Anybody who has ever watched a Jacques Cousteau special has seen the divers racing around in them at high speeds. We had our own zodiac captain, and since he zipped around in the lifeboats, he was named Captain Zozo, although his real name was Yves Cougoulic. Cougoulic, thirty-four, was tall, dark and looked like one of the three musketeers. Binoculars hung around his neck, so he could see details and possible dangers clearly. His mustache curled up at the ends, and he was extremely fair-skinned.

If he was out in the sun too much, Zozo's face turned bright, screaming red. He also had a tendency to blush easily, and it was hard to know if his scarlet color was provoked by emotions or nature.

The zodiacs were expected to transfer crew members back and forth between the *Abeille* and the *Nadir*, and they often did this in the roughest of weather. They functioned as seagoing shuttles, every morning and every night. It took two trips to carry over the crew and all the camera equipment to the *Nadir*.

Captain Zozo adored driving the zodiacs at full bore. I loved it too. When he would run the zodiacs at top speed, it was as joyous an experience as any roller coaster ride. There was a bond between us, because we both loved the feeling of high speed, the sensation of whitecaps hitting us in the face as we bounced over waves.

When we began, there were those on the *Abeille* that indulged in exaggerated and protective chivalry. They had no idea I was a sheriff, skydiver and scuba diver, or that I'd spent the last fifteen years of my career working with crews on ships. So the men tried to escort me all the way down the ladder, off the side of the *Abeille*. They wanted to hold my hand as I descended, afraid I might not be able to handle myself on the narrow rungs over an ocean that was generally turbulent and had high swells.

Having been on hundreds of boats, I tried to explain in my clumsy French that I was fine and leaped into the zodiac, anticipating a thrilling ride. I had been riding zodiacs since 1972, and yet the men's courtly, instinctive behavior continued, with offers of "Hold on to me, Jennifer," or "Be careful," even though I was maneuvering the rungs as capably as they were.

They meant well; some were honestly concerned. But I kept resisting their offers of help until finally, after several days, they got the message.

Never in all my oceangoing experiences was I part of a project that had so many captains.

With most expeditions, if you're on a ship and you say 'let's talk to the captain', you're talking to one individual and one only—the top dog. In our case, it was like a Hollywood film that has more producers than cast—a typical situation today. This was Hollywood's nautical equivalent. But as it developed, each captain actually had a specific and valuable service to contribute.

Captain Rowarch tried to clarify it for me.

"First of all," he pointed out, as I tried to get the players straight, "Louis Deshommes, also known as Loulou, is the *Operating* Captain of the Abeille—which means he pilots the ship, sets its course and is in charge of the actual maintenance and overall operation of the *Abeille*. Captain Clet is his counterpart on board the *Nadir*. He navigates the *Nadir* and also is in charge of its actual day to day operation."

Rowarch then got around to identifying his own position. "I'm the captain also on this ship, but I'm a captain who represents Taurus International, the people who leased these two ships, so it's up to me to make sure

that both of the other two captains carry out their responsibilities—as outlined in your contracts with Westgate and
Oceanic Research and Exploration."

I felt somewhat as if I had stumbled into a Jim
Carrey movie, but one produced in France.

"Is this clear?" he asked me.

Before I could answer, he went on.

"There are only two more captains," he joked,
stroking his silver mustache. "Captain Paul Henri
Nargeolet—P. H.—and he is in charge *specifically* of the
submersible *Nautile* and its operation. He has nothing to
do with the *Abeille* or the *Nadir*, only the *Nautile*. And
then—*last*—we have Captain Keranflech, who is the
supreme entity representing Ifremer. Ifremer stands for
Institution Francais Pour Recherche Exploration de la
Mer. Which means—the French Institution for Research
and Exploration of the Sea."

And Ifremer, he concluded, is subsidized by the
French Government. So any instructions which come from
the French Government or Ifremer must go through
Keranflech, and be transmitted to all the other captains."

The word 'chain of command' gained a new meaning, and I had a momentary fear that he would ask me to
repeat it. I felt like a waiter who had already rattled off the
specials, and dreaded being asked to repeat them again lest
he forget everything.

I had to know, "Is there anyplace the buck stops?
One ultimate supreme leader?"

He said, "That depends on who you ask. Since I'm
the one talking to you—it's me."

Personality conflicts are always bound to arise on a
ship. The best of friends can become mortal enemies by the

time a voyage is completed, and there have been many cases where people were tied up or incarcerated by captains to prevent murders—some of which do take place despite every effort to stop them. The first major personality conflict on the *Abeille* was between Peter, our photographer and Mark, our video technician.

I had the greatest respect for Peter's talent and I genuinely liked him as a person, but it was imperative that he find a way to get along with his assistant.

"You just don't understand what's going on," he told me, when I commented—as tactfully as I could—about the constant arguments. "It's Mark's attitude, not mine. He's not willing to take instructions from me, and I'm supposed to be his superior."

The quarrels continued. They constantly clashed over technical aspects. Mark and editor Joey Weiss had set up a certain type of time code system and Peter violently disagreed with their method. Time code is a procedure which editors utilize, in order to know exactly where the picture is at what second of the tape. It runs constantly at the bottom of the tape from the moment you start shooting till the instant you stop. The numbers appear in a band identifying hours, minutes, seconds and milliseconds. Even though these continuous figures are visually present when the tape is being shot, the editor has eliminated them when the final tapes are shown on television.

Peter and Mark were both extremely knowledgeable, technically. But both parties felt there was only one way—his way—and neither would concede the possibility of a gray area, nor that the other might have had a valid position. The big problem was that the disagreement had gone from abstract to personal.

Good-natured Randy, Peter's assistant, felt it

would work itself out, and Ralph insisted that there was no problem. I would have been happy to remove myself from the battle zone, but as Expedition Leader, I couldn't.

"Peter," I told him, one night in my cabin. "You're putting yourself in jeopardy. All this fighting will hurt the overall morale of the ship."

"Why don't you talk to Mark?"

"I have. I told him the same thing."

"Is there any complaint with my work?"

"No," I said. "That's just it. You're a fantastic cameraman and I don't want to lose either one of you."

I tried to warn him, not just as one professional to another, but as a friend.

Tension eased at mealtimes, when we enjoyed Camille's latest dishes—one day brochette of beef with bearnaise sauce, served with pommes frites, the next day salmon with hollandaise, and for dessert a chocolate fudge sundae. Sometimes these fantastic feasts didn't go down too well, especially when the boat swayed and the crew's stomachs lurched with it.

Everyone had ideas about what the prime focus of the dives should be.

"We've got to find the hole," said Ralph.

I disagreed. "No, the propellor's more important."

"We don't know if there *is* a hole," said Nargeolet.

"Then it's up to us to find out," Ralph insisted.

"Never mind the hole. Never mind the propellor. We still haven't been paid for the safe," said Captain Keranflech.

After that, everybody talked at once about the different goals—the Rubaiyat, one of the lifeboat davits, the valises.

"All this talk about a safe," said Rowarch. "Survivors claim it's empty."

"It better not be empty," I said. "Not after all this fighting about it."

From there we moved to the chief order of business, artifacts—and which ones were to be targeted and brought up from the ocean floor. Although my job, with Captain Nargeolet of the *Nautile*, was to make those choices and select the people for the daily dives, I found myself flooded again on all sides by varying opinions.

Even Joel had suggestions.

"As long as you're recovering artifacts," he wrote to me, "why not try to recover a musical instrument from the band?"

It was a haunting idea—to have one of the violins or cellos that the musicians had played during those last, hopeless hours on the *Titanic*.

His statement lingered with me, and that night I had a dream, in which Joel was one of the musicians on deck, playing the last, melancholy strains of *Autumn* and *Nearer My God To Thee*. When I woke up, I felt a cold chill at the thought of losing him. I understood dreams well enough to know that they weren't literal translations of thoughts, but representative of feelings. And my feelings were that I missed Joel, and dreaded losing him under any circumstances.

I called him ship to shore, and the sound of his voice reassured me. Everyday reality on land was reassuringly familiar: he had gone to a movie with Kevin, helped Brent with a term paper and written a new song for a children's television special entitled *The Original Top Ten*, an animated musical version of the Ten Commandments.

"And I hope you're obeying them all," I kidded him, "especially the one about 'thou shall not commit adultery.'"

"You have my word. And how's Ralph, by the way?"

"Don't worry," I told him. "There's no time for that kind of thing here. Everyone's too busy."

"No one's ever too busy for a little hanky panky," Joel laughed. "But I'll send you a copy of the song, to keep you on the straight and narrow. It's called 'Be Loyal To The One You Love.' Since it's a show for kids, we couldn't use that big bad word adultery."

"By the way," Joel said, before hanging up. "I'm sending you a little present. But you've got to promise me one thing. Don't open it up until you're on the submersible, going down to the *Titanic*. No matter how curious you get, once you receive the package, *don't open it.*"

"I promise," I said, but I couldn't help wondering what the mysterious package would contain.

Chapter 13

First Woman to the *Titanic*

As planner of the dive schedule, I had to be careful. My role was to choose *other* people to dive down to the wreck and relegate my own desires to the back burner. Day by day, I watched Ralph, Adam, Randy, Peter and Mark disappear from the ocean surface, dropping downward into history. How I wished I could join them. It was Captain P. H. Nargeolet who solved my dilemma by inviting me to make the 12,500 foot dive. P. H. knew how dedicated I was, and how much this dive meant to me, and he saved me the discomfort of asking and possibly being turned down.

Nargeolet was, and remains, one of the heroes of my life. Master submersible engineer, a blend of limitless courage, integrity and kindness, he represented the best that France—or anywhere else in the world—had to offer. All these qualities, combined with charm, dark good looks and a winning smile, added up to a prototype of what the modern-day adventurer should be—and the modern man.

"You are a *real* professional," he told me, and I

knew it was his highest compliment. I wanted, more than anything, to be regarded by these men as a professional—not somebody who did things well *for a woman*. A few days earlier, one of the crew had used that very phrase, and he had sincerely meant it. But phrases like that still drew a line between the achievements of men and women, implying that a man could do more, but women, after all, did have their abilities.

P. H. was completely different. He defied all clichés generally attributed to French men. He wasn't chauvinistic, he never said a patronizing word. He never said 'sweetheart' or 'honey', or explained things to me in a pleasantly tolerant way. It reminded me that there was no such thing as 'the French are like that,' 'the Americans are like this'—pigeonholing of groups and cultures was always inaccurate. What mattered in the end was the individual.

On the morning of August 9, I stood on the deck of the *Nadir*, waiting for word to begin. Due to a 'minor malfunction', the dive—originally scheduled for 6:00 AM—was now being delayed.

The delay gave me time to think, to dwell on the poignant history of the *Titanic* and to review in my mind that tragic phrase *If only*.

If only they hadn't called her unsinkable, which appeared in retrospect to tempt the fates; to "fly in the face of God," as survivor Eva Hurt had put it.

If only the ice warnings had been taken more seriously. On April 14, *Titanic's* wireless operators had received at least six messages which described the ice directly ahead.

Incredible as it now seemed, one message wasn't

posted on the bridge until five hours after it had been received.

The next message wasn't delivered to the captain for *fear of interrupting his dinner.*

Twenty ships had seen ice in the area, and some were forced to stop by gigantic icebergs. The mystery remains: why were these icebergs so extravagantly underestimated by men who should have known better?

Glacier icebergs are usually flat white in color. They can be dazzling white on occasion, when the right conditions of light reflect from air bubbles under the surface. Denser than the tabular icebergs specific to Antarctica, they resist weathering. Black icebergs are dark in color, their dark hues caused by embedded mud and stone, or because of final air expulsion as they melt.

The iceberg that shattered the *Titanic* was black, and no one spotted it until 500 yards away. Most Atlantic icebergs travel from Greenland. The largest one ever witnessed was 208 miles in length, and the majority of them are four-fifths beneath the sea.

Beyond the dismissal of iceberg danger was that most famous *if only*—the behavior of the British freighter *Californian* which, on the night of the disaster, was stopped in an ice flow and was only ten to twenty miles from the *Titanic*. While the great ship sank, the *Californian* sat, her captain and radio operator asleep.

If only they had been awake...

The sound of pilot Pierre-Yves' voice brought me back to the present. "Just a little while longer, Jennifer," he said. It had already been five hours, and now I was becoming alarmed. Would the dive be cancelled, and with it my one opportunity to see the lost liner?

Once again, I tried to occupy my mind by recalling the *Titanic's* history. I thought about the crew members of the *Californian*, who indicated they were in sight of the *Titanic* and witnessed its distress signals but ignored them. To this day, no one knows why.

So many things had gone wrong. The circumstances lent credence to the general feeling that the *Titanic's* demise was fated. Certainly an early 1898 novel by Morgan Robertson seemed to underscore this premise. The book concerned the story of a great ocean liner crossing the Atlantic on its maiden voyage, striking an iceberg on a cold April night and sinking. Robertson's description of the ship's size, location and sinking turned out to be an almost total duplicate of the incidents involved in the *Titanic* disaster, yet the book had been written 14 years before the *Titanic* went down. The name of the ship in Robertson's novel, incredibly, was *The Titan*, and the book itself was called *Wreck of the Titan*.

Once the *Titanic* struck an iceberg at 11:40 PM Sunday, April 14, 1912, and Captain E. J. Smith knew they had a maximum of two hours before it sank, the final *if only* appeared—if only there had been enough lifeboats to accommodate the 2,227 passengers on board. Instead, the lifeboats numbered only twenty—sixteen standard and four collapsible, deemed sufficient by the Board of Trade. Ironically Thomas Andrews, the designer of the *Titanic*, had originally submitted a plan for sixty-four lifeboats, but this was reduced to thirty-two, then to sixteen.

It was later determined that Andrews' original estimate was almost exactly on the mark—the *Titanic* would have needed sixty-three to rescue all the passengers.

The great ship sank at 2:20 A.M., Monday, April 15, 1912. It was a cruel fate for a boat described by her builders, Harland and Wolff, as the biggest, best and most secure vessel afloat. Her first class accommodations were the most luxurious ever installed on a ship of any size up to that date.

At 882 feet long and 92 feet wide, the *Titanic* was —at the time of her launching on May 31, 1911—the largest man-made object on the face of the earth to actually move. It was a triple-screw vessel, whose manganese-bronze center propellor was sixteen feet in diameter. The *Titanic* was powered by massive boilers and 159 furnaces that consumed 650 tons of coal per day.

Titanic's first class suites were the most palatial passenger accommodations of any liner ever built. In addition to elegant Louis XIV and Louis XVI style furniture in rare woods, the suites featured mahogany paneled walls, fireplaces and private baths with marble wash basins and cabinet showers.

The great ship also featured two "Millionaire suites," which cost $4,350 on that first voyage. That was for a one-way crossing of the Atlantic—the most ever charged for a cruise. In today's currency, the same ticket would cost approximately $80,000.

First class passengers enjoyed a fully equipped gymnasium with electrical camel ride, Turkish baths and a swimming pool.

Another element that made the *Titanic* story so legendary was the passenger list—a who's who of American business fortunes, adding up—in today's currency—to a net worth of a quarter of a billion American dollars.

Colonel and Mrs. John Jacob Astor were on their honeymoon when the calamity occurred. Also among the doomed magnates was Isador Straus, founder of Macy's, J. B. Thayer, President of the Pennsylvania Railroad; Mayor Archibald Butt, Aide to President Taft, Benjamin Guggenheim, the noted mining tycoon; Washington Dodge, head of the wealthy American banking family, Margaret Tobin Brown, million-airess from Denver and later the heroine of the Broadway musical, "The Unsinkable Molly Brown."

One of the survivors, a Mrs. Charlotte Cardeza of Philadelphia, listed among her lost belongings fourteen trunks, four suitcases, three crates and a medicine chest, all of which contained seventy dresses, ten fur coats and ninety-one pairs of gloves. William Carter, a man from Philadelphia, listed equally devastating losses: a new red Renault automobile valued at $5,000.00, sixty shirts, fif-teen pairs of shoes, two sets of white tails formal wear and twenty-four polo sticks.

Captain E. J. Smith, the man entrusted with the safety of so many immensely wealthy passengers, had never been given this kind of responsibility before but at 62 years of age, having accumulated twenty-five years of experience with the White Star Line, he appeared totally up to the task. During the two hours and forty minutes that the ship was sinking, the luckless Captain walked the decks of the ship, encouraging his men to stay at their posts and keep the ship's power and lights on, and to say goodbye.

Captain Smith's reputation later suffered a mortal blow. Investigations accused him of ignoring the ice warn-ings so he might set a Trans-Atlantic speed record. But the major blame was placed at the feet of Bruce Ismay, man-ager of the White Star Line. It was Ismay's decision to reduce the number of lifeboats and binoculars, so that more money could be lavished on needless luxuries. He was also the one who urged Captain Smith to continue at high speed despite the known threat of icebergs. As a result, 1,522 perished of the 2,227 passengers and crew, and the total number of survivors was only 705. As I waited for my rendezvous with history, I envisioned it all: the gleaming iceberg looming, the passengers dancing, the crash, the orchestra playing its final melody as the ship went down. Now I was about to see what I had for so long dreamed.

At 2:35 PM, having been assured by our technicians that the submersible was in fine working order, I began my descent to the *Titanic*.

Armed with camera, tape recorder and the small package Joel had given me, dressed in a blue fireproof suit, I crawled through the sub into a tiny hatch. Our twenty million dollar submersible, was ready to proceed.

I climbed in first; Pierre-Yves followed. The pilot, P.H. Nargeolet, remained seated in the opened hatch until the sub moved aft to the launch crane.

Soon we were at the launch, getting ready to take off. I could see Peter with his camera, shooting the sub from above.

The *Nautile* is kept in a protective hanger in the middle of the ship on a special launch/recovery wagon which uses tracks and a huge chain drive to move it to the fantail. Just before it starts to move, one of the support divers climbs aboard. It's his job to hook up a huge cable attached to the "A" frame, which will lift it into the air, and then to disconnect it and the various launching lines once it's in the water.

This diver in black wetsuit rides atop the *Nautile* as it lifts into the air. It's an exhilarating moment, seeing him astride on a huge, seaworthy bucking bronco thirty feet in the air, offering a kiss in the air, a "Bonne chance, Jennifer."

Once the *Nautile* is secured to the "A frame" the launch director gives the pilot an okay sign and he climbs down into the sub, closing the hatch. Then the A-frame lifts our eighteen and one-half ton sub up high over the fantail and drops us into the water.

For a brief moment I could see some of the crew staring from the stern and the realization hit: there was no turning back. Within seconds after being dropped into the water, the divers removed the tow line and completed a final inspection. I caught one last look at the divers outside the hole, peering in, making funny, cartoonish faces at me. They made a signal on the other side of the portholes that everything was A-OK. At that point, the descent began as the pilot released the air from the buoyancy tanks.

The divers traveled with the sub about one hundred feet from the surface, and then waved their goodbye, and the ocean suddenly went through a kaleidoscopic change of colors—from intense turquoise to royal blue, dark Navy and finally, total black.

Nautile is constructed to operate safely for up to 130 hours. The dives are designed to last from eight to twelve hours. Moved by one axial motor, two vertical thrusters and a lateral thruster, *Nautile's* top speed is 2.5 knots, and its underwater range at one knot is fifteen miles. Power is supplied by batteries of fifty kilowatts. In addition to sophisticated communication systems, the *Nautile* always carries scanning sonar, a DXC 3000 TV camera, two still cameras and six external lights.

Contributing to the lack of space was equipment on every side—two monitors to my right and a monitor on my left; underwater navigation equipment for the interrogation of the acoustic transponders, which was used to

The *Abeille*, as seen from its sister ship, The *Nadir*. The *Abeille* was Jennifer's home at sea for eight weeks, and was sturdy enough to weather two hurricanes.

Submersible pilot Pierre-Yves Le Bigot sitting on top of Ifremer's eighteen and a half ton, twenty million dollar miracle machine, the *Nautile*.

Putting on this survival suit was part of mandatory life boat training aboard the *Abeille*. Jennifer is smiling because she accomplished this awkward and difficult feat in two minutes.

This silver-plated chocolate pot held by Jennifer was once used in the first class dining room.

Ralph and Jennifer, holding the bell that *Titanic's* Frederick Fleet rang three times to signal disaster.

Titanic first class china made by Royal Crown Derby. This fragile piece miraculously withstood the sinking.

Inside the *Nautile*, which has only a six foot diameter for three people and stacked top to bottom with monitors and video equipment. It was the nautical equivalent of a space capsule.

Jennifer standing next to the official board on the *Nadir*, showing the date and location of her dive.

Yann Keranflech, Yvon Rowarch and Paul Henri Nargeolet, Jennifer's three captains, congratulate her after her dive.

When Jennifer Carter emerged from the submersible after her dive to the *Titanic*, she was pelted with beer, sawdust, kitchen scraps and eggs – an initiation rite that seemed to her barbaric, but made her a part of the Ifremer team.

The starboard propeller lies half buried on the ocean floor.

Photo: A Scene from the IMAX® Film *Titanica*, a feature-length adventure. ©Imax Corporation/Undersea Imaging International, Inc. & TMP (1991) I Limited Partnership

The bottom portion of the telegraph stanchion, with a brittle starfish draped over the top. It offers a haunting juxtaposition of metal and marine life.

Photo: Emory Kristof

Photo: Ralph White

The bow of the *RMS Titanic*, with rusticles flowing off it and sediment covering the bottom two-thirds.

Photo: Ralph White

Aluminum megaphone that was used by Captain Smith. Aluminum is one of the most difficult substances to restore.

A woman's leather shoe lies as a solemn reminder of the lives lost.

An engine telegraph lies on its side in the debris field; its final position is marked "All Stop."

A mysterious hole on the starboard side of the bow. Some experts feel it is the result of an explosion, caused by air pressure when the ship hit bottom.

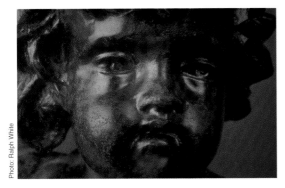

Few artifacts made as much of an impression as the cherub, which once stood proudly at the bottom of the aft Grand Staircase.

This vase with dragon heads on the handles was once in the First Class Lounge. It was recovered during Jennifer Carter's dive.

Jennifer Carter holding a Baccharat crystal decanter. Her index finger is pointing to the White Star Logo.

An EDF representative measures sterling silver tray that was found shiny and uncorroded. EDF – Electricite de France – was in charge of cataloging and restoring all artifacts retrieved from the *Titanic* debris field.

Producer Doug Llewelyn and Jennifer Carter, discussing whether to cancel a dive due to an upcoming storm.

With winds over 100 mph and waves over 70 feet high, Hurricane Arlene posed a near-lethal threat to the expedition, the ship and the safety of the crew.

A testament to the technological mastery and human skill displayed by the Ifremer pilots who operated the robot-like arms which lassoed the safe and brought it to the surface.

The *Titanic* safe became an object of intense national fascination, as well as an issue that divided French and Americans. Here P.H. Nargeolet is seen bringing the retrieval basket on board containing this key item.

The heatedly sought after safe was almost empty. Those on the 1987 expedition believe that the contents of the safe were emptied into this valise.

Some of the jewelry that was discovered included diamond and onyx cuff links, watches, stickpins, a sapphire and diamond ring as well as a small silver box.

calculate the submersible's position without the intervention of the *Nadir*; data acquisition equipment, including a set of sensors used to record altitude, pressure, temperature, heading, time and speed. The sensors were connected to a data acquisition unit which stored the data for subsequent analysis. There was also equipment for the acoustic transmission of television pictures, a system using acoustic waves for image transmission.

The interior cockpit was small, but nothing had prepared me for how claustrophobic it actually was. I struggled to find a comfortable position. There was a small pad beneath me, but it was so thin it didn't keep the metal bar that runs across the bottom of the sub from pressing painfully at my body. All the instrument panels were so close to my arms and feet that I worried if one move in the wrong direction would inadvertently shut down the controls of the re-breather apparatus which provided our air life support system.

Pierre-Yves, the co-pilot, was able to view a video of everything happening outside from a monitor in front of him. There were other monitors where he and P.H. could see the stills and the DXC 3000 camera. *Nautile* reminded me of being inside a space capsule. I had enjoyed that opportunity while filming at NASA for WQED, while in the planning stages of shooting a segment for one of my productions, *The Oceans,* part of a series called *Planet Earth.* On that occasion, it was brought forcefully home to me that three quarters of the planet is water, and how extraordinarily little we know about what lies beneath our vast seas. Now I was gaining some of the elusive knowledge about life that existed at these unexplored depths.

I kept watching the monitor that displayed our

depth, and as we passed 328 feet, I thought of the Frenchman Jacques Mayol, an amazing diver who I had met working on *Mysteries of the Sea*. We had had footage of him diving to that depth, in a breath-hold dive off the island of Elba which had lasted three minutes and forty seconds, an extraordinary feat that took years of training. At that same depth, Jim Jarratt had located the Lusitania, wearing an 800 pound armored suit—called "The Iron Man" at the time, and later updated, redesigned and named the Jim Suit after Jarratt.

Then we passed 728 feet. We were moving at one hundred feet a minute, and I remembered the record that the world-renowned diver Hans Keller of Switzerland and writer Kenneth MacLeish had made in Lake Maggiore. Most scuba divers keep at depths of no more than 120 feet, occasionally venturing to 200. It was remarkable to me how much further we could go with a submersible.

At 1,250 feet, one of my idols, Dr. Sylvia Earle, the celebrated aquanaut and scientist, came to mind. In *Mysteries of the Sea,* she had made a dive off Makapuu Point in Hawaii, in a Jim suit—a bulky, bulbous suit of armor not designed for her 110 pound weight. She was able to walk inside this tethered one-atmosphere suit on the ocean floor and explore marine life.

At 1,700 feet, we passed the distance where Comex divers had gone, setting records for their deepest working saturation dives. We were also well beyond the estimated depths of nuclear submarines.

By 3,028 feet, we had reached the depth achieved by zoologist William Beebe and engineer Otis Barton, known as the fathers of submersibles. I had read Beebe's book, *Half Mile Down,* many times, and treasured his quote about the oceans: "The only other place comparable to these marvelous nether regions must surely be naked space itself, out far beyond atmosphere, between the stars... where the blackness of space, the shining planets, comets, suns and stars must really be closely akin to the world of life as it appears to the eyes of an odd human being in the open sea, half a mile down."

I understood just how Beebe felt. I, too, felt like a pioneer, an explorer in new and uncharted territory.

At 8,040 feet, we were at the depth where the Bathyscaph Trieste had explored the site of a sunken nuclear powered sub, the Thresher.

Since we were floating through darkness, I decided it was time to open Joel's mysterious package.

Unwrapping the envelope, I found a cassette, with just the words "I love you" written on it. I slipped the cassette into my tape recorder, and heard his voice speaking in the tiny enclosure.

I can't say I wish I was with you, but I want you to know I admire your courage and your magnificent spirit of adventure. It was at three in the morning—God, I thought only advanced neurotics did things like that—when this came to me, and it seemed to express how much I love you and how privileged I feel that you're my wife. It's a part of a whole symphonic piece I've written, called "Titanic Adventure" but for now you'll have to settle for just me playing it on the piano.

The concerto Joel called *Titanic Adventure* came on—a theme he had composed. As it unfolded, chills ran through me. The music was simple, yet it conveyed tenderness and passion. Joel was articulate, but his true language was the music he created. I listened to the theme twice more, then removed my earphones so P. H. and Pierre-Yves could hear it.

"Ah, so romantic," said P. H. "Love music in a submersible."

"Sounds like a good title for an album," said Pierre-
Yves. "Much better than 'We All Live in a Yellow Submarine.'"

Although Joel's music had warmed my heart, my
heart was the only warm thing in the now-freezing sub.
There's no heating or air-conditioning inside the *Nautile*,
so when you're at the surface, it can be eighty to ninety
degrees, with eighty percent humidity, but as soon as you
drop to the bottom, the temperature plummets down to
thirty-two degrees.

As we descended, I felt no sensation of movement,
no sense of falling, just stillness, being completely still in
the water. Only the reading on the monitors testified to any
movement at all.

It was beginning to grow colder, and I felt the onset
of a slight headache. I still had difficulty moving my body
anyplace where it didn't hit hard metal. Then I shivered
when I made the mistake of resting my head right up against
the edge of the porthole, which was icy Titanium steel.

A loud alarm sounded, and I jumped in shock, trying to see what had happened. P. H., noticing the fear in my
eyes, quickly explained that there was no leak and no
change of pressure. *Nautile* was just letting us know that
we had almost reached the bottom, that we were about a
thousand feet from our goal, and almost one league
beneath the bottom of the sea.

In that brief moment I realized that even though
Jules Verne was a prophet—and my earliest hero—there
was actually no place at the bottom of the sea that was
20,000 leagues, let alone twenty. The deepest was two.

Suddenly the lights flashed on, all 4,000 watts of

them, and it seemed as though the *Titanic* had appeared with blazing clarity in her own swimming pool. Instead of the murky, mysterious remains I had expected, the dull shades of black, gray and brown, details and colors of the ship were brilliantly clear, red, orange, gold, green and many different shades of blue.

I know you'll find it for me. I know you'll see it. The words of survivor Edwina Troutt MacKenzie played in my mind, like a distant music box. *I don't know if I'll be alive by then. I hope I am.*

P. H. surprised me by maneuvering the submersible to the area of the stern lights. We were a short distance from the starboard propellor.

"Look, Jennifer," he said.

This was his gift to me, and I knew the significance of his gesture. It wasn't just that he had made me the first woman to see the *Titanic*; but we were the first people to see the propellor of this great ship.

I knew from Bob Ballard's book, *Discovery of the Titanic* that his expedition had never been able to view the propellor, and when Ralph, Randy, Peter and Adam had made their dives, they hadn't dived in this area. Up to now, we had been concentrating on the bow.

Tears came to my eyes. Well, Joel, I made it. Kevin, Brent and Derek, I know you'd be as thrilled as I am if you were here. Then, after so many years, I thought of my long dead father. I knew he would have loved diving in this submersible, and as an engineer, he would have appreciated the technological expertise utilized to develop such a remarkable mechanism. I think, if he had been alive, he would even have been proud of me for accomplishing it.

Seeing the ship up close brought the reality of lost lives into sharper focus. The thought of the lives of those in first class, in steerage, as well as the cooks, carpenters, stokers and stewards. I envisioned the tragic third class passenger at the piano in the steerage dining room, singing an Irish lullaby as the water began rising around her.

I could envision the lifeboats with 473 empty seats rowing off from the ship, leaving behind to die those that could have been saved. I wanted to cry again for the lost children and the eighty-one third class women that perished, all because those belonging to the upper tiers of society felt their wealth and privilege came directly from God, rendering them superior and more worthy.

I pulled myself out of my thoughts to concentrate once again on the mission and to witness Robin's baptism. Robin is an ROV (Remote Operated Vehicle), a small plastic box-like structure with eyes that are powerful lights and a video camera that taped everything it saw. It was remotely controlled from the inside of the *Nautile* by the pilot operating a joystick, and attached to the *Nautile* by a long umbilical cord. The Robin was essentially a robot, just like in the movie *2001*, small enough to enter the *Titanic* and detect places I could never possibly go, view things I could never possibly see.

Robin is equipped with high resolution television cameras and still photographic equipment. Because of its size—two feet long, about two and one-third feet wide and just under two feet high—it fits easily into small spaces to photograph them, such as down the cargo hold. It's similar in concept to the J.J., the ROV used by Bob Ballard in his 1985 expedition.

We were employing it to maneuver in and around the propellor, to take shots of the propellor from all angles. The umbilical cord could extend to 230 feet, and the Robin had its own four oil filled electrical thrusters, each with a five kilogram thrust. There were three lights on the Robin in front: one 100 watt quartz iodide and two 250 watt quartz iodide. These supplied the light for a color low light television camera and two black and white still picture cameras. It also had a flashhead, and traveled at a speed of one knot.

The Robin's home was at the lower front end of the *Nautile,* underneath the portholes. It took the place of the sample recovery basket when a dive needing the Robin was planned. P.H. had spent considerable time working with this miraculous instrument, testing it out on its debut dive, sending it out the full length of its 230 feet. The umbilical cord coiled like a yellow snake as it unfolded, while the Robin photographed the stern area around the propellor with video and still cameras. Then P. H. turned the Robin 180 degrees around and took video and stills of our submersible. It was strange to have this robot photographer filming us, documenting our experience on the bottom.

Then, without warning, disaster loomed. As we moved in for a close-up of the propellor, rusty tentacles reached out to envelop the *Nautile.* I saw that we were stuck underneath the twisted remains of the stern. No one breathed. P.H., Pierre-Yves and I knew that a move in any direction could seriously damage the craft. And yet, if we didn't attempt to free ourselves from the overhang, we would be trapped with a rapidly diminishing air supply. Rescue, as I had been told when signing a myriad of release forms, was impossible. Any submersible capable of joining the *Nautile* at this depth was more than seven days away.

P.H. and Pierre-Yves transmitted the situation to Captain Keranflech on the surface. It was startlingly clear and eerie to hear every word Captain Keranflech was saying, even though we were two and a half miles down. With his input and the little time we had to evaluate the risks, it was decided to make a lateral move, operating the thrusters at full bore. The lights blinked off ; a fraction of a second later they flashed on again.

As I tensed up, fully aware of the critical danger, P. H. guided the sub with excruciating care, skillfully extricating us from the deadly overhang. Endless minutes later, the sub escaped into clear, unobstructed waters.

Nobody acknowledged out loud what a close call it had been, but I knew how near I had come to sharing a watery grave with the ill-fated *Titanic* passengers.

After finishing, P. H. pulled the robot back into its little house beneath us. It was time for us to tour the *Titanic*. P. H. lifted the sub off the bottom, and maneuvered it over and around every single portion of the stern. I was able to see the crusted four story high boilers and the immense variety of sea life that dotted the ship. Snow-white anemones and galatea crabs crawled out of little holes, their miniature homes inside the ship. Here and there an alabaster starfish, a deep sea variety known as brittle stars which had long spindly arms, crawled into view.

With the exception of the four story high boilers, recognizable to me through old Harland and Wolff archival prints, nothing else was clear; the stern was a twisted, unrecognizable mass. It looked like a war zone. The metal was so distorted and grotesque it appeared as though devastating explosives had been set off, creating untold destruction and cutting the ship in half.

The sight of anemones and crabs was an incongruous contrast to the shambles of the stern—a shocking contrast between life and death.

Because of my scuba diving background and the

undersea films I had produced, I had an insatiable curiosity about the ocean creatures that inhabited this surreal world, creatures that managed to survive at such bone-crushing depths.

We were now into the debris field, where we were planning to recover certain items. My overwhelming first impression was of a vast, desert-like expanse between the stern and the bow, unique because of pitch black coal strewn all across it. Over 3,000 tons of coal had been used to fuel the ship, and since it took 650 tons a day, most of the last day's coal was there.

Singular pink stems of coral stuck from pieces of coal. They were spiny corals and the effect was somewhat like a quill pen in an undersea desk set. The corals reminded me instantly of Dr. Sylvia Earle's observations, when she made her Jim suit dive off the coast of Hawaii. I had followed her conservation efforts and dives in various types of submersibles. Sylvia had described this kind of coral, some of which grew to three feet tall.

Pieces of porcelain appeared. Then a broken plate from third class.

I saw the beautiful curlicue shapes of a cast iron deck bench, but the wooden bench portion had totally disappeared, feasted on by wood boring molluscs. These molluscs had eaten away most of the wood on the ship, including carved paneling, luxurious wood furniture and the staircase. The fish and the crabs ate the molluscs in this underwater cycle; the only wood that remained seemed to be teak, owing to its density. Objects such as china, crystal, silver or brass—all materials capable of withstanding enormous pressure—also remained.

More marine life sprang into sight—grenadier fish—sometimes known as ratfish—more anemones, crabs

with antennae twice the length of their bodies, their eyes
beady and pink. The large majority of marine life looked
albino, as though the depths had washed their color away.
One exception was a large collection of blood-red shrimp,
a color I had never seen before.

I knew that at such extreme depths, sea life existed
in great quantities around deep sea vents; but I wasn't prepared for such a distant geological area to be the spawning
ground for this infinite variety of marine life.

Bedsprings and bottles, chamber pots and china—
the contrast was bizarre and beautiful. I caught a glimpse
of a sterling silver platter, the glitter of twisted gold-plated
chandelier fixtures, the glow of lovely cut crystal decanters.
We picked up two of the gold-plated lamp fixtures, the
chamber pot, a few of the wine bottles with corks still in
them, a silver gravy server, a copper stockpot, a teapot and
a chocolate pot, and placed them inside the recovery basket close by. We secured a beautiful blue and white plate
with flowers in a vine pattern decorating the outside rim.
It was particularly entrancing to me because I had a collection of blue and white china at home, and this plate
reminded me of my own cherished treasures.

We picked up a burnt sienna vase with dragon handles that may have come out of the first class lounge.

Even though it seemed as though we had just
reached the bottom, many hours had passed, and I asked
P.H., "is it possible to see the bow before we have to return
to the surface?" He nodded. An expert at piloting, he
maneuvered the sub from the debris field down the starboard side, where the rusticles hung. Thin orange-red icicles of rust, they reminded me of contemporary sculptures
in the Museum of Modern Art, flowing tentacles extending
great lengths along the edges of portholes, windows and

over the edges of the ship. Peering again at them more closely, they looked similar to the stalactites I had seen while cave diving in Bermuda.

The legendary ship was adorned like a Christmas tree covered with icicles. Orange icicles hung everywhere, dripping down. Yellow silt covered some of the rusticles.

Captain Rowarch was right, I thought. *You don't care about the cold, you don't care about the lack of food, you don't care about anything because being on the bottom is so fascinating that every other thought vanishes, every memory fades into the distance.*

By this time I had been on the ocean floor for seven hours, so busy I hadn't noticed that tiny drops of moisture caused by the condensation of our breath were now running like rain water on the sub's interior surface.

The batteries were spent. It was time to go back.

Inside the sub, as we ascended, Pierre-Yves turned off the lights, and we began viewing the video tapes. We saw the material that was taken on the bottom by the DXC camera and then looked at what the Robin had recorded. P. H. and Pierre-Yves filled out the report. As we watched the tapes, reality hit me: I had done it. My childhood dreams, my lifelong obsession with the sea had brought me to the pinnacle. I had seen the *Titanic*. Never I had felt so exhilarated.

Back above water, I climbed from the submersible onto the gantry and was welcomed with a cry, "Here she comes... the first woman to dive the *Titanic*." All the French captains were at the top to meet me, each one congratulating, hugging and kissing me on both cheeks. They shouted, "Jenn-ee-fer... Jenn-ee-fer." Before I could revel in the compliment, I was forced to endure a rite of passage. Condoms dangled from the ceiling, and I had to bite into them. One was filled with milk, the other with wine, and one with beer. As I completed this ritual, the cheers became louder. Then, as I descended the steep ladder from the gantry, the final shock came—a huge bucket filled with a combination of beer, eggs, sawdust and coffee grounds with kitchen scraps thrown in was dumped over my head.

Gooey, foul-smelling liquid was raining in my eyes, streaming down my cheeks.

When Keranflech, Rowarch, Ralph and Nargeolet cracked open eggs on my head, I didn't flinch; I knew this was an initiation ceremony, a rite which proclaimed me "one of the crew," an insider, one of the group. Since I could barely see, Ralph took a hose with a high-powered nozzle on it and squirted it at my head until some of the bilge was washed off.

Nargeolet then drew out a long, sharp diving knife and slashed open a bottle of vintage Mumm's Cordon Rouge champagne. The captains surrounded me and they all raised glasses in a toast. I toasted them in return. They were the finest group of men I'd ever worked with, the finest crew I'd ever met. I concluded with a toast to the French men, thanking them for making it possible for an American woman to be the first to dive down and see the legendary ship.

I thought the initiation was concluded, as we stood around laughing on the stern. But Pierre-Yves suddenly grabbed Nargeolet, dragging him, pushing him off the stern into the water. Everyone in the crew laughed hysterically at this last event. Then someone grabbed me and hurled me off into the water. I joined the captain in the frigid North Atlantic.

As I came to the surface, I heard hooting and hollering. I was breathless and dazed by my baptism, but relieved when they quickly fished me out and lifted me into a lifeboat.

The next day I received a fax from my employers, Llewelyn and Joslyn:

Congratulations from all your friends at Westgate Productions on being the first woman to dive the wreck of the R.M.S. Titanic. We are very proud of you and there is champagne awaiting your return.

I had had enough champagne to sink the *Abeille* and *Nadir* combined, but I would have felt just as elated if I had been cold sober. Suddenly I remembered Edwina's voice.

When you find it, I want to see the pictures. If I'm alive, will you bring them to me?

How I would have loved to bring our photographs and video back to Edwina. I knew that her belief in this day had sustained her and kept her alive for so long. However, she had finally passed away on December 3, 1984, after hanging on past her one hundredth birthday. All I could do was whisper, "Today was for you," and hope—wherever she was—that she could hear me.

Chapter 14

Hurricane Hell

Although human beings and the sea are natural allies, they're natural enemies too. They share a deep but perilously ambivalent love that caresses, enervates, and sometimes kills. Hurricanes at sea are the most negative and dangerous expression of that ambivalence.

Hurricane season begins on June 1 and ends in November, but hurricane activity reaches its full, ferocious height in September. August rarely equals September's howling fury, but a hurricane at that time can still bear down violently and claim a devastating toll in property and human lives.

Damage done by wind rises with the square of the wind velocity, so a seventy-five mph wind has a 2.25 greater potential for destruction than one measuring fifty mph. What distinguishes a storm from a hurricane is determined by the speed of these winds. Once they reach seventy-four mph, the storm attains hurricane proportions, although seventy-four mph is only a stage one according to the Saffir-Simpson Hurricane Damage Potential scale established in 1971. Stage two has a range of 96-110 mph, stage three escalates from 111 to 130, and stage four—131 to 155—is as deadly as most hurricanes ever become. There are stage fives, but the United States has only endured two of these killer storms in the twentieth century. Their mad, malevolent power has been likened in strength to a dozen atomic bombs.

When Hurricane Arlene began dropping dangerous hints of the disaster to come, I still had the blessed protection of innocence. I had encountered a terrifying storm in Cozumel, fifteen years before, and had considered it as shatteringly powerful as any I'd ever experience in the future. The Cozumel storm lasted twelve hours and my comment to Ralph after the screaming winds had subsided was, "Well, tell me that's not the worst thing you've ever been through."

"I *could* tell you that," Ralph said to me, as rain splashed noisily on the windows of our hotel room, "but I'd be lying. There's worse. Much worse."

I didn't know that some hurricanes last for twenty-eight days, and they can dump forty-three inches of rain.

There was no indication that August 13 would bring more than the typical, sporadic rain and wind to which we had all grown accustomed. The sky, in fact, was clear that day, the sun uncharacteristically bright. Only strong winds rocking the *Abeille* contradicted this benign image.

"I don't think we'll be diving tomorrow," Ralph said offhandedly.

"That won't make Westgate too happy," I said, anticipating their irritation if we lost time.

"It won't make them too happy if we have an accident and people die."

"No one's dying," said Peter. "Look at the sun."

Randy agreed. "You could go surfing by that sun."

"Ralph's exaggerating again," Adam chimed in.

We were all so sure of ourselves, and so sure that Ralph was being melodramatic, that the first sharp, choppy waves took us by surprise.

Then, as if on cue, rain started to fall, and the sun vanished. Clouds blew in so quickly, they seemed to swallow the sun up whole.

I still felt confident that the storm would exhaust itself in a short while. There was nothing particularly threatening yet about the rain. We had been experiencing heavy swells since leaving St. John's, and the ship had been rocking heavily back and forth since the crew boarded it.

However, by early next morning, as the *Nautile* was being prepared for launching, Captain Nargeolet came to me and reluctantly announced that the day's dive was being cancelled.

"We have to be ready when the storm attacks," Nargeolet said, and his words brought an ominous, unsettling vision. This imagery seemed to foreshadow a contest between two warring factions, the ship and the storm, readying themselves for battle.

At first the crew expressed more relief that the dive was cancelled than anxiety about an oncoming hurricane. In our race to acquire as many artifacts as possible and assemble as much film footage, no one had been getting enough sleep.

"This might be a good chance to write a letter home," I said. Randy and Adam agreed and we all went to our cabins.

With the first words on my stationary, "Dear Joel" my hand slid across the paper and the pen made a gashing, crooked line on the page. I started again:

The winds are kicking up. They say we're in for a hurricane.

The erratic motion of the ship made it difficult for me to keep writing.

Then the *Abeille* began to shake like a toy boat on the nose of a sea monster. By afternoon, the gusts were up to 68 mph, and word from the wheelhouse confirmed what everyone suspected: It was going to be a big one.

Call it temporary insanity, curiosity or my propensity for flinging myself into the center of the action, I raced to the portside with my Nikon and my video camera. The portside was directly in front of my cabin and totally exposed to the elements. Mammoth waves that seemed the height of office buildings were flinging themselves at the sky. I wanted to capture those towers of white spray on film. My adrenaline was pumping at the prospect of recording each detail of this experience.

I was wearing a yellow rubber slicker with a hood, white rubber boots that came up to my knees and a pair of jeans. I stationed myself with my legs wide apart to insure my stance. But the hammering winds were brutal, the waves increasingly mountainous, and the gale literally knocked me over as I lurched to port, sending me slipping across a drenched, slick deck. I reached out, realizing in that second that if I didn't grab hold of something, I would slide straight overboard.

Frighteningly close to falling off the side into the angry sea, I managed to pick myself up and grasp for a railing, Christian, the first mate, saw me struggling to recover my balance and force myself upright. He had just come from his cabin, on the way to relieve Captain Louis Deshommes, who had finished night duty.

He pulled me to my feet, put a line around my waist—fastening the other end to himself—and in his gruff, Bogart manner, the manner he adopted to cover his concern—he said, "You must swear to me you will never, *ever* do this again. You don't know how dangerous it is. And never be outside without someone to accompany you to and from your cabin when there's a storm this bad. I know storms after fifteen years at sea, and this one's vicious—it's coming on fast."

Christian accompanied me to my cabin and waited while I strapped on an orange rubber life vest, the vest we were all required to wear in stormy weather, and I followed him to the wheelhouse. His speech became quicker, more tense, as he told me of his proposed navigation plan.

"When you reach hurricane level, you have to position the ship directly into the wind and the waves. If the ship broaches to, and lies broadside to the waves, that's when you can be flipped over completely and sink. All ships have a certain amount of roll from which they can't recover. The wider they are, and the lower to the ocean, the more stable. Actually, the *Abeille*'s better in a storm than the *Nadir*. We're forty-four feet wide, she's thirty-nine. But even an ocean liner can be swamped by a rogue wave. Did you know that the Queen Mary nearly capsized not far from this area, when a wave hit her wheelhouse windows?"

"Then why am I standing in front of the wheelhouse windows?" I joked.

"Don't worry. Our windows were replaced and reinforced just a year ago. And remember, this ship is designed for the North Sea, and that's even worse than the North Atlantic."

I decided, before the storm reached maximum turbulence, that it was best to telex Westgate; besides, it would keep my mind off the roaring waves that were pounding us. I sat in the chair, in front of the *Abeille*'s old-fashioned telex machine. It reminded me of an ancient underwood typewriter that my grandmother had once had. This machine wasn't nearly as easy to transmit on as the INMARSAT satellite machine utilized by the *Nadir*. Their system had a computer, keyboard and monitor, where you could compose your text, and a separate fax machine to send it on. It was easy to operate, compared to the *Abeille*'s antiquated setup.

Nadir's INMARSAT also allowed us to telephone directly to land, an ability lacking on this ship.

Every five to ten seconds, the *Abeille* would roll, first to port—causing my chair to slide all the way over to the extreme end of the wheelhouse—then, moments later, it would slide all the way back to my position on the starboard side in front of the machine. At first, Christian laughed at my plight and I shared the laughter; but as the winds gained force, they became so violent that my chair was knocked over repeatedly. I was thrown to the floor, along with my notebook containing the text I was struggling to transmit—four times before I decided to cut short this insane attempt.

I left them with a line saying it would be impossible to reach us, since we would not be able to make it to the *Nadir* to transmit our daily faxes. I also said they couldn't reach us by telex.

What is it about Captains and First Mates that make them so calm under pressure? Both Louis Deshommes and his First Mate Christian never demonstrated the slightest agitation, no matter what crises arose. The same traits were exhibited by Captain Clet, Captain Keranflech and Captain Nargeolet: Utter, steely calmness in the midst of a storm. They were as apt to react emotionally as anyone when chastising a crew member for carelessness or not following the rules of the ship. But in the face of physical danger, they became models of stoic efficiency.

My thoughts turned to Joel. He may not have been a ship's captain, he may not have been an athlete or an adventurer, but I always noticed his strength and composure during any crisis. It was one of the qualities that had drawn me to him in the first place.

I admired this courageous serenity and hoped I would someday achieve it.

Struggling to keep my footing, I hurried to the galley to check on my crew and all of our equipment. Randy, Peter and Ralph were tying everything down with bungee cords and rope.

"Let's lash down some of the doors and store everything that's breakable," said Ralph. I grabbed lines and tied them tightly around any object that could slide and cause serious injury.

I had never thought it would happen, but I finally was able to use my Girl Scout training tying knots—something as a ten year old I had thought was silly and unnecessary.

Suddenly like a macabre slapstick comedy, everything in the *Abeille* came flying loose at once. Pots flew in the air, followed by toasters. Our television set hurtled to the floor from its bracket in the wall and Randy jumped out of the way just in time to avoid being struck by the industrial steel refrigerator as it collapsed from its mounts.

"There goes dinner," Randy joked, as we studied the wreckage.

"I guess this is what they mean by a mess hall," said Ralph.

Waves sixty feet high crashed against the *Abeille*, forcing her downward on the starboard side. The ship listed severely, then righted itself.

Randy and I were thrown across the width of the galley, after fighting a losing battle to stand in one place. My body smashed into the butcher's block cutting table that extended the length of the galley. The blow knocked all the breath out of me and I gasped, from both the crunching impact and the unbearable shooting pains in my shoulder. I was certain I had broken my arm, so excruciating was the sensation that shot like lightning bolts through the left side of my body.

This is the worst of it, I thought. *In a few minutes, the storm will subside.*

Wishful thinking, of course. The remarkable fact about a violent hurricane is a sense you have that it has reached an unthinkable peak—only to discover that the madness has barely begun.

We all braced ourselves for the grotesquely powerful waves fiercely battering our ship. The *Abeille* tipped to port, then shot upright again.

"Time to get out the rubber suits," kidded Randy.

I had an incongruous vision of balloon-sized survival suits, recalling our giddy, hilarious game only two weeks before. The mind leaps erratically during a crisis, and I also thought of Joel, parodying Leslie Nielsen's line in "The Poseidon Adventure"—"Oh, my God, I've never seen anything like it. An enormous wall of water, coming right toward us."

We had both laughed when Joel did his sober, square-jawed impersonation of Nielsen. I wasn't laughing now. I recalled Joel, urging me not to go on this expedition.

Simultaneously, an assortment of sounds accosted us: screeching groans from the ship, the incessant, ever-increasing howl of the wind, the cacophonous clamor of items crashing to the floor.

Peter reached out, holding me fast as the next wave hit. He kept me from falling against a table. I felt an unexpected closeness to him. Whatever our problems, we had bonded in some basic way. I had no idea of his personal conflicts or inner demons, but I knew he had fought his way through them and would be a continuing asset to our voyage—if we survived.

"This must be one of the worst goddamn storms ever," said Randy.

"Oh, no," said Ralph. "Hazel in New York City recorded one hundred thirteen mile an hour winds."

"How come you're an authority on hurricanes?" Randy asked. "Did you work at a goddamn weather station?"

Ralph, enjoying the opportunity to demonstrate his knowledge, continued.

"Hurricane Carla was a big one. And remember Claudette."

"Never met her," said Peter.

"Good thing," Ralph said. "She dumped forty-three inches of rain near Alvin, Texas."

He went down the list, quoting statistics about Donna in 1960, Ginger in 1971, Alicia in 1983 and Diane in 1955. By the time he started describing the financial damage inflicted by Agnes ("6.4 billion"), everyone cried 'enough' but Ralph plunged on. As a Californian, I knew about the Richter scale for earthquakes, but Ralph was thoroughly familiar with the Beaufort scale and the Saffir-Simpson scale, and their ratings for storms in Martinique, Galveston, Haiti and Honduras.

"If you start telling us how many people died in each one, I'm diving overboard," said Randy.

"Over twelve thousand in Galveston Texas."

Peter made a mock fist and Ralph shifted gears.

"I'm guessing this is a stage four on the Saffir-Simpson," he said. "Winds above one hundred thirty."

"Why the hell do they name hurricanes after women?" Peter wondered aloud.

Ralph even knew the answer to that one.

"It happened after World War Two. Meteorologists started naming the storms after their wives and girl-friends."

"If we get out of this in one piece, we'll name it Jennifer," said Randy.

"I just hope I'm alive to enjoy that," I said.

I thought of a line I'd once read from a Jack London story, *Fog*.

It's nasty weather like this here that turns heads gray before their time.

Suddenly, eerily, we were all enveloped in silence. Time seemed to stand still; the wind had abated. The moment had a supernatural quality, a suspension of all time and space.

Motionless, I waited with the others, inhaling deeply, fortifying myself with air.

When the next wave came, it seemed double the force of any that had preceded it, a blunt, merciless shudder that reverberated thunderously through the ship. It lifted us up, then dropped us down, and it seemed impossible that the *Abeille* would not burst and split into a million pieces. We all fell to the floor.

I expected to feel my panic double, commensurate with the power of the wave, but instead, a strange, fatalistic calm began replacing my anxiety.

Captain Rowarch stumbled into the galley.

"That damn wave hit so hard that two lifeboat canisters were knocked loose into the sea," he said.

This time, mercifully, there were no people underneath, no victims of their crushing weight. No open-mouthed, terrified men and women as there had been on the Majestic Explorer, rushing about in disorganized bedlam, making sounds, as Jack London had put it, "like the squealing of pigs under the knife of a butcher."

Whatever we had to face, we were facing it as a professional crew. The storm refused to abate; it kept gaining intensity. We had lashed down as many movable objects as we could—all of our video transferring equipment, VCRs, screening monitors—and were told that nothing more could be done; the lurching of the ship was so strong all we could do was return to our cabins, stow our gear and hang on tenaciously to anything stable so we weren't hurled around. Captain Rowarch felt that, despite our efforts, there was still too much danger of being hit or killed by objects that might break loose.

There was nothing more we could accomplish, but I felt a comfort in remaining with my crew. Nevertheless, we realized that Rowarch, with his vast experience, knew best, so we each staggered back to our cabins.

Alone, I asked myself: *How do you just lay still and wait out a storm?*

Sleep was impossible. I flipped through three books I had brought along with me: Conrad's *Lord Jim,* which I had loved as a teenager and was interested in re-reading; *Titanic - Triumph and Tragedy* by Eaton and Haas; and *Atlantic High,* by William Buckley Jr. I picked the latter up first because of my admiration for Buckley as an author and as an expert on the sea.

I loved his use of language, and one phrase struck me as a perfect description of our own disastrous weather: *One of those noisily chaotic sequences at night in uproarious seas when suddenly the sail lets go... the entire vessel vibrates with the whipping canvas.*

At two o'clock in the morning, when I completed the book, I knew it was still useless to attempt sleep. My senses were too heightened, my mind too ready to react in case of further emergency or evacuation. The storm had not subsided; the pounding was even more intense than when I first hit the bunk. The sharp, ear-splitting *crack,* like the loud snap of a whip, continued through the night. As we lurched up and down I was convinced the whole ship was breaking in half.

Finally my fear overtook all efforts to conquer it. I couldn't shake the conviction that I was doomed, that I'd never see Joel and my sons again. It was inconceivable that any man-made creation could triumph over the savagery of nature. I ran to the closet and pulled out my survival suit. No one had issued any orders to do this, but I wanted to be prepared in case the *Abeille* was no longer capable of defending itself against its relentless enemy.

Forcing myself into the suit, I lay back down in bed. I didn't zip it up in the back or put on the hood. But even so, after twenty minutes of being encapsulated in a rubbery cocoon I felt trapped and boiling hot. My body heat had accelerated and there was no place for air to vent.

Preparation for emergency be damned, I thought. I'd better tear this thing off before I roast to death. I began shedding it, and once again had trouble wriggling free. The wriggling was compounded by a ship in spasm, lack of room and the necessity of clutching on to the edge of my bunk at all times.

Whenever I became drowsy, I was always awakened by the *crack* of ship against water, the deafening sounds that thundered through my brain.

Time inched by, but by morning, the insanity of raging seas had tapered off into an uncomfortable but not life-threatening storm. P. H. told us, by ship's radio that the *Nadir*, despite some broken items, had withstood the battering.

And Ralph had another lady to add to his list— Hurricane Arlene. She had lasted thirty-six hours.

Chapter 15

Mystery of the *Titanic* Safe

We had survived Hurricane Arlene, though the storm had nearly capsized and destroyed our boats. Our attention now turned to the fact that Arlene, in addition to its danger, had also been a raging inconvenience from a business standpoint. The dives and retrieval of artifacts had been delayed for three days, upsetting investors who had put money into our expedition. I could almost sense an attitude of, *I'm sure it wasn't that bad. Did you have to go for three days without a dive?*

Another hurricane—this one whipped up by the press—continued to haunt us. Criticism about the collection of artifacts remained a major theme in newspapers and on television. The grave-robbing issue refused to go away.

"We need good publicity from a reputable source," I told Ralph. "A spokesman people know and believe."

I knew someone who fit that perception. His name was Don Barkham, and his public relations firm represented political and business as well as entertainment figures. Don was admired for his efforts to protect the environment on land and sea. He also had a convincing and charismatic media personality.

In addition to his publicity value, I viewed Don as a friend. A short redhead with ocean-green eyes behind small, gold-rimmed glasses, he had humor and charm. A year earlier we had met when he did a brief guest appearance on one of my documentaries, and that meeting had evolved into what I considered a warm comradeship.

Everyone at Westgate and Taurus International agreed that Don could help to defuse the blistering attacks, so I called from the ship, reaching him at his plush offices in Manhattan.

After exchanging warm pleasantries, I asked him, "Will you join us in St. Pierre in five days and handle our public relations?"

He enthusiastically agreed adding, "Well, then, I'll look forward to diving to the *Titanic*."

I wanted to say *wait a minute. We're hiring you for publicity. There are a limited amount of dives, and we've lost a lot of time during the storm. I can't guarantee you a dive.*

But I didn't. Once he was on board, I'd see what I could arrange. His presence was important enough to shift our schedule around and give him a chance to dive.

Meanwhile, on August 15, the French decided to bring up the safe, on American assurance that the funds had been wired.

Among the thousands of artifacts that were certain to fascinate the public, none had as much potential impact as the safe. Our men had visions of opening it and finding clusters of priceless rubies, diamonds, emeralds and currency. The investors were hoping to build an entire publicity campaign around these glittering contents before they were donated to prestigious museums.

As the safe was brought up, I held my breath. It was made of fireproof brick, and there was a brass handle on the front identifying its British manufacturer. The safe was halfway deteriorated, open on all sides. We waited for coins and jewelry to pour out.

Patrick Dallet, one of our divers in charge of logging artifacts reached inside. Captain Rowarch and I watched as Patrick's hand pushed into the muddy interior. His fingers came our dripping with grayish brown slime. He held them like a sieve, letting the slime drip through in the hopes that gold and jewels would be left behind. But there was nothing.

"Try again," said Randy. "The Astors must have put something in there."

"We're not asking for the rubaiyat," said Pierre-Yves. "But a ring or pen, no?"

"No baubles, no bangles, no beads, just borscht," Ralph quipped, staring at the soupy mess.

Patrick sunk his hands again into the dark, sticky, dilapidated safe.

"Rien," he said. "Nothing."

I looked at the stunned faces of everyone watching. Peter was filming our reactions, capturing every open-mouthed, puzzled, disappointed expression.

We all felt betrayed by the deteriorating safe, as if it had deliberately raised our hopes only to dash them. It appeared the king's ransom in jewels was only a figment of our imagination.

"The whole world is waiting to hear about this," I said. "What are we going to tell them?"

"Never mind," Captain Rowarch said calmly. "It's

still the most valuable artifact we've found so far, and the most valuable videotape." As he explained, the retrieval of the safe demonstrated the dexterity of the *Nautile* pilots and the *Nautile* itself to tie a knot underneath the ocean at 12,500 feet and then lasso the safe and pull it into the recovery basket.

What made it even more remarkable was that recovery of the safe had been unsuccessfully attempted before. Bob Ballard's crew had tried to lift it in 1986, without success. Our expedition had done what people all predicted was impossible. Although the safe had no money or jewels, it had a vast symbolic power. It was the one item the public was most curious about, and a *Titanic* mission would have been regarded as a major disappointment unless it had been discovered and raised.

This achievement also showed what extraordinary care everybody was taking, the precedent-setting technological achievements of Ifremer and the French in creating such an astounding vehicle, and the remarkable talent of those who operated it.

Nevertheless, we couldn't help feeling disappointed.

I faxed Westgate, trying to be truthful without sounding too negative.

You should be aware that the safe is so deteriorated it's in a state of collapse, with only five sides still intact—and they are extremely weak. If you wish to show a safe similar to this in good condition, you'll have to contact the original maker in England, Thomas Perry & Sons. Maybe a model or replica of this fire-resistant clay safe could be bought or made for the show because this one can't withstand further transport without falling apart completely.

After sending the fax, I began to wonder—in our disappointment and haste, had we made absolutely certain the safe was locked up? As an artifact of such historical significance, I wanted to make sure it was thoroughly protected. I asked Captain Rowarch later on if the safe had been locked up.

He wasn't sure, so we decided to check. It wasn't. We untied it and took a last look inside before putting it under lock and key.

"Wait a minute," I said. "Isn't that something sticking out in the mud?"

We turned on our flashlights, and I stuck my fingers deep into the oozing, ochre clay. I touched a chamois bag and pulled it out. Patrick had obviously overlooked it.

Inside the bag were four coins, one of which was gold.

Excited about my discovery and feeling more than ever an integral part of our expedition, I went to tell Ralph. He wasn't there, but I found Peter and Adam and brought them downstairs.

"You've got to document this," I said, thrilled, and within seconds, their cameras were recording the bag and it's contents.

Captain Rowarch put the chamois bag into a tupperware container and sealed it. Then we gave the bag to Captain Louis Deshommes to lock up. At 2:00 AM, I prepared a telex for Westgate, explaining my discovery.

The next morning Joslyn called, expressing his enthusiasm and thanking me for finding the coins.

His next comment, however, made me feel sad. No sooner was I congratulated for my part in finding the bag of coins when Joslyn informed me that a new cameraman was coming on board and Peter would be leaving in a few days.

"I'm sorry to hear that. Peter's doing a great job," I told him.

"It doesn't matter. Mike Seligman wants Bobby Keyes. He's worked with him in the past. Bobby's already been hired."

I had no objection to Bobby; I'd heard of his great reputation. But I thought of Peter, the night before, shooting pictures of the safe. I thought of how much we'd been through together, even in so short a time. I imagined his disappointment. But the powers that be had spoken, and I had to tell him he was being replaced.

Hurt as he was, he wasn't surprised.

"I was under a lot of pressure, and physically still recovering." He went on to explain about a near-fatal accident he'd had months before the *Titanic* expedition. A magnificently accomplished mountain climber, he had been hit by falling rock, sustaining a serious head injury.

"The injury left me with murderous migraines," he said. "And it changed my personality—I got mood swings. I was angry half the time, and I didn't know why. I'm just getting over it."

There were no words to say. I hugged him, reminding him that many of his wonderful pictures would still be used; that he was still one of the principal figures in the *Titanic* story.

Our crew had become a family. There's nothing as close as a group of people at sea, working together for a common goal, an inexplicably powerful bonding that takes place when you're parted from everyday realities on land. Your only realities become the cresting waves and the open sky, your only emotional priorities the sailors on whom you depend for support and sometimes for your very life.

I realized then that even if I never saw Peter again, he would forever remain a member of that family.

Peter's departure wasn't the only dark cloud forming. The French wondered if their bonus would be withheld now that the safe proved to be such a major disappointment. Dormant, long-buried resentment surfaced, a re-kindling of the anti-American bitterness that had flared up following Bob Ballard's Expedition.

Hostility had risen over the issue of who was going to get credit for the pictures. According to Ballard's account at the time, a newspaper report in the London Observer had proclaimed that Ballard and his crew were salvaging the *Titanic* wreckage, an act he had publicly disapproved of from the beginning. To prove he was only taking photographs and not bringing up artifacts, he released footage of the ship's boiler and a company celebration following the expedition's success. These images, Ballard felt, would begin to tell the true story of his finding and filming the *Titanic*, not keeping souvenirs.

"The next thing I knew, Woods Hole was on the phone, not to congratulate us, but to complain about the apparent exclusive we'd given out."

The images of Ballard and Jean-Louis Michel's discovery had been televised, much to the anger of the United States networks who still didn't have them. These stations threatened Woods Hole with lawsuits. To appease them, more images were released simultaneously to the French media and North American television.

Woods Hole released all of Ballard's material, and according to his story, "That night... French television viewers saw our newly minted *Titanic* images on their screens before Ifremer could release them. They had been picked up from the American networks via satellite."

Ifremer was enraged at Woods Hole's actions, resulting in an explosive conflict over who owned the expedition's pictures and how they would be used. Ballard's partner, Jean-Louis Michel, Ifremer's representative on board, was caught in a squeeze, suffering the pressures of his employers back in France. As a result, the French-American connection was dealt a severe blow, paving the way for resentments that once again hurt morale on our voyage.

Although Ballard's actions were motivated by integrity and not self-interest, the unfortunate circumstances of his media debacle had far-reaching effects.

Those ill feelings between Americans and French were evident when we discovered that Peter's footage of the safe was missing from the equipment room.

Peter was devastated. This footage was the most historically valuable of any that had been shot, a fitting testimonial to Peter's abilities and his contribution. I could see how desperately he wanted the crucial missing tapes to be found.

I didn't believe for an instant that one of my crew was responsible, but I followed Westgate's orders to search everyone's belongings. Meanwhile, the suppositions from Americans and French began to fly.

Was it someone on the *Nadir,* in an attempt to keep an item that gave him bargaining power if the investors didn't pay the promised bonus money? The safe itself had drastically diminished in value. Now that it no longer held the promise of priceless treasure, it was no longer a powerful negotiating tool; but Peter's footage was.

Or could it have been someone who was still angry

because of the way Ifremer had been neglected in all accounts following the 1985 expedition—anger many crew members had frequently voiced to me, especially concerning the limited press their hero, Jean-Louis Michel, had received during the worldwide media blitz of that year, an omission heightened by the fact that Ballard's name was the only one dominating headlines across the world.

As a Los Angeles Sheriff, I knew how easy it was to find motives for every single person on board, from the cook to the Captain. I felt as though I was playing a real-life version of the board game *Clue*. Still, I had a job to do, and the responsibility for finding out who had stolen the footage.

I went to everybody in my crew and told them I needed to check their belongings. I checked their duffel bags with them. I combed the drawers underneath their bunks, and the original bag used to transport the tapes from the *Nadir* to the *Abeille*. I scoured the equipment room that held the tape, making an exhaustive search.

Nothing turned up. The friendly camaraderie between us turned chilly. Everyone began suspecting those individuals they had a grudge against. The French didn't want to be tainted with an image of thievery, especially considering the unfavorable publicity still inundating newspapers; nor did the Americans want a damning image of greed and acquisitiveness.

Then, one morning, the footage made an unexplained reappearance, sitting in the equipment room as though it had never been stolen. Satisfied with its return, the captains urged all of us to concentrate on our work and forget the whole matter had ever occurred. No word of it crept into the paper, no hint was mentioned on television.

If I hadn't been the one conducting the cabin-to-cabin investigation, I would have thought I'd imagined the whole crisis.

Why make a big deal? was the general reaction. *After all, we have the footage now.*

Everyone was satisfied to accept the fact that it was an oversight, even though the footage had clearly been moved and then restored to its proper place. Whoever took it had obviously thought better of the idea, and the matter was dropped. But the safe—once again—had exacerbated tensions between the *Abeille* and the *Nadir*.

Beyond that, it raised the question: where *were* the jewels and all the currency everyone had expected? Where had they gone to—and was there any chance of finding them?

Chapter 16

Rendezvous in St. Pierre

Every few weeks the *Abeille* sailed to St. Pierre de Michelon for refueling. Much as I loved the sea, the sight of St. Pierre, south of Newfoundland in the gulf of St. Lawrence, a small charming French community dotted with houses spread across rocky cliffs, was a welcome break. Most of the harbor was filled with dinghies and bright-colored fishing boats, rather than the enormous freighters and ocean liners found in St. John's. With a population of roughly 5,000, it has a gentle, refreshing beauty.

On August 14, the trip promised to be particularly interesting. Taurus International had arranged for Brigitte Renaldi, a French journalist, to cover the events of the expedition, and I was supposed to meet her in the bar of the Ile de France Hotel.

Like the town, the Ile de France Hotel was small but charming. Tucked into the heart of the city, with twenty-four rooms, a cozy bar with wooden beams, wooden stools and little Captain's chairs, it offered a feeling of both camaraderie and seclusion.

Brigitte was waiting near the front door when I walked in.

"Jenn-ee-fer," she said, in a lilting French accent. "I'm so pleased to meet you."

I studied Brigitte carefully. Every woman on earth notices when another woman is thinner, and Brigitte was thinner than me. Even though I was in top shape because of exercising and running, I had never been Audrey Hepburn, and Brigitte possessed the kind of slender body that French designers adored. With an angular face, high cheekbones, brown eyes and hair pulled into a ponytail, her physical attributes suggested disarming simplicity although her softly accented voice rang of sophistication.

I'm supposed to be wary of you, I thought. Not just because you may be a potential rival, but because the Americans hate having you on the expedition and they're afraid you'll steal their press.

From the beginning, Westgate Productions made certain that all our activities were shrouded in mystery. We were forcibly directed not to speak to the media, not to reveal what artifacts were brought up or any other detail of the expedition. This was such a serious edict that we had to sign a piece of paper, agreeing we would not release any information to press or public. Through Westgate's confidentiality agreement we were completely muzzled.

Westgate felt the television show we were filming, *Return to the Titanic,* would be able to unveil new secrets the public hadn't heard. Brigitte, as a journalist, threatened that secrecy. Her job would be to interview the crew members and play these interviews daily on France's Europe One.

"If she's female and she's French, she'll get any piece of information she wants," Ralph had told me before this meeting.

I wondered if she would be a responsible reporter or if she would do a sensationalized treatment of our activities. Would she sniff around and find out that Peter's tape photographing the safe had been stolen? Would she discover the antagonism between the French and Americans and exploit it controversially, blowing it up into a scandal?

"I have so many questions," Brigitte said, an innocent remark; but it confirmed my worst fears. *What questions?* Maybe Westgate was right to be wary.

I didn't let on, by word or hint, that her presence was wildly resented by the Americans. I didn't let on that Westgate had told me, "She is *not to dive under any circumstances.*

She seemed—from a first impression—to be an agreeable, exceedingly pleasant person who would cooperate and write favorably about our venture. But I knew a quote from director Elia Kazan that shed light on the psyche of journalists in general.

"*Observe* a writer... You will believe what everyone else does: that he is a perfectly friendly and agreeable fellow. Then read what he writes about the affair. You'll find that he saw things you didn't and had reactions you didn't suspect."

What reactions would Brigitte have? There was no point in trying to guess. She was a stranger, a professional with her own way of seeing, her own journalistic approach.

As I continued our conversation, I never felt I was being pumped, never felt I was the target of a journalistic investigation. Brigitte spoke about the *Titanic* and her fascination with the ship's legend. It was safe ground, a subject we could both explore comfortably while measuring each other.

Toward the end of the conversation, I had the weirdest feeling that I was being watched from a distance. Looking around, I saw nobody familiar.

"Are you meeting someone here?" Brigitte asked me.

"No. I just had a spooky feeling. Maybe the *Titanic* does that to you."

Brigitte leaned forward.

"What's it like with all those men?"

"Well... they're very professional," I answered. "Except that lately I notice a few more shirt buttons open, and more of them are stripping to the waist. They're all filled with... how do you say it in French?"

"*Luxure. Desir lascif.*"

"That's it."

"Let's hope they always feel that way," Brigitte said, and we both laughed.

I tried to relax, but the feeling of being silently observed grew stronger.

Brigitte went to the ladies room and a middle-aged waiter walked up to me and handed me a note.

Meet me in Room 28 as soon as you're through.

I had come to St. Pierre with my whole crew. Any of them could have written this note. Was it Ralph, playing a joke?

When Brigitte returned, we said our goodbyes and I told her I had to make a phone call before I left. I took a few last sips of my drink and pondered whether to visit Room twenty-eight or return directly to the ship. In the end, my curiosity outweighed my trepidations.

I knocked on the door.

"Who ees there?" said someone, in a peculiarly unconvincing, comedic accent.

"Jennifer."

The door opened, and it was Joel.

I must have looked hilarious, open-mouthed like a giant grouper. Joel pulled me into the room and kissed me, smothering any comments I might have made—and I knew, instantly, that the male crew of the *Abeille* weren't the only ones who were filled with *desir lascif.*

"Do you have to go back to the ship tonight?"

Since Joel's hands were still roaming my body and his lips were hot on my ear, his attitude about spending the night was crystal clear. "Remember, you came here for refueling."

"Well, now I'm fully charged."

"I think," he said, "that we could rev your engine up a little more. So you can get through the next month alone."

I loved his banter; but I knew that underneath the breezy wit he was serious. Not that anything could have torn me from his side. As we lay together, I had a sudden inner retreat to childhood, an image of Joel stowing away and spending the rest of the expedition with me. I thought of him, playing piano for his supper. But the vision was laughable. An oil support ship like the *Abeille* didn't have piano bars or singers doing Andrew Lloyd Webber over rough seas.

I told him about my dive, and how I had loved his concerto, how it had so powerfully intensified the excitement and happiness of that experience. All my reactions

were written in a letter I hadn't yet sent, but it was so
much more satisfying to let him know in the sensual con-
fines of a small French hotel room.

When I woke up the next morning, it was 5:00 AM
and completely dark. Joel appeared to be sleeping. I got out
of bed and began putting my clothes on as I gazed out the
window upon the moonlit streets.

"I like watching you dress," he said. "I've missed it."

"It won't be that much longer." I said, turning
towards him.

He didn't get up. "You know what? There's something wonderfully sinful about this. You creeping out of
here in the dark, as though I was some illicit lover in a
strange town. Usually it's the man in movies, going to sea,
leaving his lover behind. We're just playing it in reverse."

"I wish I didn't have to go."

"Then don't." I was startled. "Just kidding."

"You're not kidding," I said. "What's on your
mind?"

The room, such a source of comfort seconds before,
suddenly felt stifling. Strange, unexpressed tensions filled
the air.

"You're in another world," Joel said. "I'm not part
of it."

"It has nothing to do with us."

I remained standing by the window. He slipped on
a shirt and jeans and walked over to me.

"But you miss it. You're married to Woody Allen,
and maybe sometimes you're wishing I was Chuck
Yaeger."

"He's too old for me."

"I'm serious. Expeditions—diving—river rafting—
all of it. That's not what Jewish boys from the Bronx do."

"They could," I said, "if they wanted to. But I never cared if you were an explorer or a soldier of fortune. I love you exactly the way you are. I wouldn't change anything."

"Anything?"

"Well, maybe the fact that you forget to throw out razors when they're used up. But that's it."

Our light, funny patter was helping us through a rough spot, but I realized for the first time that Joel sometimes felt isolated and shut out by my world of adventure.

"I'll never go on an expedition again," I said.

"You will," Joel protested. "I want you to have freedom."

We held each other tightly and then I had to go.

Walking through the pitch-black streets of St. Pierre toward the *Abeille*, I felt tears welling in my eyes. I was glad no one could see me crying. I was also glad, in that trying moment, that I was a temporary sailor and that after my great adventure I'd have the person I loved and my wonderful children to come home to.

Chapter 17

Sailing with the Enemy

Along with an optimistic, excited Brigitte, we were joined on the return trip to the site by our Public Relations representative and on-camera spokesman Don Barkham. I was happy to see Don, and he was warmly congratulatory about how "I had come up in the world." In 1979, I had consulted with him on a television special. He was well known for his publicity campaigns, and had been very kind and generous with his advice.

"Tell me," he said, still smiling, "what exactly do they ask of an expedition leader on this trip?"

I explained my different roles.

"Well, having a woman makes wonderful P.R.," he said.

Something about the phrase 'having a woman' struck me as faintly patronizing, but I put that down to over-sensitivity.

"I don't know," I said, trying to seem as casual as he did. "I haven't seen my name in the papers lately, and there's no glamour in having to working eighteen hour days."

Trying not to read undue meaning into his remarks, I reflected back on my previous encounters with Don. He had always been supportive and validating, but I couldn't help feeling vaguely uneasy.

"I'll say one thing, dear. Working hard hasn't made you any the worse for wear. You still look lovely."

Suddenly Brigitte cried out with delight. A sea turtle swam by us, plunging under the water and leaping back up, pushing his head above the surface. It must have been four feet long, not counting tail or legs.

"He looks so *tame*," she said. "He's not afraid of the ship. I suppose no one has ever frightened him."

A little further on we saw Atlantic bottlenose dolphins. They followed the bow of the ship, swerving in and out, leaping joyously into the air. The dolphins and turtles cheered us; they came on cue, as if acting as a welcoming committee.

Brigitte and Don arrived at the perfect time. The next day, August 16, was a historic moment for our mission. As I wrote to Westgate:

Congratulations. The dive today is beyond your wildest dreams.

Everyone - from captains to crew - also feels that this dive offers the solution to the Great Safe Mystery.

We found a leather valise, and this valise evidently holds the answer to the empty safe. We believe it to be the purser's bag, which contains the contents of one of the two safes on board the Titanic. That's why the safe we brought up had so little inside it. If there's another safe on the Titanic, it's logical to assume that one was emptied too, because of the valuables we've now retrieved.

The bag resembles a brown doctor's satchel. The

handles where a hand would grip the case are missing. Otherwise it's in excellent condition. I wondered if it was jerked out of somebody's hand during a panicky moment. Had there been a struggle, a battle for its contents, that had broken the handles off?

It was strange, because everything about the bag was in such good condition, considering the seventy five years it had been underwater. The reason for this, according to the EDF officials in charge of restoring our artifacts, is because of the actual tanning process of the leather, the tannin used which preserves it from water and decay. This tannin hopefully will preserve all leather items we bring up.

There were two keys inside, one very long, perhaps 5 to 6 inches. What does the key open? Could this have been the key to the lock on the other safe? Could it have been a key to John Jacob Astor's million dollar suite?

We found many many packets of currency. The valise was probably stuffed full when dry. The packets of currency came from all countries -- French francs, German deutschmarks, English pounds, American dollars in all denominations, along with other currencies. This huge amount of money from so many countries would indicate that they were indeed the contents of the Assistant Purser's safe, and that whoever emptied the safe obviously drowned or dropped the bag while struggling to survive.

We also brought up a brass badge with crown on top, size approximately two to three inches high and one and a half inches wide. The badge reads:

Hennings Masonic Depot.

Little Britain, London

The huge amount of valuables the safe was presumed to hold are here: Rings -- three that are particularly stunning. The first is a large blue sapphire with diamonds surrounding it; the second has three huge diamonds, two on either side of a pear-shaped one in the middle; and the last is a ladies ring that's oblong-shaped, with a series of small diamonds in a circle in the center of the ring. A gold necklace with at least three huge nuggets attached; most of the crew felt this necklace belonged to Margaret Tobin Brown, because of her husband's vast mining fortune.

There are also seven stickpins, some with large diamonds, a necklace with a starburst design, and another one with a very antique setting that looks like four petals in the center surrounded by half circles of either diamonds or small marcasite stones.

We found a man's gold ring with a diamond as well, and two pendants not attached to a necklace -- one an English gold coin, another a heart.

A woman's black beaded bag, filled to overflowing with gold coins. I'd estimate at least forty of them.

Finally, we found three watches (one stopped at 12:50PM), pearls, pins and brooches, a $20.00 American gold piece, many silver coins, and a gold necklace with heart pendant.

Our new Director of Photography, Bobby Keyes, was enthralled by the dazzling array of artifacts we had already retrieved. Bobby was very different than Peter, both physically and in temperament. Where Peter had been intense, Bobby was easygoing, an amiable jokester with a perpetual smile on his face. Stocky, strong from constantly moving heavy video cameras on his shoulders, he had worked extensively with our producer Mike Seligman on past Oscar and Grammy shows.

I had expressed my doubts to Mike about using

anyone on this expedition that was accustomed to doing only studio work, but Bobby was skilled at handling location documentary assignments with the same ease as structured studio jobs; Since he was equally versatile at both he had no problem coping with the rigors of working on a ship's unstable, slippery surface.

Bobby and I developed a wonderful camaraderie. Don, however, often stared at me intently, and I wondered what he was thinking.

"You must be so tired," he said.

"Tired? I'm not tired at all. I feel great."

"I was wondering... how is it you became expedition leader?"

I filled him in on my history. "I've led expeditions for National Geographic—hired crews, organized, leased boats, arranging for transport of tons of photographic equipment, arranged for carnets and clearances—seeing to it that the equipment passed through customs in Japan, Greece, the Red Sea, Israel, Egypt and Mexico." I told him I'd dealt in the past with ambassadors at embassies and heads of consulates.

"Really? I had no idea."

I told him that Westgate Productions and the whole crew had taken a vote and decided I had the experience to take the Expedition Leader position.

"I'm still surprised," he countered quizzically. "This is the kind of thing Ralph does really well. Does he mind having his protégé in a leadership position?"

"I'm not his protégé," I said. "Maybe ten years ago I was, but I've graduated. We all have to start somewhere, and over the last ten years I've paid my dues."

He wouldn't let the subject go. "It's just that it's

awfully hard for a woman to be in charge of so many men, don't you think? Men in these kinds of situations don't take direction well from a woman."

I thought: *The men in my crew are always willing to take direction from me. Maybe that's your problem. I don't order them around. We work as a team.*

I felt he was needling me, under the guise of concern. I didn't know why; I'd done nothing to threaten him. If anything, I'd been a champion of his talent. I had been the one who suggested Don as our media representative.

Later that evening, I spoke to Ralph about Don's attitude.

"Don acted as though you resented me for being Expedition Leader, that *you* wanted the job. Did you tell him that?"

"That's crazy," Ralph insisted. "I don't want to be everybody's chief nurse and bottle washer. I'm here as a submersible cameraman."

"I think I'm a little more than a chief nurse and bottle washer."

"I know. I think you're doing great. Look, who's always been your biggest fan?"

Not long afterward, Brigitte told me that Don had referred to me as 'an ambitious woman.' Every woman knows that when a man uses the word *ambitious* about a female, it's not meant as a compliment. He isn't praising her competence or her background, he's politely damning her for pushing too hard, being unfeminine and competing with men.

"Besides," Brigitte said, with the clarity of vision that comes when you're not directly involved, "This man works with actresses who play sexy and feminine all the time. He doesn't like it that you're strong and direct. He'd rather see you bringing the men their coffee."

My uneasiness was heightened later that afternoon when Don and Ralph chose to meet with Nargeolet and discuss the dive plan without me.

"You were busy," was all Ralph said, when I asked him why I had been excluded. I mentioned it to Don, and he said he wanted to get a feel for the way the ship worked. If he was going to represent us, he had to understand all the people and the problems on board.

Temperament by the cook, Camille Stephan, a seemingly minor issue, provoked our next unpleasant encounter.

Don, Ralph and I were having a difficult conversation with Captain Rowarch. Ralph had again invited Don to the meeting, which was inappropriate; he had just come on board, and his peripheral role as press spokesman for the voyage didn't entitle him to an active voice in the *Abeille's* political conflicts.

"I'm very disappointed," Rowarch began. "I feel the Americans are working against us.

We still haven't seen the bonus money for the safe. If it's not here soon, we're going to turn around and leave the site for good."

I could see that he meant it. He was unaffected by the usual arguments that the financial delays occurred because there were so many investors and so many sources to gather the money from.

"You told us that bonus money would be here, Jennifer," said Rowarch. "Remember, since we found all these valuables in the valise—valuables which must have been inside the safe before they were removed—bringing up the valise is the same thing as bringing up the safe, with all this international currency and jewelry in it."

I knew the funds would come; I knew my employers were honest. My only fear was that it would be here too late, that money would arrive at an empty site, shorn of our ships and submersibles.

Rowarch and I had an ideal working relationship. Early on he had said, in front of a group of the men, that I was an excellent expedition leader and perfect for the job. Now I promised to use my influence to help resolve the impasse.

It was at this critical point that Eric, the young steward, walked in.

"Camille is very upset," he began. "*Very* upset, because you're not down for lunch. He's gone to a lot of trouble to prepare today's meal and he's insulted."

Things, I thought, *are getting out of control.*

"Since when," Rowarch said, "does the cook dictate behavior to the captain? Since when is a sensitive discussion interrupted because the cook wants appreciation for his new recipes? He'll have to wait. We're not finished here."

The momentum and good will of the discussion was dissipated by the news that the cook was annoyed. When the conversation ended, we went for dinner and I could see Camille fuming. Only after we all made a particular fuss over his veal marsala did his grimly accusing look turn into a beaming grin.

"Westgate has to act quickly, or this mission could fall apart altogether," I said to Don and Ralph.

"You're over-reacting," they both replied.

"There are still crucial things that have to be filmed underwater," I objected. "We all know dives are valuable and expensive; the estimate of cost to make one dive varies from thirty thousand to fifty thousand dollars, depending which captain you ask. And we have to make the remaining ones count."

I was concerned that there wasn't enough time to accommodate the people we had already slated: Yves-Cornet, head of Taurus; Veronique Chappaz, wife of Taurus co-owner Robert Chappaz; Ralph Rosato, the attorney for Westgate; Brigitte; and Don himself.

In five days, Cornet, Veronique, Ralph and Don were scheduled to leave. If one day of bad weather came upon us, a dive or even two would have to be canceled. Knowing this, everyone wanted to be first, to avoid missing their chance, and it was up to Rowarch, Nargeolet, Ralph and me to make those choices.

When I consulted Westgate, they gave me the final word: Cornet, head of Taurus had to dive. Veronique Chappaz had to dive because it would mortally insult her husband, head of Taurus, if she was passed over; and Don Barkham, as media representative, had to have his chance. Ralph Rosato would dive if we had no further storms.

Storms affected more than just the dives and the divers. They also threatened retrieval baskets filled with artifacts.

That afternoon, our divers were working against perilous conditions. The seas were running twenty foot swells, driving rain pelted us like bullets and winds howled with a fury exceeding thirty knots.

After going out in the zodiac, the divers went

underwater and attached netting over the retrieval basket. This was to make sure the artifacts were held securely in place and to prevent them from falling out when they reached the surface in the event the basket tipped. The divers then started towing the basket through rough currents while it was still underwater, pulling it to the aft end of the *Abeille*.

The crew on board the *Abeille* had dropped the line, with a huge hook attached, and divers fought to attach the hook to the basket. The slamming winds and raging sea made it almost impossible to keep the basket under control.

I was relieved to see them finally succeed in hooking it to the line. They then gradually began to lift it hydraulically from the water. It took twice as long as usual, because the basket was heavily loaded. I estimated that it weighed more than 500 pounds. Once it was lifted above the water, the winds made it swing like a pendulum on a clock, first to port, to starboard, then fore and aft.

All of us on board the *Abeille* were drenched, even with the protection of foul weather gear.

I turned to look at our cameraman to see if he was getting all this, failing to notice that the basket was coming right at me. The wind had changed direction.

"Jennifer, watch out," screamed Bosco.

I ducked, but not quickly enough, and it grazed the side of my head. The blow was painful, but I knew I was fortunate, because it had not hit me head on. The basket then hit the side of the ship and the line snapped.

I jumped aside as the packed basket crashed downward, almost crushing me and Captain Rowarch before it plunged into the ocean, taking all the artifacts with it.

"Il etait moins cinq," Rowarch exclaimed.

"That *was* a close call," I agreed.

"Are you all right?" Ralph asked me.

"I'm fine. Better than the artifacts."

My head began to throb, but I found myself more concerned with the lost basket. It had hurtled down, returning to the bottom. I could picture it, dropping through the darkness, as if being reclaimed by the *Titanic*. It was the great ship clutching tenaciously to its belongings, and no mere crew members and divers were going to claim the prize without a fight.

Eerily, right after that incident, headlines suddenly erupted all over the world—MAJOR ACCIDENT ON *TITANIC* EXPEDITION. Somehow the rumor had begun that two people on our expedition were seriously injured, and speculation ran rampant that one had been killed.

Nobody knew how the story started, but it once again allowed the media to be critical of our "reckless endeavor."

I tried to get through to Joel, but the lines were tied up by terrified wives, relatives and friends, desperate to learn if a loved one had been the victim. Since the supposed victim was unidentified, reporters had a field day with lurid speculation and conjecture, offering lines such as "Unknown person on expedition joins *Titanic* victims."

Accusations and counter-accusations sprang up on board. Once again the Americans blamed the French; the French blamed the Americans. And Brigitte became a natural target, since she was the only journalist with direct access to the press.

"Nargeolet looks at me as though I'm responsible," Brigitte told me. "I was there with my hands in my pockets, wanting to *scream*. A curse on these rumors that poison the atmosphere on the boat."

I believed her. She had nothing to gain by creating antagonism.

When Nargeolet and Deshommes conducted an investigation, they came to the conclusion that my near-fatal mishap was the likely trigger that had started it all. Shortly after the incident, a rumor had spread that 'Jennifer and Rowarch had an almost fatal accident.'

Nargeolet's supposition—which made sense—was that someone on the busy CB radio had picked up pieces of the statement—'fatal' and 'accident'—and dropped the 'almost,' in transmitting information about the event through static. The snapping of the basket had been exaggerated and these two shreds of information, tied together, had resulted in a horror story that panicked loved ones and strangers alike.

I finally got through to Joel on ship-to-shore radio, reassuring him that I was all right, and no one had been hurt.

"Kevin and Brent were already packed," he told me. "They were ready to leave school and fly down there. Listen—if you promise not to die before this is over, I'll learn to scuba dive."

"I don't *want* you to scuba dive," I told him. "I want you to do only two things: play piano and take me away for wild, sexy weekends."

"You don't care if I skydive either?"

"How could you skydive?" I asked him. "You won't fly on a commercial jet without taking valium."

"Well, anyway, I love you. Please take care of yourself."

"I love you too."

Ralph's girlfriend Astrid, a beautiful, devoted

woman who wrote to him every day and was willing to accept the fact that he was gone so often on expeditions, also called for reassurance and told him she worried about him and asked him to be careful.

I sought calm so that professionalism reigned in the midst of hysteria. The crew complied. The personnel on the *Abeille* and *Nadir* continued to work hard; they had a job to do, and nothing was going to deter them from doing it properly. Yves-Cornet dove, as planned, and Titanic 87 continued on schedule.

By the next day, the furor was still raging, and the general mood was also aggravated by oncoming fog. A basket filled with artifacts, still on the ocean floor but set to be released, was delayed for over two hours because of inclement weather, and when the basket did come up, the stratus cumulus clouds on the surface of the water were so dense that the divers couldn't find it. It took hours for the basket to be located, a basket containing a huge binnacle (a housing for the *Titanic's* compass and a lamp), the *Titanic's* telephone, two telegraphs, the telemotor which would have held the ship's wheel that Captain E. J. Smith commandeered, a ship's light, bottles and plates. Most fascinating, dozens of blood red shrimp covered the telegraph and all the other artifacts. As I wrote in my fax of August 20, but couldn't send until the next day:

It's like Christmas, New Year's Eve and the Fourth of July. Send off the fireworks, open the champagne. We now have every major navigational instrument on the Titanic.

That night I wrote Joel expressing my anxieties about the dangerous conditions:

I must say that being over the Titanic is a very

unnerving experience. I don't consider myself a nervous person, but there's something about being over the wreck that makes you believe in superstition. It makes you believe in supernatural powers. I can't help but wonder what kind of powers lie beneath the waters here, powers that took the Titanic, and if those powers will take more lives again.

I'm still recovering from my near miss, and relieved to say that rumors of my death have been greatly exaggerated. But some of the operations are extremely dangerous on board these two ships. I'm not talking about just boarding and unboarding. I'm talking about the cables and the huge weights on the end of the cables that go swinging about wildly, about to hit anybody in the head.

I'm talking about just the sub operation of releasing and gathering the sub. I'm really alarmed that we might injure somebody by the time this two month expedition is done because it could easily happen, as I now know from personal experience. I hope not; I pray not. I wouldn't as Expedition Leader, want to have a death on my shoulders. I don't know if I could live with myself.

It was a rough day, long and tough. Not just the terrible weather, or the ever-present fear of people being injured, but everything takes so much time. So much of the time the batteries go dead, or motors are out, or the Robin starts malfunctioning.

This job is far more time-consuming than I ever expected. Because of my role as Expedition Leader, there's no rest. It's constant planning, constant coordinating. In the morning it's getting the crew together, laying out the game plan, and after the dives are completed and we're through with dinner, it's screening all the videos that have been shot, logging them in—writing a full description of each tape, as well as planning the next day's dive, what artifacts will be recovered, who will dive, what equipment needs replacement—you get the idea. And, of course, the preparation and transmittal, the typing up of the daily fax to Westgate, detailing everything we've done and plan to do the following day.

My crew makes life easier. Randy, Adam, Mark and Bobby are the hardest working, most capable and most cooperative men I've ever met. They break their backs to do a good job, and this expedition would never have moved ahead so well without them. They hung together and pitched in during the hurricane, like sailors who had been at sea for a dozen years, and whenever I need them, they're always right there.

Even so, because of the heavy responsibilities, I never get to bed before twelve, most nights two or three. And when I do, I lie awake and think about the Titanic. I can't shake it off. Even when I sleep, she haunts my dreams. Ralph feels the same way, and so do most of the others on board. I know Nargeolet does. This mission isn't even over, and they're talking about the <u>next</u> one, about coming back to this site and diving to the wreck again. It makes me think of Bob Ballard's words, "I can't put her aside. She won't let me." I want to feel, when I leave the expedition, that I can go back to a normal existence, without Titanic fever, without the image of this doomed ship controlling every facet of my life.

Sometimes it truly scares me.

Despite my early trepidation, I was happy that Brigitte had joined us on the expedition. In the short time she had been on board, we had become close friends. She was proud of her people, and felt that they acknowledged the contributions of women more readily than Americans.

When I saw a copy of her first broadcast for Radio One, I realized that she had included a description of me. It was interesting to see myself through the eyes of a person from an altogether different background and perspective. Her copy read:

Jennifer is passionate about diving, wrecks, submarines and research. Her head, her brain, her reflexes, her gestures are all turned toward this mission she has to pursue. To bring the mission to fruition, to retrieve the artifacts to, photograph as many objects as possible, to survey the divings, the shootings, always demanding more not only from the searchers and the French pilots. So preoccupied by her work that nothing else matters.

Brigitte arranged for me to speak on Radio One, and it gave me a chance to express my feelings to the French people:

"I'm thrilled to be working as the Expedition Leader of the American Film Team, because it's a wonderful opportunity to show a side of France that Americans are unaware of. Most of the publicity in the United States about France is strictly a romantic image. When Americans think of France, they think of Paris, the Eiffel Tower, the Arc de Triumph, high fashion models, perfume, wine, cheese, fabulous restaurants and famous chefs. We're only beginning to learn about the achievements of French technology. This two hour show, *Return to the Titanic,* will for the first time focus not only on the story of the *Titanic,* but on the progress being made in underwater research and the accomplishments of *Ifremer.*

"It is only due to their amazing engineering that we, as a team, are able to film the *Titanic* at this depth and recover the artifacts safely. I'm proud to be the first woman to dive this deep, but I'm even more proud of the French and American people who made it possible for me. The submarine *Nautile* is capable of exploring ninety-seven percent of the total ocean floor, and can work at depths of up to 6,000 meters.

"For over fifteen years I've been making documentaries and many films on the ocean. This dive was the culmination of my dream to explore the ocean at its deepest reaches. I'm a scuba diver and have dived all over the world, to depths of forty meters, and dived with all types of sharks, whales and dolphins. But this thrill makes the others pale by comparison.

"When I was a little girl, reading Jules Verne's novels, I never dreamed that someday I too would be fortunate enough to see some of the things he prophesied come true.

"When all the artifacts go on display in a worldwide tour, the public will no longer believe press reports claiming that the French and Americans on this expedition are grave robbers. They'll see for themselves the history of this ship come to life, and their children will learn from the tragic circumstances of the *Titanic* that arrogance and greed can only lead to disaster."

My speech was enthusiastically received in France, and Brigitte told me I had become well-known overnight as "Jennie of the *Titanic*."

Chapter 18

Fog Bound

Ever since an iceberg destroyed the *Titanic*, icebergs have come to represent in the minds of most people the most fatal threat to life and safety on the seas. In the history of the sea, fog, however, is an even greater menace. It has destroyed more ships than any iceberg, coral reef, or storm wind.

Fog is silent compared to other natural catastrophes—it doesn't lurch, blow, erupt or crash. But a fog's insidious approach in no way diminishes its impact. Fog is relatively unknown at the equator and in the trade wind belts, but it's ominously familiar in the middle and high latitudes. In the Newfoundland Banks region, the Labrador current and the Gulf Stream converge. When the frigid water of the Labrador Current is overrun by warm air from the Gulf Stream, dense masses of water vapor— fog—appear. These fogs near the Grand Banks are considered to be the most persistent on earth and are known as advection fogs; a thick, stew-like mix occurring when a warm humid mass of air travels across an ice-cold surface.

The higher the concentration of water vapor, the denser the fog becomes, with a consequent loss of visibility. At zero-zero visibility, the fog is an army-like aggregation of hundreds of thousands of water droplets in the surface air so minute that it would take twenty one billion of them to fill a tablespoon.

The story of the Italian luxury liner, the *Andrea Doria,* and her fog-blanketed collision with the Swedish liner *Stockholm,* on July 25, 1956, is a prime example. As a devout student of sea lore, I was able to call the captain's name instantly to mind—Captain Calamai, a fifty-year-old veteran who had one crossing to complete on the *Andrea Doria* before his retirement. The parallel to Captain Smith of the *Titanic* was too startling to ignore: Smith and Calamai were of late middle age, both commanded ships that were labeled unsinkable, and both encouraged their ships to move at a rate that carried elements of risk.

Captain Calamai appeared, on the surface, to be less vulnerable to disaster than Smith. This was forty-four years after the *Titanic* sank, and the *Andrea Doria* had sufficient lifeboat space for 2,000 passengers. Her crew of 572 was also schooled in emergency procedures, and all of the equipment had passed inspection from the United States Coast Guard.

The fog had been lethally teasing and playful—lifting and coaxing the ship to pick up speed, then rolling in again more thickly than before.

When the *Stockholm* suddenly turned directly toward the *Andrea Doria,* and it became appallingly evident that she was going to smash right into her, Captain Calamai made a mistake born of misplaced pride and ego—he elected against turning directly into the *Stockholm,* which would have reduced impact. He couldn't bear, after a lifetime on board the beloved ship, to consciously bring that kind of destruction on her.

With this tragic suspension of judgment, the *Andrea Doria* and the *Stockholm* crashed into each other and fifty-one people died—five crewmen from the *Stockholm* and forty-six from the *Andrea Doria*.

As the person responsible for my crew's safety, I had to decide, along with Captain Nargeolet, whether to let the dive scheduled for August 19 commence as planned. I had been warned at six-thirty that morning by Captain Deshommes and First Mate Christian that any dive would have to be delayed, or possibly canceled because of the seriousness of the enveloping fog.

"Not because the *Nautile* cannot be dropped into the ocean," explained Christian, "but because it's not safe for Captain Zozo to take the zodiac into a fog with no visibility. Not only is the *Nadir* invisible, you can't see ten feet in front of you."

I shuddered when they told me. Don Barkham was scheduled to dive, and matters had been so tense between us that I dreaded telling him he couldn't dive as planned.

"Do you think there's a good chance it'll clear?" I asked.

"We can only wait."

Less than five minutes after their departure, Don knocked on my cabin door. He was already dressed in his fireproof blue suit, and his manner was friendly and engaging.

"Don't worry," Don said, before I could voice my objections. "I've already spoken to the *Nadir*, and there's no problem with the submersible going down."

I explained to him, as courteously as I could, that

the submersible wasn't the problem; it was the zodiac. The reason the *Nautile* presented no difficulty going down was that the A-frame hydraulically lifted it up and over the stern fantail, then gently dropped it right into the location where it was to descend to the bottom. The only crew that had to leave the ship were two divers, to unfasten the cable and lines once the *Nautile* was dropped into the water, and they were no more than thirty feet, in a straight line, from the stern—well within a safe distance.

Our ships maintained a normal separation of as little as 500 feet to a maximum of two miles depending on dangerous weather conditions. Even if they moved the ships to a one mile gap, it would be too much for the zodiac to attempt without the use of vision.

Don's participation wasn't the only issue. He wanted—and had been promised—a film record of his dive. He hoped the footage would be included in our television show. This would have meant requiring our camera crew to make the dangerous crossing via zodiac as well.

"Jennifer," he said angrily, "Get one thing straight. You may be in charge of the crew, but you're not in charge of me."

A voice inside of me said, *you're cutting your own throat. He's going to bad mouth you all over the ship. He'll destroy you unless you give your permission.*

I was intimidated, but I had the lives of eight men in my hands. If anything happened to them, I would always know I capitulated under pressure in order to be political, or to avoid hostility.

"I can't risk my crew's lives or yours," I said quietly. Then, with Don trailing, I went to ask Captain Rowarch, whose levelheaded caution I'd come to respect, if Zozo used any kind of nautical equipment that could safeguard him and his passenger, and prevent their getting lost.

"No," said Captain Rowarch. "There's too much variance in using a compass. With zero visibility, it won't do you any good with two ships this far apart, and it's entirely possible that Zozo and whoever is on board with him could be lost at sea."

"What are the odds?"

"Fifty-fifty."

"What about in an hour or so?" I asked. "If some of the fog lifts."

"Forty percent. Maybe thirty percent."

I knew that was still too risky, and I was certain that John Joslyn and Doug Llewelyn would oppose any plan that put our men in danger.

"What about bringing the *Nadir* and the *Abeille* closer together?"

"We can't take that chance. They might collide."

I decided, along with the captain, to delay Don's dive, to see if the fog dissipated.

Don was as obstinate as ever. If we lost this day, he would lose his dive. He demanded a second opinion.

When you're in a position of leadership, you move along in a smooth, prescribed pattern. Years before, I had read a description written by an airline pilot, "Flying is 95% boredom and 5% stark terror," and I now understood exactly what he meant. The tests of authority are those rare and often lonely instances when you have to make a decision that is uncomfortable, steeped in gray areas, and beyond that, unpopular. A crucial decision means having to risk standing alone. Barkham was an influential man. I didn't want to alienate him. But my responsibilities had to come first.

"Let's talk to Captain Nargeolet and Captain Keran-flech," I suggested, wanting to gather as much information as I could before making the final decision. We went to the wheel-house and spoke to them via the ship's radio, attempting to get a definitive opinion. Neither would commit to a clear-cut yes or no. Yes, it was dangerous, they said, yes, we could lose crew members at sea, but Captain Zozo was a miracle man with the zodiac, and he *could* conceivably maneuver it through the impenetrable, blinding wall of fog.

"But Jennifer," said Nargeolet. "Whatever you decide, it has to be now."

That slim strip of window, the concession that it would *possibly* be all right, gave Don his opening. He shut his ears to all the warnings expressed. Fanatically focused, he had set his mind on diving and saw me as the only obstacle to his achievement—and his future glory.

"Zozo has agreed," he told me. "He's willing to take me over. He's not about to give in to any female cow-ardice."

"Female cowardice? Is that what you call wanting to insure the lives of my crew?"

"Oh, come off it," Don snapped. "There's no threat to anyone. If there was, Zozo wouldn't be willing to trans-port me."

"Zozo's a *daredevil*," I said. "He loves taking chances. He's like a cowboy on that zodiac."

"He knows his job—which is more than I can say for you."

I tightened my fists but kept my temper. Lives, not one-upmanship, were at stake here, and that was where my responsibility lay. "If Zozo's willing, I can't stop you," I said. "But I'm not sending my crew."

"Jennifer, I'll make you sorry for this," Don

threatened. "When you take me on, honey, you're way out of your league."

"Don't call me honey."

"I'll call you what I like. Listen—you're a woman doing a man's job. You don't have enough experience to be an Expedition Leader. And don't tell me about your days at Geographic. You weren't supervising fifty men on a National Geographic shoot. Don't you realize that's unnatural—a woman organizing activities for fifty men? It was insane to structure things that way in the first place. Have you ever heard of a case like this before? No. And there's a *reason* you haven't—because only a man can understand what other men need, and what they want. You'd be doing everyone on this ship a big favor if you stepped out of the way, and there's not one man on board who doesn't agree with me. Not one!"

That parting shot shook me. Was it true? Did my crew really see me as Don did?

I clung to hard evidence, certain realities which flew against every accusation he made. On all my projects and former expeditions, I had worked with men, and the collaborations had been marvelous: Nick Noxon and I, at Geographic, had been creatively in synch from the first day. The same had been true with Mel Stuart on *The Amazing Animals;* Al Giddings, Jim Lipscomb and Executive Producer Peter Guber on *Mysteries of the Sea;* Ralph on many commercials for Sea World, documentaries and the Loch Ness Monster Expedition; Martin Carr at Smithsonian World. I couldn't recall one moment of major friction with any of them, and most important, *they had all rehired me after the first projects were completed.*

Despite that, I was shaken but determined not to show it. Arguing was pointless; it would only force a second round of attacks and sexist remarks. I grasped for a sane resolution and my thoughts spun around and fastened on Ralph Rosato, John Joslyn's friend, who happened to be a lawyer. I respected Rosato; he was intelligent, friendly and supportive.

After explaining the situation, I asked him to draw up a legal paper absolving Westgate and me of all responsibility, in the event that anything happened to Zozo and Don. Rosato, as Westgate's representative, was happy to draft the agreement, and concurred that it was absolutely necessary. Don had no choice but to sign it, taking full responsibility for his own life and for Captain Zozo's.

My concession wasn't enough. He still wanted the camera crew to immortalize his *Titanic* dive.

"I won't do that—I can't."

Don's face turned scarlet. He took such a deep breath that I expected to see him explode on the spot.

"I want that crew."

"No. And it's not because I'm against your having a dive. It's nothing personal."

"I think it *is* personal," Don said. "I think you made up your mind the first day I was here to stand in my way. But remember—this is only the first round." He strode out of the room.

Rosato, who had been standing by witnessing the signing of the agreement, was amazed at Don's venom.

"This guy doesn't make idle threats," he warned.

"What could I have done?"

"Not a damn thing," said Rosato. "But that doesn't matter to him."

Don made his dive without a camera crew, and he survived the crossing.

He came up to me after returning to the *Abeille* and said, "You see, Jennifer? You were all wrong. Look at me, I'm fine. Zozo's fine. And the camera crew would have been fine too. You really should leave, Jennifer. You're in over your head."

Suddenly I felt insecure. I remembered Don's remark that everyone on board agreed with him. I had to know if his statements had been propelled by jealousy and resentment, or if they had some basis in fact. I've already prided myself on being a realist, and have never wanted to live on illusions.

Gearing myself up for whatever lay ahead, I spoke to the *Abeille* crew one by one—Adam, Randy, Bobby Keyes, Ralph and Mark. Each of them looked surprised, and I could tell—before they even spoke—that these negative feelings had never even occurred to them. I polled the captains too—Rowarch, Nargeolet, Keranflech, Deshommes and Christian, the first mate.

They told me I was doing a great job, and Christian even went as far as to say that my efforts were the glue that held the whole expedition together. That was an exaggeration, but I loved him for it.

Captain Rowarch invited me to his cabin for an aperitif. Drink in hand, he said, "Jennifer... there are always people who want to make trouble. No matter how many expeditions you ever go on, you'll find at least one person who threatens the good will and morale of all the others."

Rowarch's fatherly manner was comforting, and I felt a need to confide in someone.

"It's hard to pretend sometimes. When you're supposed to be in control, when the responsibilities are all on your shoulders, it's hard to hide when you're hurt, or insulted. Of course, Don makes it sound as if my decisions are made because I'm weak and scared and because I'm a woman."

Rowarch smiled, a little sadly.

"Because you're a woman? Then what's my excuse? I have to pretend too. I have to put up a strong front sometimes when I'm crumbling inside. So does every captain who ever lived, everybody who leads. The test of leadership is pushing *past* those feelings. It's acting like you're not afraid when you're scared to death. It's taking over and reassuring others when *you* don't know what the hell to do. You did the right thing today, Jennifer," Rowarch told me. "Just because Don and Zozo didn't die or get lost at sea doesn't mean you made a mistake. It could just have easily gone the other way."

"Don will never forgive me."

"Look at it like this—for what he did, he should never forgive himself."

I was struck by the compassion and wisdom of this man. Listening to him, I understood more fully than ever what a leader should have—the kind of strength and humanity Rowarch had, that I had also found in Keranflech and Nargeolet, Christian and Deshommes.

It was a standard I could only hope to reach someday.

Chapter 19

Who Loves Ya, Baby?

Fax to Westgate
August 20, 1987

> *The most beautiful and emotionally moving artifact we've recovered was brought up today—an angel, a bronze cherub from the aft grand staircase. It's eighteen inches high. I estimate its original height at over two feet, because a glass torch with a light in it was once attached.*
>
> *This bronze angel is so breathtaking it could be the centerpiece for the whole exhibition. Also retrieved: a complete marble basin with faucets, an electric panel with indications of where watertight compartments were. I believe it's the panel with switches that closed and opened the watertight compartments, which were designed to make the Titanic unsinkable.*

It was easy—and frightening—to imagine that during the sinking, desperate people grabbed onto the angel for luck—a rumor that had found its way into *Titanic* folklore. The angel appeared to have wings that were clipped in the tragedy. All of us could imagine the almost religious fervor people felt when they touched this angel.

Having known Edwina Troutt MacKenzie, I wondered if she had touched the angel during those last minutes before her rescue.

The image gave me chills. More than any artifact brought up so far, it took me back, as in a time capsule, to all the passengers who started out with such high hopes and dreams, and then were suddenly confronted with the stark horror of imminent death.

The angel represented something deep and meaningful from the past; the world of Hollywood represented all that was fleeting and ephemeral in the present.

Of course, our mission had a dual purpose. The first, the historical mission, had been made possible in large part by its second purpose—the film. Tribune Entertainment, backer of our upcoming show *Return to the Titanic,* had chosen Telly Savalas as host, and Westgate had suggested leasing a yacht for him and bringing him out to the ship, where he would stay for three days. And since Savalas thought it would be an exciting adventure, he proposed bringing his wife, his children, their nanny and other relatives. He needed five rooms.

If a man at sea was asked his opinion of Hollywood stars, he would smile, the lines in his weatherbeaten face would crease and he would say they were a bunch of flakes—that is, if he was polite. If he wasn't polite, the answers would all be phrased in four letter words.

If he was asked to give up his cabin to accommodate a television star, the smile would disappear and his face would darken with resentment.

My crew was no different. They were knocking themselves out during the day, and then relegated to tiny cabins, two to a room, sharing showers and trying to squeeze their muscular bulk into beds that barely accommodated me—and I was half their size.

A crew at sea does serious work; work requiring labor and sweat, work that taxes their physical stamina to the limit. They perceive actors as dilettantes by comparison, walking in front of a camera, saying their few lines and then disappearing into a dressing room with beautiful female co-stars.

No one's mood was particularly good on August 20. The weather was foul, the waves kicking up as if to remind us not to be complacent. The heaping swells seemed to be saying, *Don't turn your back on me. I'm out there, waiting. I can rear up at any time when you least expect it.*

Turbulence was a daily part of our existence, and we never knew from hour to hour whether dives would proceed as planned, or be aborted at the last second. Under these circumstances, no one wanted to deal with a pampered television star.

At the first hint of this, and the rapid realization that they would have to surrender their rooms for Telly, all the men on the *Abeille* grew apoplectic. A few toyed with the idea of throwing him overboard if he put one foot on the ship; others amused themselves by planning the sadistic jokes they would play on him.

Yves Martinon, second engineer, who was completely bald and had a face shaped exactly like Telly's—who could have been Telly's double—swaggered into dinner one night with a large lollipop in one hand and a cigar dangling from his lips. He wore dark glasses, his shirt was unbuttoned to the navel, and three gold chains hung around his neck.

He shouted Telly's signature line, "Who loves ya, baby?" and a chant rose through the galley. "No one here!"

In French, Yves yelled out, "Okay, which one of you are giving up your cabins for me and my family?" To which the room went totally silent.

For days afterward, a routine developed. Somebody would say, "Who loves ya, baby?" and the answer would inevitably be, "Not me."

I called Westgate and told them that anger was building, that it would be far preferable if Telly did his scenes in Paris—anyplace that didn't require him to disrupt the lives of our crew. They were adamant; he was our star, and stars had to be given VIP treatment.

"You're putting your head on the chopping block again," Ralph said. "You know I care about you, Jennifer, but not everything's a big deal. You have to decide which battles to fight—some are worth fighting, some aren't."

Maybe that was a weakness. It was certainly a *political* weakness. But my nature was to leap in when I saw an injustice. I responded instantly to situations and acted on them. Ralph always emphasized protecting your flanks, and I know he was advising me for what he perceived to be my own good.

The *Abeille* crew was grateful, and I became more conscious than ever of one facet of leadership: your crew comes first, before everything. It was a lesson that received daily re-enforcement through my dealings with Captain Rowarch.

But Ralph was right in recognizing the consequences of standing out on a limb after you've sawed the branch. As I explained in a letter to Joel at this time,

Rowarch got reamed by Westgate for opposing Telly's plans to stay on the Abeille. The Nadir doesn't want him; they have even less room than we do. Rowarch wasn't put off; he said he was going on record that he doesn't want Telly out here on the ship. He feels it's insane to leave the Titanic site on the third, get back to St. Pierre on the fifth to pick up Telly and his family, and not return to the site until the seventh. We would lose four to five days that could more profitably be spent recovering artifacts, and that's far more important to an expedition than catering to Mr. Kojak.

Although Westgate was still holding firm to their plans for Telly, the situation did accomplish one positive thing: it allowed the crew to let off steam through obscene humor. We had all become so *serious,* so dead set on diving, so preoccupied with the *Titanic.* The spectre of this liner 12,500 feet below the sea was always with us, serving as a constant reminder that all the artifacts had once belonged to people who were now gone, and that we had to preserve them as a memorial and remembrance of those lost.

Chapter 20

Party Time

We had been at sea for over a month, experienced a cataclysmic hurricane and relentless slurs from the media. All of us missed our loved ones, and felt terrible that the unfounded accident rumors had caused our families so much panic on land.

We needed a boost for our flagging spirits. In the last week of August we got one.

William F. Buckley Jr., columnist, television personality and Sailor Supreme, had written a column praising our expedition. It was the first unqualified pat on the back we'd received since *Titanic 87* was initiated. It occurred to me, reading his eloquent defense of our goals, that he would be the perfect spokesman for the expedition—more articulate than Don, a genuine intellectual and a name recognized throughout the world. Yves-Cornet of Taurus International agreed with me and encouraged me to contact him.

Acting on instinct, I called Buckley's office in New York. His extraordinarily capable, supportive associate, Frances Bronson, answered the phone and promised to relay my message. True to her word, she passed it on and when I called again, he was there to discuss my offer—would he be interested in spending a week on the *Abeille*, observing all the daily mechanics of our operation, studying the dive operations in detail and perhaps making a dive himself?

The idea delighted him, as I had expected. He contacted Westgate, and arrangements were made for him to come on board the next time we refueled at St. Pierre.

I didn't know how the men would react, since Buckley's most high-profile claim to glory was through his controversial television show, *Firing Line*. To my surprise, they knew him primarily as a *sailor*, as a man whose first love was the sea. Many of them had read his books on the sea—*Atlantic High, Airborne* and *Racing through Paradise*.

The prospect of his arrival overcame any gloom about Telly Savalas, and all of us felt excited and positive. It didn't matter that the weather was still acting up, and half our conversations were conducted at tilted angles from the listing ship, to the accompaniment of howling winds and contentious waves.

We were ripe for a good rowdy, hell-raising party.

It wasn't just a party for the *Abeille;* everyone from the *Nadir* came over, despite the high swells outside: Brigitte, Nargeolet, Pierre-Yves, Keranflech. The French were especially high, because the bonus money for the safe had finally been paid, and I was relieved because it reinforced their trust in me and in the good intentions of Westgate.

Wine flowed freely; all of us sang *We all live in a yellow submarine, Sloop John B*—with heavy emphasis on the lines *I wanna go home, I wanna go home*—and we sang and danced sailor jigs, going around in circles, linking arms at the elbows, first in one direction, then changing arms and going the opposite way. Brigitte and I linked arms with Pierre-Yves, Ralph and Bobby in a chorus line, and Randy played the famous French song from the *Folies Bergere,* as we kicked our legs up high, imitating and parodying can-can dancers.

The *Abeille* rolled to starboard and back again. We slid across the floor but our spirits were so high we kept dancing. At the end we turned and flipped up our derrieres, imitating how women always did it in French revues.

Nargeolet and Keranflech had brought over the best bottles of wine from the *Nadir.* Not to be outdone, Rowarch, Deshommes and the chef Camille had taken out a case of the *Abeille's* finest French wine. It became a competition, a wine-tasting contest between ships.

All the captains were blindfolded and asked to sample a wine from the *Abeille,* then from the *Nadir,* without knowing if they were tasting the wine from their own ship or wine from the competing ship. When they announced their preference, occupants of the winning ship roared loudly, stamping, screaming, jumping up on tables. People starting placing bets: *Nadir* or *Abeille.*

Over the screams we heard the wind roaring outside. Water sprayed against the portholes. Nobody cared. Each time a winner was announced, wine would flow to every member of that ship. By the time the overall winner was chosen, we were too drunk to know the difference.

Mark was photographing us in states of uncontrolled laughter, good-natured pushing around. Somehow the unstable, bouncing ship only added to our sense of freedom. Randy had a guitar, and we were able to sing with accompaniment. Bobby sang an Irish lullaby, *Too-ra*

Loo-ra Loo-ra; Pierre-Yves did spoof versions of *Like a Virgin* and *Voulez-vous coucher avec moi;* Ralph Rosato, in a musical Italian tenor, belted out the Barbra Streisand-Donna Summer hit *Enough is Enough,* making everybody howl with the opening lines, "It's raining, it's pouring, my love life is boring me to tears." Brigitte's contribution was *La Vie En Rose* - and Randy, per his nickname, bowled us over with an imitation of King Kong on top of a building, snatching Brigitte in his long arms, climbing to the top of the table and emitting an ear-splitting Tarzan jungle cry.

"Why don't you sing Joel's song from *The Poseidon Adventure?*" said Ralph. "It's about a ship turning over and killing everybody. That should be a barrel of laughs."

I had heard Joel sing *The Morning After* a hundred times, but never to a crowd like this.

There's Got to be a morning after
If we can hold on through the night.
We have a chance to find the sunshine
Let's keep on looking for the light.
There's got a be a morning after
We're moving closer to the shore.
I know we'll be there by tomorrow
And we'll escape the darkness
We won't be searching anymore.

There was an explosive round of applause—more for my guts than my performance.

The *Abeille* rose and plunged, but everyone was so determined to let loose that they forgot to be scared. As a capper to the evening, I presented T-shirts I had made up in St. Pierre as a commemoration of the trip. I leaped up on a bench and tossed them out. Now thoroughly inebriated, the men began to rip off the shirts they were wearing and replace them with the new T-shirts.

Nargeolet was first, egged on by his pilots. He laughed un-self-consciously, treated us to a view of his superbly conditioned torso and put on the new shirt.

"Wait a minute," shouted Ralph, "Jennifer's not wearing one. And neither is Brigitte."

Brigitte needed no second invitation; she flung off a long-sleeved, Navy blue and white striped knit top, tossing it into the outstretched, raised arms of the men. They grabbed for it eagerly, cheering as though they were watching a strip show.

"Now Jennifer, it's your turn."

All I could do was take a deep breath and go with the moment.

The *Abeille* veered sharply to the right. I waited for it to steady itself, then took out my final contribution—an inflatable mermaid, over five feet long, that I'd found in St. Pierre. Ralph grabbed it and blew it up to appreciative whistles, and all the men took turns dancing with their new companion.

It was at that moment that Don Barkham walked in. I didn't realize it at first, until Brigitte motioned to me and whispered, "Look who's here."

I didn't have to be told. I had noticed Don's absence earlier, with a sense of relief. I wondered if his arrival signaled the end of everyone's buoyant spirits. Everyone knew the conflict that existed between us. He had gone to every single person at the party, suggesting I be relieved of my duties.

The room grew as quiet as a mortuary. Even nature turned down the volume. The wildly erratic waves grew calmer, the wind seemed to recede in the distance.

Then, suddenly, my crew came over and lifted me onto their shoulders. They carried me across the room, shouting, "Jennifer, Jennifer," and their chorus was taken up by all the other guests. Glasses were lifted, toasts were made, and Rowarch said, "To the brightest and most beautiful Expedition leader that's ever graced a ship—our Jennifer—the Queen of the *Abeille*—the bright star of the *Nadir*—the light of our ships, the light of our hearts, the inspiration to us all."

His words were more effusive, more validating, than any I could have asked for. Once and for all, I knew I had my crew's support, and they had made it clear to Don.

Don stared directly into my eyes. For a second I thought he might hold out a hand. But he gave nothing. The fact that the members of the expedition had pointedly rejected his claims only made his anger worse. He stayed for a few minutes, had a quick drink and departed.

"Good riddance," said Brigitte.

The storm was roaring now, and we had to break up the party so the *Nadir* crew could make it back on the zodiac without falling overboard.

I had filled Joel in on my altercation with Don. He listened lovingly and patiently and sent back a lyric that said it all:

> *Mister Don —you've done your job*
> *Tried to gather up a mob*
> *Hitler could have learned some things from you.*
>
> *Such a slimy, evil stunt*
> *Fed the pack and led the hunt*
> *Out for blood - you've had your twisted coup.*

Character assassination
That's your stock in trade.
Lies are your fixation
Someday you'll be paid.

Cruelty is your mistress
Hate is your crusade
Pounding the defenseless
That's the game you've played.

Mister Don—go on, big guy
Kick someone and make them cry
That must be the kind of fun you dig.

Mister Don—a macho man
Is it fun to plot and plan
Hurting someone makes you feel so big.

No one is suspicious
They just know your charm
And if you're acting vicious
You think, 'what's the harm'?
Let's get off on cruelty
Drink a toast to hate
And if a life has been destroyed
What the hell, it's fate.

Mister Don—Pseudo star
Don't you know how small you are
Preening like a peacock in the sun?

Mister Don - how you connive
You may get your chance to dive

But you'll wind up empty when it's done.

Mister Don - Mister Don

The words perfectly captured the way Don—my friend—had acted.

The situation involving Telly Savalas coming on board, a seemingly trivial issue, veered quickly from comedic to a conflict of catastrophic proportions. Part of the problem was an oil-and-water combination of ingredients built into our expedition.

Most expeditions are carried out in a clearly defined atmosphere. They have a goal: to conquer a mountain, to discover a shipwreck, to travel to never-explored regions, seek new scientific information, unearth new archeological finds. The people involved are driven by that one goal. The world of motion pictures is completely foreign to them.

Suddenly these same adventurous individuals are placed under a Hollywood microscope. Every move is observed and recorded. Every dramatic incident is devoured by a hungry camera. These adventurers love the outdoors, they thrive on the physicality demanded of them. They don't know—and don't care about—the artificial world of multiple takes and hot, intrusive lights.

Titanic 87 wasn't only a blend of two different, occasionally warring factions like the French and the Americans; it also had a schizoid combination of film-makers and professional seamen. Given those built-in differences, it was amazing that everybody co-existed as well as they did.

Had Telly been a different kind of star—someone

less "hip", someone who seemed regular, rather than show business, his intrusion into our daily routine might have been overlooked grudgingly, but with basic good nature. Had he proposed coming alone, instead of bringing a dozen other people, the men on the *Abeille* and *Nadir* would have swallowed their bile. But his guests, though family, had the sound of an entourage, and the request for special privileges rankled deeply.

As a result, resentment flared up on board. All the men flatly refused to surrender their rooms, or to squeeze themselves in with other people, sacrificing even minimal comfort.

I conveyed the seriousness of the situation when I faxed my bosses at Westgate, explained that the men weren't happy about it, and suggested that Telly be filmed in some other location. But they adhered strictly to one of the iron rules of the motion picture world—never offend the star.

Even so, this was an unusual set of circumstances—the real star was the *Titanic,* and the co-stars were these remarkable men who dove down and risked their lives to find and secure the artifacts.

Christian came to my room one night and expressed his feelings.

"When I was a young man I ran off to sea," he confided to me. "Everything on land seemed so false to me, and there was something pure about the ocean. I know its faults. Sometimes I feel that the love I have for it is a curse. But it's *honest.* And there's something so dishonest about having a star on board. I don't mean like Mr. Buckley. I don't know much about him, but I know he's one of us."

I understood everything he was saying. Whatever he was in private life, he had retained an idealistic innocence about the sea. How could I explain that the world of idealism and commerce often met head on and had to co-exist. How could I explain what I knew—that shows demanded stars, that networks fought for high ratings, that the world of motion pictures and television, exciting as they were, lacked the purity he was speaking of?

"You knew we were making a film," I said carefully.

"But will it be a good film? Will it do justice to the subject of the Titanic?"

"We're all working to make it the best film we can."

He was so genuinely distraught that I couldn't do anything to raise his spirits. Knowledgeable as Christian was about ships, about weather, winds, waves and navigation, he was seventeen at heart.

The rumblings continued. Nargeolet and Pierre-Yves agreed with Christian, but they were less threatened, since the plan was to place Telly on the *Abeille*.

Captain Rowarch stood by his men. To me he seemed made of steel. When it was suggested that the men on the *Abeille* draw straws to determine who would give up their quarters, they said no.

"What are you going to do?" I asked them all. "Throw him off the ship?"

"Maybe."

I doubted if they would resort to violence, but I did know they would make his life a living hell, and the overall morale of the ship would suffer.

"Rowarch's got guts," Ralph said to me.

"He's the bravest man I ever met. He's everything a captain should be."

We stood on the bridge, watching the unexpectedly calm ocean, savoring the first unclouded sky we'd seen in weeks.

"You and I have come a long way," Ralph said.

The rare, relaxed serenity of the moment brought me back years ago, when he had taken a raw, inexperienced, insecure young woman and shaped her, opened her eyes to undreamed-of possibilities.

"I like you when you're like this," he said. "Easy. Relaxed. That's the real Jennifer."

"No," I told him. "That's only *part* of the real Jennifer. The other part—the part that's intense and meets things head on—I know it drives you crazy sometimes, but that's the real Jennifer too."

"You could have played it differently with Don," Ralph said. "You could have sweet-talked him. What if he starts badmouthing you throughout the industry? You're gonna run into this guy again and he has lots of influence." He shook his head, as if bewildered. "What is it about you, that you're *always putting your head on the chopping block?*"

"Ralph, you know I invited him on board this ship. I wanted him to make the dive but I had no choice."

He was quiet.

"I'm human. I want to be liked. I don't want to make enemies, any more than you do. But if I had it to do over, I'd do it again."

The Telly Savalas situation was growing more heated, and even Captain Rowarch began to backtrack. Resentment was turning to rage. I saw it every time I told my crew that Westgate intended to adhere to their original plan.

In the end, it wasn't Westgate who determined the outcome. It was Telly Savalas himself. He decided he wanted to shoot the sequences in Martinique, where the *Nadir* planned to stop on its way back to France. It seemed inevitable, once he made that decision. Martinique, not Newfoundland, would have always been the choice of a star.

Chapter 21

Treasure and Treachery

I was so relieved that the Savalas situation had been successfully resolved that I slept soundly for the first time in weeks. Even the lurching of the ship didn't jar me awake.

When I finally opened my eyes, I didn't jump up, military-style, as six weeks of the expedition had conditioned me to do. The invisible bugle played dimly in the back of my mind, but I ignored it. I was going to allow myself the luxury of awakening slowly, the way I did at home on a restful Sunday.

Above all, I wanted to meet the day without a single thought, a single image of responsibility. But when I saw a note slipped under my door, I knew that its contents were going to snap me awake with a single glance.

I picked it up, letting my tired eyes rest on its contents.

Are you sure you have all the artifacts? Check again.

The tone of the line sounded like a parody of a spy novel. I read it three times, then showered and got dressed. Before going to Captain Rowarch, I had to make certain the message wasn't a practical joke. There were several jokers on the expedition: Pierre-Yves, Ralph, Randy.

I wanted to go down to the equipment room and check the artifacts, but I didn't want to go alone. I needed backup, in case valuable treasures were missing. When I ran into Bobby Keyes, our cameraman, on the way to the galley, I knew immediately that he was the perfect choice.

Bobby was one of those rare individuals without a calculating or manipulative bone in his body. He had so much talent he didn't need to be jealous, and a sunny nature that defused tension wherever he went. He inspired unquestioning trust.

I explained the problem, and he voiced my first reaction, "Someone is pulling your leg." Still, we went below, into the bowels of the ship. We climbed down a companionway ladder and entered a dank, humid, oppressive room, a storage room for diving gear that also housed every artifact the expedition had discovered. Diver's wetsuits hung, dripping and drying out.

The crew never saw it; it was off-limits. Captain Rowarch and Christian rarely went there either. No one relished being in such a grim, smelly area. The artifacts weren't endangered by this environment. since they were stored in plastic containers and kept in water. Artifacts were measured, logged into a book, given a number, then placed in plastic containers and kept in water. The containers and water insured their safety, even in this dank, unpleasant atmosphere.

We found Bosco and Belle Bougie, the two boatswains. Both were short but strong, and Belle Bougie—whose real name was Pascal Bertin—was appropriately nicknamed. Belle Bougie means beautiful candlepower in French, and he had a smile that lit up a room. Bosco, whose real name was Jean Roblin, was twenty years older, with thick wire-like gray hair. He exuded the confidence of a thirty-three year veteran at sea. They were checking the zodiac motors. I told them I had to make a brief check of specific artifacts for Doug and Don. They helped Bobby and I to find where things were located.

I was struck again by the voluminous amount of egg plates we'd gathered—151 of them—so many that the crew had called our enterprise an "eggspedition". Every possible play on words was used, from eggs-traordinary to eggsceptional. At dinnertime, we would go around the room, and each crew member would take a turn. The one who came up with the most egg words was the winner.

"I'm eggs-asperated," Ralph would say, and Randy would follow with eggsited, until every egg word was exhausted. To make the game more of a challenge, we switched to doing sentences with two or more eggs words, such as "Captain Keranflech is an eggsemplary eggsecutive officer."

By the time the game was done, we'd all be falling over in gales of eggscruciating laughter.

The acquisition of egg plates also drew its share of ridicule. George Tulloch, a new player on the scene and freshly appointed head of ORE (Oceanic Research Explorations) had told Westgate he wanted every egg plate on the ocean floor; Keranflech felt we shouldn't bring one more egg plate up, that we needed more variety in our artifact selections. Nargeolet was willing to follow whatever orders were given, whether Tulloch's or Keranflech's, but he too thought we were going eggstravagently overboard on our egg plate emphasis.

What had originally attracted Tulloch to egg plates was a wonderful still shot that had been taken on the bottom, of a crate of egg plates that had landed totally intact from the *Titanic*. The crate was no longer there, because wood-boring molluscs had eaten it, but the egg plates were all stacked up, as though ready and waiting for the chef to serve a special breakfast of Eggs Benedict.

The still was aesthetically striking—it was one George intended to release at the press conference coming up—and it was a natural idea to use it as a centerpiece in a museum exhibit, surrounded by all the egg plates. The only problem it presented was one of time; the more hours we expended on retrieving each and every egg plate, the more dives were used up and the less hours we had for other things.

Our list, compiled by Keranflech, Nargeolet, Rowarch, Ralph and me, contained egg plates, but also included suitcases, valises, china, silver platters, any navigational ship's equipment, davits for the lifeboats, portholes, ornamental items such as vases or ceramic ware that were definitive of the period.

One idea we had all agreed on at the inception of Titanic 87 was that no shoes or hats would be touched, since they had been an integral part of human beings that had descended to the bottom. We felt that a suitcase was a different matter; it wasn't part of an individual's personal clothing, and could have just dropped out of the cargo area or any part of the ship. Despite accusations made in the press, there was a genuine concern and respect for those who had died on this site. Every person on board felt this way.

Perhaps the most important aspect of my responsibility, I felt, was contributing to the decisions that determined what our pilots recovered, what items would make a beautiful and meaningful exhibit. We still had not retrieved the exquisitely designed leaded cut glass window from the door entering the first class dining room, and we felt that would be a major and significant achievement.

The artifacts had become almost human to us. Stealing them was a violation, a rape that insulted the memory of the ship's victims. Whether egg plates—a source of humor—or vases—a source of beauty—these artifacts deserved our respect.

If a thief was going to steal anything, the overabundance of egg plates made them a perfect target. They were the items to count first.

Another reason egg plates were so simple to take was that they couldn't be distinguished from the modern day egg plates utilized on the ship. The vast majority of artifacts bore no resemblance to contemporary items. They had the White Star Line logo, or they were representative of the early twentieth century period.

The next logical step, once we confirmed that certain items appeared to be missing, was to consult Captain Rowarch. Bobby and I both agreed that it would be pointless to involve anyone else in our crew; it was sure to destroy morale.

Sitting in Rowarch's cabin, watching him read the note, I felt sympathy for him. He believed passionately in his men, and major theft would cast an unavoidable cloud on his command and call his efficiency into question. Robert Chappaz, the head of Taurus International and Rowarch's employer, was known by reputation as a powerful perfectionist.

"I can't accept this," Rowarch said.

"You have to," I said softly. "We have to investigate the possibility." The three of us returned to the equipment room and Rowarch checked all the items against his list. When the checking was done, his face had turned grayer than his hair.

I believed that third class china, as well as egg plates, were among the missing items, as well as a golden Greek orthodox cross. I asked him which ones were gone, and he said he'd tell me the exact items once he made his final count and his list.

Robert Chappaz was arriving in St. Pierre on the first of September. When he reached the site, Rowarch promised to talk to him.

On August 29, just before we departed for St. Pierre to refuel, Brigitte came aboard the *Abeille*. She was smoking furiously, her hands trembling as she held her cigarette.

"So you're leaving to pick up Monsieur Buckley," she said.

"Yes."

"And they expect me to leave with you? Without my dive?"

The rain had begun to fall lightly, but we continued to stand on deck.

"How can I leave without seeing the *Titanic*?" Brigitte said. "If I do that, it will haunt me my whole life. To be *so* close, and not see it. So close." Her expression of anguish changed to anger. "Those bastards. Those *dollar* makers," she said. "What can I do?"

I showed her a copy of the fax I had received on August 24, which read:

Please respond to my telex, regarding trip ending August 24 for Europe One and confirm that personnel has disembarked.

I explained to her again that they were afraid to have an article about the dive hit the world press before the show was aired.

"That makes no sense. Buckley is coming on board, and he's going to write about his dive."

"Yes," I admitted, "but he's on our side. They know he's going to write something positive."

"And I won't? Just because I'm French, they don't trust me. Look at my Radio One reports. Have I said anything wrong up till now?"

I knew, from all her broadcasts, that she was an expert journalist with no thought of slinging mud, and her reports from the ship to Europe One had been accurate and carefully researched. They had, in fact, created a frenzy of excitement in France about the upcoming television show.

"I know about the missing artifacts," she said.

"How?"

She smiled. "I'm a journalist. It's my job to know these things. Don't you think I could use that if I wanted to? But I wouldn't. I'm not here to destroy a legend. I'm here to help the Americans and they don't see it."

There was nothing I could say. I couldn't give her false hope and tell her Westgate would bend. They were dead set against it, immovable. Taurus and Ifremer had sanctioned Brigitte's presence on the ship, against Westgate's wishes, and there were still vestiges of that French vs. American distrust.

"Well, don't miss the boat," I told her. "We leave at eleven, and if you miss it, we'll have to go without you. It would be *terrible* if somehow we left, and no one could find you on board the *Nadir*. If, for instance, you were in the library, or holed up in your room. Then you'd be here for the rest of the expedition. And anything can happen during that time, don't you think?"

"Yes," she said, her lips curling into a slight smile. "I must be ready on time."

"So you'd better start packing now."

"I'll do that," she said, hugging me.

When the *Abeille* left for St. Pierre at midnight, for our expedition's final refueling, Brigitte wasn't on it.

I couldn't help identifying with her desire to be a part of history, to have an experience of a lifetime. William Buckley would be diving within a few days, and then writing a newspaper article about his reactions; details of a *Titanic* dive would no longer be a secret. Nor would Brigitte's report even be heard in America.

Most of all I knew, even if the others didn't, that Brigitte's story would be a tremendous asset for us all. There was still no guarantee that she would dive, but by remaining on the *Nadir* for the rest of the trip, she had a fighting chance.

I stood on the deck, watching the ship pull away from the site, and thought of Joel. He had once again arranged to come to St. Pierre to see me, and his presence would make it easier to deal with some of the up-and-coming personality conflicts and political pressures looming.

Miraculously, thus far on our expedition, the participation of five captains didn't impair the smoothness of its operations. But other captains of a different kind were beginning to pile up. In addition to Westgate, we were now expected to deal with Chappaz and George Tulloch of ORE. All of them were meeting us in St. Pierre and coming out to the site. I couldn't help feeling some trepidation.

These multiple participants had exerted their influence via long distance. Their new orders, counter-orders and revised orders had been a challenge to execute, especially when they conflicted with each other. But at least it was done without face-to-face encounters.

Now, on the last leg of our expedition, they were converging on us all at once, accompanied by investors.

Each person saw himself as the prime mover of the expedition. Robert Chappaz was a self-crowned king, a man of intelligence and charm but enormous ego; George Tulloch was a man of vision, who perceived himself as keeper of the flame, protector of the *Titanic* legacy and the individual sent to make sure that artifacts became part of history and were displayed in exhibits all over the world.

Tulloch's commitment was clear from his comments to the press:

"You don't spend ten years on something like this because of the business," he said. "You get to know more about the people who were on board, you start falling in love with the people and their stories... and you realize how crazy the world is for this subject and therefore how important it is to do it right."

He had put together a group of investors, and they were to accompany us on our final return to the site. Tulloch, through his company ORE, had raised more than two million dollars toward financing the expedition.

Westgate Productions also cared about protecting the legacy, and they were equally concerned that the quality and appeal of their documentary did justice to its subject.

Everyone had high-minded motives, but different methods of achieving them.

I silently said a prayer of thanks for the presence of Captain Rowarch at the helm. With his help we could bind the wobbling, splintered factions.

It was thirty-six hours to St. Pierre, and I decided

to go to my cabin and organize my dive schedule for the coming week. I ran into Captain Rowarch coming down the companionway.

There was a difference in his bearing, I thought. *His shoulders seem stooped, his eyes look blank and tired and he isn't smiling.*

"Do you feel all right?" I asked him.

He didn't answer, just nodded, as though any facial movement was an excruciating hardship.

"I don't feel much like talking," he told me, which was also unlike him. Rowarch was unfailingly gregarious and communicative.

"You've been working too hard."

"Well," he said, with a wintry, defeated smile, "that won't be a problem now. I won't be working at all. I have been relieved of my duties."

My body reacted before my lips could operate. I felt a knife-like wave of air, arctic air, shooting through me.

"Mr. Chappaz doesn't feel I'm the proper captain for the *Abeille*. Not since I phoned him about the stolen artifacts. He said that if I was paying attention, it would not have happened on my watch."

"Maybe when you talk to him..."

"There's nothing," he said. "I tried. I said I'd investigate, I would find the thief. And he told me, 'there is to be *no* investigation. You have nothing further to do, you're relieved of command."

I didn't know how I could go on without Rowarch. In this short time, he had become more than my captain; he had become an example. Though he wasn't old enough to be my father, he had the sort of gentle wisdom that ideal fathers possess.

"I'll speak to Chappaz," I told him. "And I'll write to Westgate."

"It is no use," Rowarch said. "But thank you. Thank you for your support."

St. Pierre was overcast the morning we docked, a perfect reflection of my mood. I made up my mind to corner Robert Chappaz alone and speak to him. He *had* to understand what he was giving up.

I was fortunate. Chappaz had come from France, and wasn't with Tulloch, the backers and William Buckley. He had come to meet the ship alone. Everybody exchanged greetings, and when I had a minute to speak to Chappaz alone, I grabbed it. Quickly, I asked him if we could meet for a drink by ourselves.

His eyes sparked, and I realized that my invitation had given him the wrong idea. But there was no immediate way to correct that impression, and besides, if it did the trick, I was willing to let the misunderstanding go on for a little while.

Robert Chappaz was a large man, at least six feet two, with dark hair and a double chin. He looked more like a stevedore rather than an executive, but his cultured speech, expensive beige cashmere jacket and silk tie belied that image.

"So tell me, my dear Jennifer," he said, leaning over toward me, "what's on your beautiful little mind?"

"I wanted to let you know, first of all, that the amount of dives we've made, and the artifacts recovered have been extraordinary. I think you'll be very pleased."

We sipped our drinks and I searched for that opening—that exact, appropriate moment—when my defense of Rowarch would make the most impact.

"It's good to know that when the men have done a hard day's work, they have someone *tres gentile* to look at. I can imagine that many of them are tempted to do more than just look."

"I've never had any problem."

"Now what's really on your mind?" he asked. "Maybe it would be more comfortable to talk if I found us a room."

"No, I can say it right here."

He drew back, and the hotly flirtatious expression in his eyes vanished.

"Say what?"

"That Captain Rowarch should be allowed to remain on the *Abeille*."

"Captain Rowarch," he said, with curt emphasis, "is no longer part of this expedition."

Before I could launch my passionate defense, he continued:

"Captain Rowarch has one flaw—a flaw that is not to be tolerated in a captain—he conducts his business as though it is a one man operation. *Anyone* who does that, my dear Jennifer, is dangerous."

"The crew trusts him. His leaving could hurt morale. Who understands the politics and the players well enough to replace him?"

Chappaz was quiet, and then I knew.

"No man or woman," he drew out the last word, "is irreplaceable," Chappaz said. "No one. An operation of this size goes on, through infighting, through political struggles, through anything—and Mr. Rowarch will be forgotten by the time the next artifacts are brought up."

"I won't forget him," I said, trying to match his agreeable tone. "I don't think the men will either."

"And now, let's change the subject," Chappaz said. "I'll be on board until the end of the expedition. I trust we will talk again, about pleasanter things."

Rowarch had been right. There was no hope of saving his job. Chappaz, although totally unequipped, now saw himself as captain. He was ready to cast himself as the star of the expedition's third act and be an eleventh hour hero.

I couldn't forget his veiled threat, the threat that announced 'no man or woman is irreplaceable,' with extra emphasis on 'woman.' But I didn't regret speaking up. I knew that Rowarch would have done the same for me.

I went to the Ile de France to meet Joel, surprised and touched that he had come such a great distance for just one day. I knew he was in the middle of scoring a movie and had a difficult deadline to meet.

When I saw him, I got another shock. He wasn't alone. Kevin and Brent were with him, and both looked so handsome and grownup that I felt a choke in my throat.

"I *know* it cost a fortune," said Joel, before I could speak. "I know we'll have to sell our house and sign away rights to any future children. But we all missed you too much."

I hugged my sons. They seemed so tall, yet they couldn't have grown that much in six weeks.

"Derek wanted to come, but he had a terrible flu and he didn't want you to get it," Joel explained.

I told them about my meeting with Chappaz, then about the stolen artifacts.

"Well, it sounds simple enough to me," Joel said. "Either play ball or lose your job."

How simple that sounded; and how hard it was for me.

"You've had enough with Mr. Don," Joel said. "Stick with this and I'll be writing Mr. Chappaz... and that'll be rough, because Chappaz is a *tough* word for a lyric. It won't scan easily. Nothing rhymes with Chappaz except Oz."

"Are you saying I should drop the whole thing?"

"I don't give advice," Joel said. "I just drop hints."

"Well, this hint sounds like a lead weight."

"You've gone this far," Joel said. "There's only two weeks left. Keep out of this guy's way."

Kevin and Brent asked if they could come aboard the *Abeille,* but I didn't think my bosses would look kindly on that.

I had the feeling that if I had suggested it, my sons would have thrown aside everything to race to the *Titanic* and share the last few weeks of the expedition with me. How I would have enjoyed that. How much fun it would have been to have loved ones by my side, viewing every dive with fresh, youthful enthusiasm, getting to know the crew and pitching in—as I knew they would—with whatever physical task was required. They were strong, athletic boys, willing to work, willing to experiment and try new things.

As though reading my mind, Joel smiled and said, "You're proud of them, and you should be."

Chapter 22

Power Plays and Politics

One of the most overused descriptions in the history of journalism and literature is the term "Renaissance Man." But within our cosmos occasionally appears a beacon of talent and intellect that blazes blindingly above the rest and justifies the accolade. Such a person is William Buckley, writer, political commentator, sailor, debater, musician—and creator of his own patented peanut butter.

I didn't have a chance to taste his peanut butter on that return trip to the site, but I did receive a generous sample of his charm and affability. There was nothing formidable about him. He was a raconteur extraordinaire, and when he gifted us with anecdotes about his past, words flowed in a rainbow series of images. William Buckley was open, down to earth and friendly, dressed in khakis, a long-sleeved broadcloth shirt, navy blue blazer and docksiders.

He was also exceedingly conscientious about answering his voluminous correspondence. When I queried him as to the amount of luggage he was carrying for the week on board, he explained that two oversized duffel bags were exclusively to house letters that had to be answered as well as reading material. His other luggage contained a computer, tapes of Bach and Mozart, navigational equipment, his sextant, jars of peanut butter and enormous quantities of clothes. Finally, there was a case of his favorite wine and a crate of fresh Maine lobsters—both gestures of good will and generosity that were certain to endear him to the crew.

Like most people who meet him, I was awed and intimidated by the Buckley image. Yet I was completely comfortable in his presence. So was Ralph. We instantly became an inseparable trio.

He was looking very much forward to his dive, and it was a relief to know that this dive had been granted the approval of all parties, French and American. Everybody was grateful that he had given us a badge of respectability. When William F. Buckley Jr. said you were undertaking a worthwhile enterprise, the world listened. Tabloid journalists and muckraking magazines faded into insignificance. And he had arranged to write a personal *Titanic* story for his syndicated columns that appeared three times a week throughout the United States.

George Tulloch, Robert Chappaz, John Joslyn and the other backers—all such contrasting personalities—were united in one aspect: they were all warmly receptive to their distinguished guest.

Buckley's presence immediately acted as a good luck charm. I went to the wheelhouse to catch up on any new telexed information and Christian, grinning, handed me a telex from the *Nadir*:

To: Jennifer Carter
From: P. H. Nargeolet

Wonderful news. The pilots and Bobby have been successful in scraping off the letters on the starboard side of the hull. The word TITANIC, which has been hidden so long by 75 years of concretions, is now visible, though not easy to distinguish.. We've have known all along this is the Titanic, but to see the letters is a thrilling verification. We have made two dives and will make one more, and when we're finished, the letters TITANIC will be clear enough for all to see.

I announced happily, upon entering the dining room, "Good news! We've cleared away the mineral deposits and found the letters. We suspected they were there, but we never knew for sure, because some Harland and Wolff photographs showed the letters and some didn't. But now we know. I just got word."

Chappaz beamed and took the telex from my hand. He passed it to Buckley, and then around the room.

Buoyed by this news, the atmosphere at dinner was convivial and festive. Everybody took turns talking, discussing their feelings about the *Titanic*. When it came to me, I said the expected words of welcome and then filled them in on the daily activities of the ship.

I covered such necessary banalities as the hour laundry was done, the time everyone was expected for breakfast, the procedure of signing a logbook on the bridge to use the phone, their lifeboat drill and survival suit training, the fact that they would all have to wear life jackets when they rode on the zodiac, transferring to the *Nadir*.

"And if you want to keep any possessions from getting wet," I said, "there are plastic trash bags available to store books or cameras. This is the best way to board the *Nadir* because of the swells." They listened with a calm, receptive ear.

It was at that moment that the ghost of Captain Rowarch seemed to loom up and invade my body.

"Not only should we be grateful for becoming part of history on this expedition," I began, "but we should also take pride in the way the French and Americans have begun to work together in such harmony."

They were smiling, still with me.

"When we started, there was a mutual wariness between the Americans and French," I said. "The attitude of the French was, they wouldn't tolerate anyone who was out for glory, monopolized the press or took credit they didn't deserve. They were suspicious and on guard because they'd been burned in the past, and it's taken all these weeks to bring about a real rapport."

The smiles were fading. I was dimly aware of it, but I felt a compulsion to keep on.

"Their technological contributions and their dedication are beyond compare, and we can maintain this delicate balance—the balance that Captain Rowarch helped to build—if we treat them with tact and diplomacy, courtesy and cooperation. It took our crew a long time to create a strong working relationship and we now have it; the trust is there, and will remain there if we keep focusing, at all times, on how the French feel and give them the respect they deserve."

Chappaz sprang to his feet.

"We don't need a lesson in tolerance," he shouted, veins bulging from his head. "These men are not our superiors—we are *their* superiors. They will do as we say, when we say it, and how we say it. We will not baby them. They're not the people putting up the money on this expedition. *We* are. They have a job to do and they will do it, and I will see to it that they do."

I was shocked and unprepared for the outburst. I had, after all, been defending the French, and he was a Frenchman.

Chappaz was waiting for a rebuttal, a statement of self-defense, but I said nothing. I listened to his stream of invective, to his implications that I was over-reaching, placing myself in situations that were none of my concern. It was obvious that this man was a power unto himself. Democracy was a foreign ideal, and he intended to rule the *Abeille* with an iron hand.

My only comfort during that humiliating moment was a look from William Buckley. He caught my eye, as if to say, *I understand what you're trying to put across, and I admire you for speaking out.*

I was also grateful to Ralph and Adam. They showed their support by standing up after Chappaz' explosion and walking out of the room.

Sometimes the only way to react is by not reacting. As I stood there, I found it difficult not to speak my mind. I wanted closure, complete resolution. I didn't realize that in many cases, total closure is impossible. Chappaz saw everything through the filter of power and money. Asking him to examine the finer distinctions of human interaction was like pushing a blind man against the wall and ordering him to see.

Everyone in the room kept looking at each other, wondering what to do next. I sat down and sipped a cup of coffee. I needed something, anything to do with my hands.

When we arrived at the site, George Tulloch asked us to wait, before going to our rooms.

"For anyone who wants to come with me to the stern," he said, "I'd like to say a prayer for the *Titanic* victims."

A group of ten followed him.

Moments like this separate the sincere from the cynical, the true believers from the fakes. I knew George Tulloch as a key financial component of the expedition, but until then I had never seen the depth of his commitment to the *Titanic* and its history. He did nothing saccharine or dishonest in his memorial that would have made a travesty of his tribute.

Instead, he made the victims human. He portrayed the depth of the tragedy, so eloquently that everyone was transported back in time. His words were a reminder that we were not simply here to have fun, have our egos stroked or treat the enterprise as a superficial adventure. The *Titanic* meant glory, but it also meant pain, and George was asking us, without saying it directly, to pray that these suffering souls had reached a safe harbor after death.

"Seventy-five years ago," he concluded, "the *Titanic* collided with an iceberg and plunged to the bottom of the sea, taking the lives of over fifteen hundred people. May they rest in peace, and know we're thinking about them and dedicating ourselves to keeping their memory alive."

Chappaz kept his head down, feigning sensitivity. His body language seemed to be saying: *I'm a man of feeling. I'm part of a noble cause.*

Nobility is the cloak every manipulator wears, and Chappaz slipped into his with practiced efficiency. George

Tulloch had established a deep connection with the ship that transcended questioning. All I could think of, beyond the victims, the *Titanic* and the circle of well-meaning mourners, was Captain Rowarch, a man of truly noble nature, whose contributions had been washed away on a wave of injustice.

Chapter 23

Buckley's Dive

William F. Buckley, Jr. quickly became Bill. I appreciated this relaxation of formality. I also admired his curiosity; he wanted to know everything about the *Abeille* and its operations.

I gave him a tour, starting from the moon pool. The moon pool is an area open to the water located amidships where a submersible can be deployed to take oil workers underneath the rigs, enabling them to maintain their equipment. Bill took copious notes. I pointed out the special quality that differentiated the *Abeille* from the *Nadir*, hydrodynamic positioning, which allowed the *Abeille* to turn in a 360-degree circle while maintaining its fixed position.

The engine room was next on our tour. This area's level of noise was so ear-crushingly extreme that we wondered how the Martinon Brothers, Gerard and Yves, who managed its operation, could avoid succumbing to deafness.

Then we went up to the pilothouse. Bill was fascinated by the navigational charts and took down the actual position of *Titanic*. He fired away questions at Christian and Louis Deshommes. When they showered him with technical details about navigation on board, he added to their knowledge with navigational information of his own. They were impressed when he told them he'd brought his sextant along and thrilled by his command of French and the sea.

Arriving at the site on September 4, even though rocked violently by a brief, sudden surge of stormy weather, I rebounded from Chappaz' attack. I felt excited by Buckley's presence, by the infusion of fresh, positive blood he brought. I wanted Brigitte to meet him too; I was sure she'd be impressed.

So, after showing Bill a collection of the finest artifacts aboard the Abeille, we took a harrowing zodiac ride to the *Nadir*. With only the weight of the two of us, along with Zozo, we were able to reach higher speeds, and I could see how much Bill was enjoying the feel of salt spray on his face.

The *Nadir* was a newer ship than the *Abeille*. Its technical rooms and its bridge were state of the art. It had an entire room filled with computers devoted solely to the analysis of the *Nautile's* dives, the *Robin's* routes and the *Nadir's* stats as well.

The *Nadir's* bridge was immaculate, reminding me of how a top naval ship would look under a particularly harsh, by-the-book commander. Every spotless surface matched the ship's snow-white exterior. Buckley got a chance to inspect the photo shop, the tool shop and the lab containers.

Clashing with the *Nadir's* picture of cleanliness and discipline was the oil that spread a thick, slippery smudge over the aft portion. Oil covered the steps of the companionway ladders and the metal surfaces on the exterior of the ship. Not a day went by that somebody didn't slide like an out-of-control ice skater on these oil pools and go crashing to the deck. When I asked about the oil, the captains explained that it was spillage from the *Nautile* when it was lifted back onto the stern, and when it received its daily servicing. The servicing often went on all night, particularly if battery, motor or other engineering problems occurred. The maintenance staff had a shift schedule that required them to sleep while the *Nautile* was down on the ocean floor, so they could resume work when it resurfaced.

P. H. told me there were backup parts for every minute piece of equipment on the *Nautile,* along with a machine shop and a staff of engineers who understood every working mechanism that made up a submersible. I also learned that the pilots of the *Nautile* had to undergo years of training, until every minuscule screw, nut and bolt was as familiar to them as their own name. The pilots were all university graduates, mostly engineers.

"Watch out," I warned Bill as we made our unstable way from one oily area of the *Nadir* to the other. Then, after my warning, I was the one who took a spill. After slipping and sliding on the *Nadir,* high-speed racing with Captain Zozo on the zodiac felt like child's play.

I introduced him to the crew, all of whom treated him with appropriate respect. But he didn't encourage a distance, he didn't want deference. He wanted to be one of us. There were no heated controversies about politics, no treatises on conservatism. This wasn't the White house, it wasn't Washington, it was a theatre made of wind, sea and sky. As he put it, "I never talk politics unless required to do so, and usually for that I require a huge fee. Probably I

don't talk politics for the same reason that, oh, proctolo-
gists don't talk about lower intestines."

Through it all, I marveled at Bill's ability to make
people feel they were the most important thing in the world
when he spoke to them. He smiled, he responded to anecdotes, he listened with complete concentration. As a producer and a person who dealt with many celebrities, I knew
how rare this was for a man of Bill Buckley's stature and
international fame. Only a handful of people have ever made
me feel so special. With Bill, you not only felt more interesting and attractive; you felt smart, articulate, capable.

You also felt the presence of a truly civilized soul.

"You know, Jennifer," he said, a few nights after I
had delivered my respect-the-French speech, "What you
did took courage. It's always been my opinion that man-
ners and civility toward your fellow man come first above
everything else."

He attributed that attitude to his mother and the
values she had instilled in him as a child in Massachusetts.
I thought of my grandmother, also from Massachusetts,
and the way she had emphasized politeness and courtesy.

"On my sailing voyages," Bill said, "I will not allow
people to behave rudely. Rudeness is unacceptable. I will
not countenance confrontations. If people behave like that,
they won't be invited along. Or encouraged to stay on
board."

I knew that morality had become a highly flexible
term, and loyalty was also highly adjustable according to
the situation. But Bill saw them as they had originally been
conceived, and he lived what he believed.

We talked about books, and he offered to exchange
his Michael Davie book, *Titanic - The Death and Life of a*

Legend for my *The Titanic - End of a Dream* by Wyn Craig Wade. He told me that as a twelve-year-old, he had traveled on a large cruise ship from Southampton, encountering a storm so crippling it did $100,000 worth of damage to the ship. Years before he had also experienced a severe hurricane in Bermuda. Neither storm had in any way diminished his love of the sea. Storms were part of the adventure. Dangerous as they can be, most seamen would reject one hundred percent smooth sailing and the elimination of all storms. If you love something, you love it in its entirety.

His dive was scheduled the first morning of our arrival. Later on, he told us all about it, eyes piercingly blue and shining, hair flopping on his forehead. The most endearing thing about William Buckley was that he retained the enthusiasm of a twenty year old. He was an inspiring example of how to remain perpetually young.

Like all of us who ventured down to the ocean floor, Buckley declined any water or food, since the *Nautile* was not designed to accommodate a "call of nature." He did carry some personal items: a rosary, two small flashlights, a dictating machine, three cassette tapes and a thriller to "distract me from the long descent and the long ascent."

Ralph, whom he referred to as a "new best friend," gave him a set of kneepads. Ralph was delighted and flattered that Buckley said he knew more about diving, history, mechanics, ships, airplanes and the sea than anyone he'd ever met.

At first he didn't know why kneepads were so vital. But he learned quickly the discomfort of lying on his nose against the porthole and having the need to place your left knee somewhere, since there was no room to stretch it out. He then discovered that the knee ended up on the narrow ice-cold titanium bottom strip of metal.

Once at the bottom, he experienced the same awed sensation Ralph and I had felt on our debut dive. He noticed immediately that no articles of personal clothing were picked up, out of respect for the victims, and saw that our pilots only secured teacups bordered in blue.

"The distinction," he noted, "is that the blue-bordered china is rarer than the plain white, which was used by the seven hundred twelve steerage passengers. The three hundred thirty seven First Class passengers had the fancier, blue-bordered china." An abundance of the white steerage china had been picked up on former dives.

He called the experience vivid, exhilarating and uncomplicated by any philosophical misgivings about the mission.

"I did not feel any kinship to the voyeur," he said. "No more than when, a year earlier, I ogled the tombs of the Nile or, a dozen years ago, the catacombs of Lima beneath the great cathedral where the bones of thousands of Incas lie."

His most eloquent answer to the naysayers, our opponents criticizing the mission, was expressed in an article he wrote while on board:

Titanic 87 has been accused of "exploiting" the event. To say that is on the order of saying that Gauguin exploited Tahiti. Or, if you strain at that, that Quaker Oats exploits Iowa. The Titanic 87 people have refreshed a legend, and are making possible scientific and historic discoveries.

Fax: Westgate Productions
        September 5th

William Buckley made his dive on September 4. His total bottom time was five hours and fifty-two minutes, and the length of his complete dive was nine-and-a-half hours. I transmitted his first two columns to his office while he was on the bottom.

Arrived on site September 4, 1987. Delayed due to extremely bad weather, Sea State 8 on most of the trip to site.

Buckley's columns were positive and supportive of our efforts. He spent his time in the southern debris field, where they recovered a bag filled with small bottles. We're unsure whether it was a woman's or a man's. Some say they could be doctor's prescription bottles; some claim they may be perfume bottles. Other items in bag include a silver ladies hat pin with a Chinese decoration—the Chinese character symbolizing good fortune— and a box for Gillette razor blades. A leather satchel was also retrieved by the Nadir during the time we were en route to the Titanic site.

This leather satchel, although in excellent condition, does not hold the kind of valuables that were seen in the first valise. Accounts of contents vary from person to person. Some people from our crew say that it contained a sort of chain with a cross or symbol resembling a Greek Orthodox cross. Others say this description is incorrect.

We do know that there was also a gold pocket watch inside, letters and some currency. Another suitcase we've seen in the debris field is still to be recovered.

Other items recovered yesterday on Buckley's dive

include: A lovely white wide-bottomed vase, with blue and white flowers on the inside and outside and displaying the White Star logo on the exterior; a saucer, the first class variety, with royal blue and gold edging; an odd shaped curved plate with gold trim and a piece of lead glass window (not the complete window that we intend to raise, only a portion of another one).

The first brushing of the bow started on August 31 and continued on September 1 and September 3. Bobby dived on August 31 and on September 3, and took video of the after-effects of this brushing.

It's possible to distinguish some of the letters, but be very careful what you release to the press on this, because when we arrived on site, we expected to see clearly those letters on the starboard side, and we still have a difficult time distinguishing them in the video footage. Stills may be clearer. It may be possible to image-enhance this video shot to see more of what appears now.

George Tulloch is diving today, launched around noon our time. Brigitte Renaldi dived on September 1.

Fate and timing helped Brigitte. When we departed, she was given her opportunity to dive by Captains Keranflech and Nargeolet, and she was impervious now to any anger, any opposition.

"All I could think of," Brigitte said, "was that we had the weight of 3,870 meters. Mentally, I added and piled up a dozen Eiffel towers."

Seeing the *Titanic,* she felt elated to be "far from the *Nadir, Abeille,* Paris. At long last I had joined the ship."

I could understand her emotions and William Buckley's. All of us would be friends forever; once you've shared something as immense as the Titanic expedition, your connection is powerful and enduring.

Bill wanted to know all he could about the *Titanic,* and I gladly shared all the information I had. When I said, "Are you sure you want to hear this?" he urged me to continue. He was particularly interested in the expeditions that had taken place prior to this one—expeditions before Bob Ballard's, that had lavished money and time on discovering the ship prior to 1985.

"It all started in the early fifties," I said, "but it wasn't until nineteen seventy-eight that they really went after the *Titanic* seriously. I know that Walt Disney and National Geographic wanted to do a film about the sinking and the rediscovery of the ship. Budgetary considerations eventually doomed the project."

I filled him in on Jack Grimm, the American millionaire who conducted three expeditions during the 1980s.

"In July and August, nineteen-eighty..."

He smiled. "You have studied this, haven't you?"

Grimm, I told him, teamed up with scientists from the Scripps Institution of Oceanography in California and the Lamont-Doherty Geological Observatory, and combed an area in mid-Atlantic aboard the ship H. J. W. Fay.

"They found fourteen possible targets, but none were the *Titanic,*" I said.

Nineteen eight-one brought Grimm's second attempt. This time he spent ten days covering an area south of what he'd covered a year earlier, but bad weather devastated the expedition. He discovered an object which Grimm announced was one of the *Titanic's* propellors, but none of the scientists accompanying him verified his claim.

After the second expedition, Grimm wrote a book

and ran a contest in the newspaper, offering clues to read-
ers for a treasure hunt; the prize was to be a seventy ounce,
14 karat gold model of the *Titanic,* approximately sixteen
inches long. When a team of three winners claimed the
prize, they decided to split up an amount equal to its value,
$25,000, and Grimm kept the ship.

Grimm tried again in 1983, but his last expedition
was no more successful than the others.

Even less successful were the efforts to raise the
Titanic that began in 1914. Bill and I talked about some of
these weird, crackpot ideas

The first was conceived by a Denver architect
named Charles Smith. Smith devised a scheme to locate the
wreck by equipping a submarine with electromagnets and
hoping the electromagnets would be attracted to the ship's
hull. The cables would be fastened to them and barges
would raise the *Titanic.*

Equally fanciful was Douglas Wooley's 1966 concept. Owner of the Titanic Salvage Company in
Hertfordshire, Wooley planned to wrap plastic containers
around the hull. The containers would be filled with gases
that would buoy the hull to the surface.

Imaginative schemes continued: the 1970s presented the world with the Ping Pong ball theory—injecting
thousands of Ping-Pong balls into the hull, making the
Titanic buoyant enough to salvage.

John Pierce wanted to wrap the legendary liner in
a huge net and fill the net with nitrogen. Water around the
ship would freeze due to the nitrogen and the liner would
rise, as easily as a toy bobbing in a bathtub.

Bill Buckley's presence on the *Abeille* affected
everyone like wine. He loosened them up and everyone on

board seemed more mellow, past grievances forgotten. It was truly a case of light and dark, his positive force against the negative force of Chappaz. Bill reminded everyone why they had embarked so enthusiastically on this expedition in the first place. He made us remember why we all, as children, craved adventure, that we were all once Tom Sawyers and Becky Thatchers before adulthood started erasing the naivete and the dreams.

Renowned author and expert seaman, William F. Buckley, Jr., with expedition leader Jennifer Carter.

Brigitte Renaldi and Jennifer Carter placed flowers, a French flag and an American flag in the articulated arms of the *Nautile*. These were taken down and placed on the *Titanic's* bow to commemorate the French-American expedition.

Party on the last day of the 1987 expedition, celebrating 32 dives, 173 hours of video, 1,300 artifacts recovered and the discovery of the hole in the starboard hull. Bill Buckley and Jennifer Carter are in the background, toasting success with champagne.

The happiest day of Joel Hirschhorn's and Jennifer Carter's lives — their wedding day.

Joel preparing for a performance at the National Academy of Songwriters concert.

Chapter 24

Misgivings

I still had a nagging suspicion that Chappaz had no intention of investigating the mystery of the stolen artifacts. Nor could I forget that Rowarch had been banished with such speed that no one could quite believe he was gone.

His attitude remained aloof for a few days, then began to change into a new, unforeseen warmth I had misgivings about. He even resumed the flirtation he had initiated at the Ile de France. Praising me for my dedication and competence, he assured me everything would be all right.

"Don't you think I want the thieves to be caught?" he said to me. "Of course I want those bastards caught. And after the expedition is over—after the show is aired, we will look into the matter, and we will put them in jail where they belong."

His hands curled into fists, and he started to breathe more heavily.

"Jennie—do you know what this expedition means to me? I've paid for it in blood, in money, in time. It's taken

over my life. Don't you think I hate anyone who destroys
its good name, who smears it, who makes a travesty of all
we're trying to do? Maybe you think I have no heart?
You're wrong. Since you told me about the missing artifacts, I've been working twenty-four hours a day to hide
my rage. Every time I look at Captain Rowarch's list, my
mind is full of revenge. I don't sleep at night. But can I
show it to the investors? Can I show my true feelings to Mr.
Buckley? It's a lonely place, Jennie. Where I stand is a
lonely place."

Now his eyes met mine in a stare that said: *we are
allies in this, we know something the rest of the world
doesn't. I am your trusted confidante, you are mine.* The
expression was so nakedly emotional that my doubts, my
distrust, melted away. Resentful as I was that he had dis-
missed Captain Rowarch, I did feel his responsibility to
the *Titanic*.

"Jennie, my darling—when we start this investigation in earnest, I'll want your help. I'll want you to tell me
everything you've seen and everything you remember.
Together we *will* find them and we will get the artifacts
back."

"That's all I care about," I said.

"I know. And I admire you. We're putting together
other expeditions in the future, and I want someone with
your experience to be part of them. I want you to be in my
corner, and give me the support you gave Captain
Rowarch. Will you do that, so we can work to solve this
terrible crime?"

I said I would.

"I'll begin asking around right away. Discreetly at
first, so we don't ruin the good times and the illusions of
the others until the expedition and the show are over—but

I have sources and contacts on this ship I can trust, who will keep their eyes open."

His intensity had overwhelmed me. I knew he had the power to smoke out the thieves. I didn't have to love or respect him. I only had to believe him. It's an uncomfortable political paradox that two people with opposing attitudes about everything can find themselves on the same side.

True to his word, Chappaz supported me from then on. He was considerate. He threw me conspiratorial looks, as if to say "You and I share a secret, and a sacred trust." He was so anxious to reinforce this connection that I half-expected him to suggest we cut our fingers and make them bleed, mixing the blood as a pact of lifelong togetherness and loyalty.

With my thoughts focused on Chappaz and the theft of the artifacts, when I first felt that telltale ache in my muscles that precedes a cold, I ignored it. The illness started as minor; scratchy throat, a few sneezes. I could live with those. I prayed, as people on the verge of flus always do, that the symptoms would nudge fleetingly at me, then disappear.

But symptoms have a mind of their own. When they decide to strike they mobilize, assemble their army and hit randomly in every direction. My weakened body and protracted thoughts were perfect targets, vulnerable through lack of sleep, with an immune system that had collapsed under the weight of too much physical hardship and personal tension. I could feel the glee of each germ, rushing to embrace its new home and take up long-range residence. My throat went from itching to red-hot, agonizing pain. Nausea turned the world a queasy green. My fever went soaring to 103 degrees, and I tried to follow the age-old remedy: Drink plenty of fluids. Before long, I felt that more water was inside me than all the water in the North Atlantic.

Ravaged as I was by a hacking cough, I wanted to conceal the worst of my discomfort from my crew, from my employers Joslyn and Tulloch, and from Chappaz. I didn't want anyone to be able to whisper about *female weakness*.

"How do you feel?" asked George Tulloch.

"Just a little cold."

Tulloch generously lent me his heavy parka. Camille fed me hot soup and Ralph commiserated; he had strep throat too, although not to the same disastrous degree. Chappaz, surprisingly, was the most solicitous of all. He gave me medicines and made inquiries like a doting parent every time he saw me.

He and Tulloch also gave me a job that wasn't too taxing; to entertain the backers and shoot personalized videos for them, The subjects included Alan Briggs, Tulloch's brother in law, Peter Rocco and Larry D'Addario, one of our expedition's major funders. Another backer, Alain Barrault—an expert on submersibles and owner of one—preferred going over to the *Nadir* to speak with Captain Nargeolet.

Despite my generally deteriorating condition, I enjoyed making the videos with Bobby Keyes. I liked Briggs, Rocco and D'Addario; they were warm and sincere and just glad to be on the site, playing a part in the *Titanic* story.

All three interviewed Buckley, feeling very much like famous anchormen. Then we had a hilarious time filming a humorous short with Larry called *You'll Find Out*, in which Larry interviewed everybody on board, asking them different questions and having them all answer, "You'll find out," questions such as 'are the rumors true that there's a killer on board this ship? That someone's going to blow the ship up? That you've got an hour to live?' Everyone participated: Ralph, Zozo, Louis Deshommes, Tulloch, Joslyn— and of course, all his backer friends. At auspicious moments, Larry would recruit one of his friends to hold an axe, and I would shoot just the axe a la Hitchcock, without seeing who was swinging it. The supposition was that a murderer was on board the *Abeille* with us, and was after Larry. At the end of the film, Larry threw his watchcap into the ocean, and I filmed the cap floating away.

For me, the game carried a strange subtext, though I couldn't voice it out loud. Everything was fine, yet I wondered if I was, in some subtle way, being axed and sent out to sea? Would they find my cap in the water?

While I struggled to feel better, other problems festered. Jovial as the investors were, tensions occasionally erupted. George Tulloch's dive was a prime example.

After two hours of drifting downward without the benefit of sight, he reached bottom, only to find his view of the ship impaired by battery problems.

These problems came at the end of a particularly frustrating week; motor and battery problems had been plaguing us, no matter how hard the technicians tried to solve them. As a result, the *Nautile's* lights kept flickering on and off, and the *Titanic* phased in and out, like a victim of arty Hollywood lighting.

I could imagine Tulloch's frustration, knowing what the *Titanic* looked like when it was brilliantly and steadily illuminated. Anticipation builds to an unbearable pitch on the long descent, and anything less than a perfect view inevitably proves a crushing disappointment.

When he returned to the surface, he found that the *Nadir's* zodiacs were out, and the *Nadir* had to request a zodiac from the *Abeille*. Tulloch was forced to bob on the surface at a ninety degree temperature, which would have tested the patience of the most seaworthy soul. It took an hour for the *Abeille's* zodiac to rescue him.

He had other complaints.

"All that oil on the *Nadir*," he said. "I nearly broke my back on the deck. Why doesn't somebody clean it up?"

But his greatest anger was directed toward the pilots. From his point of view, they spent too much time on the bottom, and didn't pick up the artifacts he told them to select. Everyone had different ideas of what artifacts to bring up—from captains to pilots, producers to backers. Tulloch had his own vision, and as a principal force behind the expedition, he wanted his ideas followed exactly.

No one knew at the time that his intensity meant more than perfectionism. Tulloch's goal, already evolving, was nothing less than to acquire sole and exclusive rights to the *Titanic* and its artifacts.

My fever refused to abate. I felt a perverse relief when the nights came and I could stop pretending, stop putting on makeup and presenting a false picture of health as I did all day while persevering in my duties. Alone in my cabin, I shook so violently from the chills and fever that my teeth rattled. It took all my self-control not to scream at the vise-like migraines that were gouging my eyes and fastening a rope of pain around my neck.

The end of our expedition was at hand, and I didn't

want the last scene of it to feature me being rolled out on a stretcher. The image was so bleak that I laughed, provoking a coughing fit.

Whenever I could snatch an hour or two of rest, I grabbed it like a drowning man clutching the corner of a lifeboat. Ralph looked in on me, and so did Randy, Adam and Bobby. Chappaz talked about the upcoming television broadcast in Paris, inviting me to attend and promising to take me around the city. "Think of Paris on an autumn night," he said, "and you'll forget your aches and pains."

The night of September 6, my fever broke. My body was soaked in sweat, but by morning I knew the worst was over.

As though in celebration, the morning of September 7 was a glorious one. Sun spilled into my cabin and I was able to wake up without hurting from head to toe. The enormous amount of items secured from the *Titanic* added to my optimistic mood.

Fax to:　　　Westgate Productions
　　　　　　 September 7

We've had a very uplifting day. Everyone excited after George Tulloch dove and recovered a valise with some of the following items.

A Waterman self-filling fountain pen, four sets of eyeglasses found within a man's silver jewelry box, containing many studs for dress shirts, cuff links, buttons, a buckle and tie clips, a gold tiger's head cravat pin with ruby eyes, five French coins, two gold, three silver; a comb, a hairbrush, shoe brush with natural bristle, white ceramic jar which holds some type of cream with the label in black letters HP TRUEFITT, 1600 Old Bond Street, a silver plated safety razor, a flask with a leather case and a silver jewelry box with monogrammed letters with one letter clearly shown, letter C.

A bundle of bone toothpicks, a shaving stick, a natural bristle shaving brush, a crown barber's supply label, a lid from a cherry toothpaste container with a woman's profile on it, and the words CHERRY TOOTHPASTE PATRONIZED BY THE QUEEN - Prepared By John Cosnell and Company Ltd., London. For Beautifying and Preserving the Teeth and Gums; steel razor blade box containing Gillette blades and a Gillette razor blade envelope with a picture of King Gillette on the front.

We believe the bag containing these items to be a French gentleman's, due to the coins being French. No currency was in the bag, but upon close examination an important discovery was made. Two cuff links with very large diamonds, perhaps more than a carat each, were set on what is believed to be black onyx and edged in gold. We think that these were meant to be used on a dress shirt.

Several plates and a sink were also recovered on George's dive.

A third Buckley column was sent today, describing his dive, and one more will be sent on Wednesday the ninth before we leave for St. Pierre. We hope to arrive there early the morning of the eleventh, then fly by charter to Bridgeport, Connecticut. From there, we will take the people by limo and the equipment by truck to New York after we clear customs. Hopefully, we'll be able to catch a flight that evening into L. A.

Mark was up all night readying the cameras for this important mission. The investors yesterday all got a tour of the sub, since September 6 was a down day, and personal videos were shot.

The Nautile will dive today, but it's almost 6:00 PM, so it will be a late recovery this evening. Electronics repairs made all of yesterday and today. The objective is to use the S.I.T. camera to make a photo mosaic of the Titanic. They will pilot the Nautile approximately fifteen feet over the top of the ship, shooting continuous stills and making many passes until the mosaic is completed.

They'll also use Robin to enter inside the ship and shoot video if all goes well. The remaining two dives here will be made by Alain Barrault on September 8 and Larry D'Addario on September 9. They will both be artifact-recovery dives. The investors yesterday all got a grand tour of the Nautile and the Nadir, since no dive was made due to repairs.

Bobby and I shot personal video material of the investors. As I type this, we just found out that the S.I.T. dive had to be aborted, and the sub is on its way back to the ship. We're all terribly disappointed, since everybody worked all last night to prepare the sub and the cameras. Mark Burnett was up all night with the engineers and the technicians. The good news is that they recovered the leaded cut glass window that we believe is from the first class dining room. Bill Buckley is a delight to the whole Westgate crew on board the Abeille. We've all found him a fascinating raconteur and a very good sport.

The Abeille will be packed like a can of sardines when we leave, since we'll probably be transporting seven members of the Nadir back to St. Pierre to catch flights back to France. This means everyone will be doubling up.

September 8

Another bag brought up with two brass buttons

with the White Star Line symbol, several pipes, a cigarette holder, a bowtie and other personal items. We wonder if the bag belonged to one of the crew because of the buttons.

The number of hours on the bottom is now at 163 hours.

Chapter 25

The Gaping Hole

Why did the *Titanic* sink?

There had been so many theories, so many explanations, and they made sense, but a piece of the puzzle was still missing: The huge, gaping hole that often was alluded to but never found.

Bob Ballard voiced the following widely held view:

"On July 22 (1985) we photographed the entire exterior of the bow and took a close look at the area where the iceberg supposedly tore a gash; from the bow to a point roughly even with cargo hatch number two, the hull below the water line was buried in the mud. Aft this point, we could see the area where the gash should have been, but no tear was available. We were well within the area damaged by the iceberg. Where was the great gash we had been led to expect? It appeared perfectly possible that the famous gash never existed."

Meanwhile, as our voyage drew to a close, everyone was preparing emotionally to separate and yet wishing we could delay or deny it. Separation from your crew is like separating from your family. There was a feeling of melancholy in the air. I felt better physically and I had assumed I'd be completely prepared for the farewells, only to discover I wanted the experience to go on. There was a sense of being jarred, of broken continuity. Something inside me felt incomplete.

We had been the first to bring artifacts to the surface, the first to discover the propellor and photograph it, the first to scrape the starboard side and see the words *TITANIC*.

But we hadn't found the elusive gash.

Then, on September 9, on the last dive of the expedition, two days before we were to return home, the *Nautile* made its greatest discovery—a huge, gaping hole twelve by fifteen feet on the starboard side of the ship.

Moving as close as possible, the camera was aimed at where we had calculated it to be, in the area of the mailroom and the boilers beneath it.

We knew from past testimony at the British and American inquiries, as well as accounts from survivors at the time of the sinking, that water had poured through the mailroom in such volume that the personnel inside were moved to make valiant, fruitless attempts to drag heavy mailbags up the companionways. There were 3,346 bags of mail on board and between 700 and 800 parcels. To the end, they were dedicated to saving the mail.

This catastrophic injury to the ship—this hole, undiscovered until now—had inevitably contributed to the ship's sinking, as the bow plunged deeper and deeper into the ocean.

"It's true the hole is above the water line," Nargeolet told us, "but it had to have escalated the pace of sinking because water was flowing in at such an enormous rate."

The misconception existed—and even today is repeated endlessly—that there are just small gashes on the ship's length of the starboard side beneath the sand and sediment. It is thought that these were the sole factors that made the liner plunge to her doom.

Until this day, nobody had seen the twelve by fifteen foot hole. Everyone had claimed it didn't exist, but now our team had found it and we had filmed its existence for all time. We had become part of the legend.

Later, Bob Ballard, who had so vocally disapproved of our expedition, graciously acknowledged the significance of our discovery. He stated, "*Nautile* filmed a gaping hole that we had missed."

The explanation that had been handed down since the *Titanic's* sinking was that there had been a three hundred foot gash caused by the iceberg. In 1996, George Tulloch took scientists to the ship and with underwater sonar and the latest scientific equipment, they were able to determine what kinds of gashes existed below the sediment. There was no three hundred foot long gash, but rather a series of holes that were more than just popped rivets. These holes, in addition to our gaping gash were responsible for the *Titanic's* sinking. We'll never know whether there was an explosion in the boilers, which could also have contributed to the sinking, and the theories will continue. Some people have stated that as the *Titanic* sank, the trapped air and great pressures at those depths caused explosive forces within the ship.

As we reflected on our achievement, we all felt supreme satisfaction. In addition to finding the elusive hole, we had done more than thirty-two dives in fifty-four days, despite the loss of time for hurricanes, storms, and battery and motor problems. Our crew had taken more

than 170 hours of haunting footage of the ship and artifacts. Over 900 objects were being brought back, 1,300 if
you count every button and piece of coal. We had taken
12,000 stills and made landmark discoveries: the propeller,
the ship's letters and the gaping hole in the starboard hull.
We had done justice to the great ship, and that was what
mattered.

Chapter 26

Coming Home

I would soon be saying goodbye to the *Titanic*, yet I felt as though I'd just begun to know her. Other expeditions were being planned, and there were more artifacts to find, more wonders to film. I longed to join those explorations. Chappaz had said he was planning another one soon and I felt optimistic, recalling his promise to make me an integral part of it.

Like so many others before me, I had become one of those obsessed with the *Titanic,* and I knew I'd never be able to let her go.

I hadn't spoken to Tulloch, Joslyn, Llewelyn and Ralph, but it was clear they felt the same. The *Titanic* had only begun to dominate their lives, and would be the future centerpiece for everything they did.

That morning the sunrise turned the sky a rich, blinding blue, streaked with pink, and the water was calm enough to send a child swimming. The crew had raised the White Star flag, a large red burgee with a white symbol in the center. We all met on the stern of the *Nadir* for a last farewell. Tables had been set up on the port and starboard side; Tulloch had brought cases of *Titanic - Triumph and Tragedy* books, so each member of the expedition could have his own. And Ralph carried flags for everyone to sign. Gifts of patches from each of the ships were exchanged. Nargeolet presented me with his Ifremer yellow uniform, which I had admired throughout the whole expedition, and I gave him a black nylon windbreaker that he had also expressed a desire for.

Belle Bougie gave me a special knife that had been engraved on the handle, a gift from the crew of the *Abeille,* and the Martinon Brothers gifted me with a kodak key chain. The *D* had been transformed into a *J* by carefully cutting out a three quarter portion from nine to twelve o'clock on the d and I now had an amusing souvenir—a Kojak key chain to remind me of Telly and the bizarre crew rebellion.

What mattered most to me were the loving thoughts and inscriptions each expedition member wrote in my *Titanic* book—inscriptions I would treasure for the rest of my life.

I took Brigitte's hand when we met on deck for the last time. We had planned a little ritual of our own. We were going to walk toward the *Nautile,* each of us with a bouquet of roses in her hand. I had bought the roses in St. Pierre, and they were artificial, but they looked beautiful to me on that final morning.

My bouquet had an American flag attached with wire and hers had a French flag. The idea was that we would join hands and then blend the two bouquets together, French and American and place it in the pincer— a tribute to the French and Americans forming an alliance that would never be broken.

We put the bouquets side by side and made them one, then wrapped them together with more wire, placing them inside the pincers. The pincers were like metal fingers holding our gift, so that it could be transported to the bottom on the final dive of that day; a mechanical robot carrying our hopes and our dreams to the ocean floor. Ralph brought a bronze plaque to commemorate the mission, which would also be taken to the bottom to share space with the flowers.

A fax arrived from Bob Ballard, asking Ralph whether *his* plaque—the one he had placed on the *Titanic* deck in 1985—had been removed. We never had any intention of removing it. We returned his message, saying that the two plaques would be left on the deck, not far from each other. Nothing would be disturbed.

With characteristic unpredictability, the weather changed, and rain was falling. I felt it on my face, on my hands. My eyes filled.

"You see?" Brigitte said. "Even the sky is crying."

I hugged her, Nargeolet and then Ralph. It was the closest moment Ralph and I had shared since our days of being so intensely in love. On our voyage to the *Titanic* we had shared a lifetime of emotions, some happy, some painful, but the strength of our friendship transcended any specific event; it had a life and momentum of its own and would never die—not as long as we remembered our days and nights on the site, existing in a world that no outsiders could fully comprehend.

Randy played his harmonica as we watched the zodiac spurting from one ship to another. He did a plaintive rendition of Burt Bacharach and Carole Bayer Sager's hit, *That's What Friends Are For.* The gently nostalgic, happy/sad melody perfectly expressed our feelings and we all sang along.

Then Randy surprised me. I had lent him a tape of Joel's *Titanic* piano piece a week earlier, and he had learned the main theme. He played it, and for an instant, I felt as if the day was a beginning, not an end, that we were all arriving, filled with anticipation, breathless newcomers embarking on a journey that would change us forever. I wished Joel were with me to share this moment.

I didn't want to leave, so Brigitte and I waited until the last crossing.

It was then that the final realization that our mission was ending struck. There would be no more joyously reckless zodiac rides, no more celebratory champagne, no more times when we were, however briefly, allowed to touch the artifacts and form a silent communion with the past. It was wrenchingly hard for me to say my farewells to Captain Nargeolet, Captain Keranflech, Pierre-Yves, Bill Buckley and to all the men I had come to love like brothers—Randy, Mark, Adam and Bobby. How I could live without my family on the *Abeille*—Christian, Captain Deshommes, Zozo, Bosco, Belle Bougie, the Martinon Brothers, Camille?

Robert Chappaz kissed me and whispered, "Remember. We have a date in Paris."

Then it was goodbye, to the waiting and now unfamiliar world of Los Angeles.

Returning from an expedition is somewhat like coming home after years of being stranded on a desert island. The buildings, streets, flashing lights, zig zagging cars seem like toys, created by an alien set designer. The sea still feels more substantial than solid ground; you rock back and forth with each step you take for weeks after leaving the ship. Your body refuses to regain its normal balance, but it's not just your physical body that hasn't adjusted—it's your emotional stability. You don't grasp how isolated you've been until you arrive at a noisy airport, strange and jarring after two months at sea. Abrasive recorded announcements like "This spot is for loading and unloading only," arouse unreasonable resentment.

In the midst of this unreality is your family. When I had seen Joel, Kevin and Brent in St. Pierre, our family unit felt natural, framed by turf that related to all my deepest current concerns. Now they seemed like strangers. I knew it was temporary; I knew these were people I loved more than anything else on earth. We all went through the motions, but to me the conversations sounded disembodied, as though spoken under water.

Joel understood. He knew I was coping with a loss, and he never tried to rip me away from my memories. Instead, he urged me to speak about them. By absorbing himself in my private world, he became more a part of me than ever.

Chapter 27

Cover-Up in Paris

Chappaz had promised to keep me informed of his efforts to find the thief, so I made sure I kept in touch with him. I planned to seem him on October 28 in France for the live presentation of our show *Return to the Titanic*, but it worried me that in the six weeks preceding my flight, he would let the whole matter drop.

There was good reason for my concern. My first three phone calls weren't returned and the excuses given by his secretary sounded increasingly feeble.

Focusing on his promises to find the thief at whatever cost, I kept trying. *I want you to help me, Jennie. Together we will put this man in jail.*

My persistence finally won out. Chappaz himself picked up the phone on my next attempt. His voice was warm and enthusiastic.

"I have good news," he said. "My private investigator is close—*very* close—to naming the culprit. Trust me, I'll have this solved in another week or two." He then inquired about Joel, Kevin, Brent, and Derek, saying all the right things and praising me again for my invaluable contribution to *Titanic 87*.

Joel heard the conversation, and I told him what Chappaz said about the private investigator and the fact that the case was on the verge of solution.

"Yes, and I'm the ghost of Captain Smith," he said.

As time passed, the likelihood of Joel being Captain Smith's ghost grew stronger than Chappaz' investigation to find the artifacts and bring the criminals to justice.

"Who's the detective agency you hired?" I asked when Chappaz and I spoke again. "Maybe I can speak to them—perhaps in some way I can help."

"I have it all in hand," he said coldly.

"Have you shown them the note? Have they analyzed the handwriting?"

"So far, no leads about the note. Jennie..." and then I heard unmistakable irritation in his tone. "When I see you in Paris, we can discuss if further. It's too dangerous to speak over the phone."

I started to answer but a sharp, sudden click silenced me. He had hung up.

It was raining when I stepped off the plane at De Gaulle Airport, but the chill of wet October didn't dampen my excitement. I longed for one final reunion with my comrades from the *Titanic* mission. Joel had been planning to go with me but a last minute script deadline made it impossible.

Brigitte and I met for dinner at the Jules Verne restaurant, the restaurant which had spawned Camille, and caught up on our month apart. She felt more familiar, even now, than anyone I'd encountered in Los Angeles. Psychologically, I still hadn't detached myself from the world of the expedition.

Our dinner was delicious, even though we both agreed that Camille's food on the *Abeille* was superior.

"They should hire him back at twice the salary," Brigitte said.

"Mais certainement," I agreed smiling.

We went afterward to the special cocktail party honoring members of our expedition at *La Villette*, the Center for Science and Industry. Brigitte knew the four officials of Ifremer and introduced me to all of them. I embraced Nargeolet, Keranflech, Pierre-Yves, and Christian. Captain Zozo looked like an orphan without his zodiac and binoculars, and George Tulloch had his family in tow, along with all the investors.

Everyone was there but Captain Rowarch, who I felt deserved much credit for making the expedition a success.

The Center for Science and Industry was so impressive that I wished Kevin, Brent, and Derek were with me to see it. The underwater section featured a full-sized model of the *Nautile,* and there were fascinating sections centering on Jacques Cousteau's contributions to diving. We saw the first diving cylinders he and his partner had invented and other exhibits chronicling the whole history of diving. CSI's ocean section was the finest I'd ever seen, more complete than the famous oceanographic museum in Monaco.

Later, as "Return to the *Titanic*" unfolded, I concentrated intently on the artifacts. I replayed all my telexes listing each and every artifact and pored through my mental files to figure out which ones were missing. I did the same thing the next morning, when we were all taken to the *Electricite de France* to see the procedures of restoration—a process by which artifacts are chemically treated to insure their longevity.

Witnessing the restoration process was tremendously reassuring. Every recovered object is treated instantly after exposure to air, to protect it from crumbling. When the relic is handed over to the laboratory, it undergoes thorough washing in deionized water so that contaminating surface salts can be eliminated. All impurities have to be removed that have accumulated in the material.

Metal objects to be restored benefit strongly from electrolysis. Sea water conducts electricity, and metal objects in the ocean conduct a tiny current causing negative ions from dissolved salts to attack uneven surfaces in the metal. Those objects that have suffered excessive decay can frequently be rescued before corrosion is too extreme by placing them in metal baths, wiring them to a negative battery terminal, and covering them with a metal cage attached to a positive terminal. The artifact's corrosion is then removed when the current pulls the negative ions and salt from it.

"These people are geniuses," said Brigitte when we saw the experts restore items that would have been expected to decay through time. Paper items such as newspapers, sheets of music, and personal letters are freeze-dried to remove water, then treated to protect them against mold and resized to restore their shape. Artifacts recovered from the ocean floor are meticulously maintained in an atmosphere of controlled temperature and kept away from damaging sunlight.

"Return to the *Titanic*" achieved higher ratings than any other syndicated show in history. The actual footage was riveting as we looked again at the artifacts: the cut glass window from the first class dining room, the bell from the crow's nest, and the cherub from the grand staircase that had touched our crew to the point of tears and obviously affected millions of others the same way in museums.

Before I left Paris, I had dinner with Robert Chappaz at Maxims. We discussed the stolen artifacts, but Chappaz seemed more evasive than ever. He reassured me again that he was on the case.

"You're not telling me everything," I said. "All you're doing is being polite until I'm on a plane headed for home."

"Jennie, it's over," he said, taking a deep puff of his cigar and blowing smoke in my direction.

"How can it be over, if the thief is still free?"

"What is it about you?" he demanded. "Why is it you never give up?"

The wine was loosening my tongue.

"Why is it you don't care? Why are you willing to drop the whole thing?"

"I would tell you more—but I don't believe you'll keep quiet if I do."

His tone was harsh, erasing the thin veneer of charm.

"Can I trust you? Can I tell you the truth?"

"How will I know it's the truth?"

"You'll know," he said. "And you can take satisfaction in this—none of it would have happened except for your pushing. But if I tell you, I want your word."

Anxious to hear the story, I gave him a promise of silence.

"We know who the thief is. Do you remember Georges Massenet?"

I nodded, remembering him vividly. A man in his early fifties, with a beard, curly black hair and a weatherbeaten face. I also recalled his enormous hands and thickly muscled, tattooed arms. He was a freelance diver who had been with is for a few weeks, not one of the regular *Abeille* crew. I had never trusted him.

"I didn't know Massenet had a prison record, or I would never have hired him," Chappaz continued. "Sometimes a man's background looks impeccable, but Monsieur Massenet was a convincing liar."

Massenet had stolen the artifacts and placed them in his safe, located in the French town of Menton.

Menton is a town in the south of France noted for its exquisite, flower-lined boulevards, cypress trees and unusually warm winters. It is also known for its gallery dedicated to Jean Cocteau and its Mardi Gras "Citron Festival," featuring 100,000 oranges and lemons on carnival floats. But this world of blindingly beautiful color and tourism was obliterated by darkness, fog and heavy rainfall when a man hired by Chappaz broke into Massenet's home to steal the artifacts and restore them to their rightful owners.

"After my investigators found out the Georges was the thief, I decided not to involve the police," Chappaz explained. "Instead I turned to some friends . . . with powerful connections. Connections the law would not have approved of, but they get the job done. The man they recruited was an expert at breaking safe combinations."

"So, did he get the artifacts back?"

"Patience, my dear Jennie." I could see he enjoyed drawing out the story, tantalizing me, poking fun at my eagerness to learn the details.

I could visualize the dark house, the violent storm and the precise, anonymous intruder opening the safe door and carefully removing the *Titanic* artifacts. But, Chappaz explained, Massenet, who was supposed to be out of the country, had changed his mind at the last minute.

He entered the room, creeping up silently behind the stranger who had invaded his territory. Massenet grabbed the housebreaker by the throat and began strangling him. He was a powerful man, and those massive arms increased their choking hold. Chappaz' agent fought for air against Massenet's lethal pressure.

Strong as Massenet was, however, he was dealing with a professional. The hired thief tore free and threw Massenet against the wall. He picked up Massenet's diving tank and smashed it against his chest. As Massenet screamed from the pain caused by his cracking ribs, the intruder reached for a nearby regulator hose and wound it around Massenet's neck. Tightening his grip, he used the regulator hose as a garrote. Massenet collapsed, unconscious, the blood supply cut off from his brain.

The intruder raced to the safe, gathered up the artifacts and fled. He left behind Massenet's money, identification and other personal effects, stealing only what had been taken from Chappaz in the first place.

Newspapers later reported that Massenet's home had been broken into, but never mentioned that the retrieved items were artifacts from the *Titanic*.

"Why did you do it that way, instead of calling the police?"

"Because we didn't want our critics to find out," Chappaz replied. "They were criticizing us from the beginning, calling us grave robbers, thieves. There would have been a scandal, and a trial."

"So Massenet just gets off, scot free?"

"Not quite. If you had visited him in the hospital, you would have found a man with broken ribs, two missing teeth and a punctured lung. Isn't that punishment enough? And remember, Jennie, he was only a hired hand, not a regular member of the expedition. There's nothing to say he would be convicted, yet bringing it to trial will make us all look guilty. The artifacts have been reclaimed. It's time to move ahead."

I knew there was more to Chappaz' motives than just the image of our expedition. It was the preservation of his own image that mattered most. He saw himself as a knight charging into a great historical battle, as a key contributor to history—even if he had to work hand in hand with the Mafia to accomplish it.

"Be satisfied," he told me, as he lay down his credit card to pay the check. "And put it behind you."

All the way home I thought of Chappaz' story, trying to achieve an overall perspective about the situation. I could exert pressure on him or the other principals involved, but what would I gain? There was no way of convicting Massenet without Chappaz' support, particularly since Massenet no longer had the valuables in his possession. Besides, I told myself, any negative publicity would only detract from the magnificent crew on the *Abeille* and the *Nadir* who had put their hearts and souls into finding the artifacts and placing them on display to honor those who perished.

In the end, there were innumerable artifacts for museum exhibits: a bell, valises, jewelry, many varieties of china from first, second and third class, a porthole, telegraphs, a telephone, a compass, the leaded glass window, and newspapers, postcards, letters, and clothes found in suitcases.

George Tulloch had dedicated himself to placing these artifacts, and all those from future expeditions, in museums around the globe. Knowing his meticulous dedication and devotion to the *Titanic* legend, I was convinced that he would make certain future surveillance of the artifacts stricter.

Joel and I had dinner on the *Queen Mary* in Los Angeles and held our own private celebration of *Titanic* survivor Edwina Troutt MacKenzie's memory. I felt sad that she had died three years before our mission. How she would have loved the sight of Ken Marschall's pictures and the photographs of *Titanic* artifacts. She had passed away five months after her one hundredth birthday, and it was almost as though she had willed herself to hang on for as long as it took scientists to find and present tangible objects to embody what had existed for years only in her memory.

Toasting her as the setting sun formed patterns on the restaurant window, I relived that night in 1982 when she had spoken so animatedly about her life.

"You were right," Joel said to me. "The good in men won out."

"I'm not sure." I sighed.

"Look. Even Chappaz, in his own way, cared about the people on the Titanic. All right, so you don't like his methods or how he hired some underworld goon to break in and take the artifacts back. At least he got them back and you can feel responsible for not letting them be swept aside, because it wouldn't have happened if you hadn't pushed him. Just remember one thing—those artifacts will be seen by thousands of people all over the world and because of that, even a hundred years from now when the Titanic's gone, the artifacts will still be here."

He was right. Beyond history books, long after the ship had turned to rubble, the preservation of artifacts guaranteed that Edwina and all the others would live forever.

The issue of the thief was closed, except for thoughts that occasionally floated through my mind. Even those thoughts faded away in 1990 when Robert Chappaz suddenly and unexpectedly died.

Our expedition finally received its seal of approval from those who were most personally involved: *Titanic* survivors themselves.

"I feel that if research and salvage of the *Titanic* will benefit all people, then such activities should be encouraged," said Louise Kink Pope, American *Titanic* survivor to the United States Congress.

Beatrice Sandstrom, a Swedish *Titanic* survivor, agreed. "As a *Titanic* survivor," she said, "I am personally pleased to see the *Titanic* story remembered by your fine efforts. Your presentation of the recovered objects from the ship will help to teach present and future generations the timeless human lessons learned from this great maritime tragedy."

Oddly enough, our strongest detractor in 1987 had spoken very differently in 1985, following his own expedition. Dr. Robert Ballard, co-founder of the wreck, addressed Congress with these words: "I am proposing that any future revisits to the *Titanic* which would involve deep diving submersibles dedicate a portion of their diving time to carefully recording and recovering those delicate items lying outside the hull of the ship itself. The artifacts recovered should be used to create a museum."

I couldn't help feeling he was right the first time.

Chapter 28

Snake in the Garden

I didn't know that my conflict with Don Barkham would resurface and become the battlefield for the second and, as Don phrased it, "final round" in our bitter conflict. When I first became aware of the projected IMAX film *Titanica*, I was simply excited by the possibilities of capturing the great ship in a large IMAX format. The IMAX film frame is the largest ever made; it uses 70 mm film ten times the size of a conventional 35mm movie frame. The breadth and grandeur of the *Titanic* had never been shown in all their tragic splendor, and director Stephen Low, the brilliant, creative and acknowledged master of IMAX productions, decided to present it in theatres with the overwhelming pictorial impact it deserved. Another Titanicphile, Stephen had originally worked in 1985 with Bob Ballard to do an IMAX portrait of the Ballard expedition.

"We had done fit checks of the camera in the *Alvin* submersible and we had some lights built in preparation for the dive," Stephen said. "But there were funding problems at the last minute. In retrospect, it was a blessing in disguise, because now technology has become vastly more advanced."

Stephen Low was renowned for filming natural wonders and making them unforgettable visual experiences. He had done this in *The Last Buffalo,* an award-winner that took viewers on a surreal exploration of the Alberta Badlands. He was also the producer/director on *Beavers* and had sent his cameras aloft to capture the flight of Canadian geese in 1984's *Skyward.*

Born in Ottawa, and the director and producer of *Challenger* in 1980, Low was widely admired for his ability to bring out the drama in non-fiction. In conjunction with his work as director, cameraman and editor, his fascination with underwater wrecks led to a scuba diving career that took him to more than fifty shipwrecks from Hawaii to Newfoundland, Lake Superior and the Caribbean. Without consciously realizing it, he was preparing for his ultimate underwater achievement.

Low's IMAX film *Titanica,* was a co-production with the Shirshov Institute in Moscow. The Russians were able to provide twin submersibles, *Mir* I and *Mir* II, both of which had the capacity to dive at least 13,000 feet. Having two submersibles, according to Low, gave him the chance to light not only from the camera position, but to sidelight and backlight as well.

The *Mir I* and *Mir II* had double the power of Woods Hole's *Alvin,* which meant a total battery power available of about eighty kilowatt hours per sub. More lights and more dive time resulted—up to twenty hours.

"The biggest single element that made this film possible was the development of undersea high intensity HMI lights," said Stephen. "*Titanica* is the first well-lit ocean film."

Renowned cameraman Al Giddings, one of the leaders of the *Titanica* expedition, had used HMIs in shallow water when he worked on James Cameron's *The Abyss*.

"I think his involvement early on was the key to the success of this project," said Stephen. "Without Al we would have been intimidated by the idea of developing deep water HMIs... since the implosion of a *single light* could destroy a sub."

Mark Olsson of Deep Sea Power and Light developed special pressure housings, reflectors and light sources, utilizing the technology developed for *The Abyss* and repackaging it for 6000 psi. Each submersible was equipped with four HMI lights, placed out on a boom twelve feet from the lens, which allowed Stephen and his crew to illuminate wide areas of the *Titanic* wreck, equivalent to about 150,000 watts of incandescent light (about 1,500 domestic 100 watt lightbulbs). These were the brightest lights ever used in the deep sea. They penetrated fifty to seventy five feet through the blackness. Incandescent lights used previously lit an area of only eight to ten feet.

"The blend of higher performance lights in addition to two powerful subs meant we could deliver about twenty times the light available on earlier expeditions. That's essential in IMAX," Stephen said.

I was excited to be chosen the Production Manager of this groundbreaking *Titanic* enterprise, and doubly excited that my son Kevin would be with me. Kevin's imagination had been stirred by my Titanic 87 adventure, and since that time—especially since his fortuitous meeting with Edwina Troutt MacKenzie—he had asked me hundreds of questions, soaking in every detail and imagining himself a part of it.

In addition to the joy of having my son on board, *Titanica* became a family reunion. Ralph was the submersible cameraman, and Emory Kristof of National Geographic was the Senior photographer. Both were the best in their field, fully capable of helping to make Stephen Low's dream come to fruition.

My participation began through the project's producer, Peter Serapiglia. Peter was Stephen's right hand, one of the best producers I've known in my entire career—organized, efficient, on top of every detail, able to handle difficult people and situations with strength, sensitivity and a sense of humor. Peter's first project with Stephen Low was as production manager on *Beavers,* following a successful producing career that encompassed suspense films such as *Dreamline* and award-winning records and music videos for CBS, RCA and Atlantic Records. He had over thirty-five documentaries to his credit, including the Oscar-nominated *Adventures in History* and the seven part series *War.*

The term "grace under pressure" perfectly applied to Peter, and in the months to come, he would need this quality on more than one occasion.

When I came to Dorval, Canada, a suburb of Montreal, to help set the whole enterprise in motion, Peter arranged for me to stay with his vivacious, charming sister, Rita Christie, and saw to it that I felt comfortable in my new environment.

Because my passion for the great ship was ongoing, the role I assumed on the *Titanica* expedition was challenging and all-consuming just as the one I'd handled on *Titanic 87.* It was my job to hire the crew that would be filming on board the ship and to plan every aspect of film equipment needed. Kevin and I set up all the logistics—from the divers necessary to the hotels required to house those who would stay on land. It was also top priority to arrange for a massive amount of equipment to be shipped to Bermuda. Bermuda was the first leg of this spectacular new addition to the *Titanic* story.

Before *Titanica* could be launched, I flew to Washington, D. C. to speak with the U. S. Department of Trade. I needed their permission before we could purchase syntactic foam—foam that submersibles must have for buoyancy.

"It's considered a highly dangerous substance," the officials told me. "The United States doesn't allow the sale of syntactic foam to foreign countries, because it can be used for spy missions."

Stephen's Russian partners had to have it; if usage was denied, the whole expedition would be aborted. I pleaded my case, against a brick wall of adamant refusals. They finally capitulated after weeks of letters in support of our mission and phone calls from numerous high-level executives.

Owing to the inherent danger of the mission, we had to prepare detailed information for the insurance company, *Lloyds of London,* supplying them with proper information about weather conditions and fatalities that had previously occurred.

A stern looking man in a pin-striped black suit and vest stared at me, as though relishing some secret bit of information.

"Do you know that *we were the company that insured the Titanic?* I've investigated and gone back into my records, and I've found that our company paid out a total of $16,804,112.00. I don't have to tell you how much that would be in today's dollars. Someone in the neighborhood of a hundred million. Now do you see why we're so hesitant?"

For once I was speechless. What was the proper rebuttal, when you're seeking insurance from a company for a *Titanic* expedition, and they tell you they lost millions insuring the original *Titanic?*

"That amount," he went on, "was divided equally among all the claimants—whether they had a claim of eight shillings and sixpence for a marmalade machine by Edwina Troutt, or the very largest claim of one million dollars filed by Renee Harris, a widow of the Theatre magnate Henry Harris. They all got the same, an amount of $663,000.00. Just so you understand—this was not the salvage value, which is normally our means of determining the owner's liability—but instead it was a total limit of everyone who put a claim in."

I knew that one claim would make a particular impression on Joel—Eugene Daly's claim for a set of bagpipes valued at fifty dollars.

"All I could do was emphasize that the *Titanic* disaster had occurred seventy-nine years before. He nodded, not accepting my logic, and pointed out another tragic submersible drama: the story of inventor and undersea explorer Edwin S. Link and his son Clayton.

Johnson Sea Link 1 was diving off the coast of Florida in 1973, when the submersible was caught in a rugged current 360 feet down while studying fishing populations near the wreck of a sunken Navy ship. The sub was thrown into a mass of underwater cables from the sunken ship, and *Johnson Sea Link 1* was unable to free itself.

All rescue attempts failed, and after thirty hours, a

hook rigged together with a closed-circuit television was lowered from a ship at the surface. It successfully lifted the submersible and brought it up, but two men in the rear compartment—Albert Stover and E. Clayton Link, Edward Link's thirty-one-year-old son—were tragically killed, victims of a carbon dioxide buildup in the compartment from a rebreather system, along with overwhelming cold.

Still, I explained, the number of accidents was small compared to other modes of transportation, above and below the water. I told them that technology had risen to remarkable heights since then, and submersibles abounded in safety and backup features. It helped that I had been an expedition leader, and had the experience of knowing what dangers had to be avoided at sea when filming.

Rita Christie, Peter's sister, was a long-time employee of Lloyds of London, and she—as an insider—pleaded our case and was a powerful influencing factor in winning them over. Reluctantly, they gave their consent to a mission they didn't really understand, after I answered twenty pages of questions relating to historical information about weather conditions and hurricanes on the site of the *Titanic* for the last fifteen years, detailed technical queries about the ship and its equipment, navigational Sonar and communications, and engine power. I was relieved I had kept all of my research books from the previous expedition, so I could refer to them as documented samples of a successful and safe trip to the site. My nautical knowledge, which had increased with this expedition, proved invaluable.

The complexity of planning a venture so large, with a ship twice the size of the *Nadir*, twice as much crew and a special crew on board documenting our whole expedition, demanded sixteen hour days. Peter and I worked together seven days a week, handling a myriad of details side by side. He never asked anything of me that he wasn't willing to do himself; I always felt tremendous sharing and support. But there was a snake in the garden, and he reared his head within the first few weeks.

Peter summoned me and said, "A fellow named Don Barkham just called. He knows people at IMAX and he's says he has good contacts for funding."

"Don and I had our differences on the 1987 expedition."

"He wants me to fire you. He says you're a dangerous woman."

I took refuge in banter. "Do I look dangerous?"

"This guy is obsessed. He's already called Stephen. He's called me three times today."

"And what did you say?"

"I told him you're doing a great job. But I don't think he'll give up."

I felt like Jean Valjean in *Les Miserables,* pursued by a modern-day Javert.

Peter stared at me. "What did you do? What could have made this guy go bonkers?"

I explained what my heinous crime was—refusing to endanger the safety of my crew to film Don's dive. "And I'd do it again," I said. "If that makes me a dangerous woman, well, I'm dangerous."

Peter contacted Stephen, and Stephen had no intention of caving in under pressure when he, personally, saw nothing wrong in my behavior or my work.

The subject of Don was dropped, and Peter and I continued with my daily activities. I hoped that Don's calls would stop, but instead they escalated.

"You've got to get rid of her," Don said, when he

saw that Peter was holding his ground. "I want her out."

When I asked Peter to press Don for details as to *why* I was dangerous, Don said, "You'll have to trust me. I know her. You'll be sorry in the end if you keep her on."

Never had I seen a vendetta this relentless. Don's lines were so vitriolic I had an image of being chained to a wall while he heaved knives at me. Twice now he had single-mindedly set a goal: to make me lose my job. Peter suggested that I might have grounds for a libel suit: I was being defamed, my job was being jeopardized by his slander.

I thought of the phrase 'dangerous woman.' What *was* a dangerous woman? Obviously, the kind of woman who had a mind of her own, who acted according to her own values and wasn't easily malleable. A woman became dangerous if she expressed too much opposition, if she didn't automatically play ball. Don had called me dangerous; on board the *Abeille* he had called me "powerful"; a third time he had referred to me as "ambitious." I wondered what sort of women he had known in his own life.

Kevin was a rock, and Stephen remained supportive. But it was Peter who took the brunt of these calls; Peter who had to endure veiled threats about his own position if he didn't cave in to Don's demands. Despite the most pressured battering I've ever seen, Peter never yielded.

At one point he faced the assaults with more strength than I did. The pleasure I took in my work, and the satisfaction I derived from being part of another *Titanic* expedition was being fatally undermined by these constant attacks. I didn't think it was fair that Peter had to suffer daily harassment.

I decided to resign. Joel had called from Los

Angeles with a message: producer/writer Keith Walker
wanted me to work on the feature film, *Free Willy*. Before
my offer to join the *Titanica* company, I had been working
on research and development for Keith's script. The subject was killer whales, a subject I'd specialized in throughout my career.

The next morning I placed my resignation letter on
Peter's desk. He came into my office after reading it, shaking his head.

"I can't accept this."

"I really feel this is the best thing for the expedition,
and for you and Stephen."

"So you're just going to let him *win?*"

"It's not about winning or losing," I said. "It's
about what's best for the project."

"If I'm standing firm—if *Stephen* is standing
firm—why should you knuckle under?"

His reassurance, his support, meant a lot to me. I
was aware, even in the midst of excruciating tension, that I
was witnessing strength of character and depth of friendship I had never imagined possible.

It was an inspiration to me that Peter remained
in my corner and withstood the blows. That Stephen,
who had more important demands, and could easily
have said, "Get rid of her," encouraged me to remain.
This kind of courage, this willingness to defend those
you believe in, is possibly the rarest commodity in all
human relations. Knowing Peter and Stephen heightened my belief in people.

"He won't stop," I said.

"Look, we've got a lot to do. I give you my word of
honor that I'll stand by you through this."

I wish I could say that the furious phone calls

ended. They didn't. Peter asked me if I was willing to have a face to face meeting with Don. Much as I hated the idea, I was willing to meet with him and talk out our grievances, try to resolve them and declare a truce. Don accepted the offer, then backed out at the last minute. I felt it showed he was more interested in vengeance than in working out a compromise.

Chapter 29

Titanica - A Return

Peter and I made a trip to Bermuda to scout the site before setting up an office there. Once our headquarters were established, Stephen and company followed. The plan was to film early underwater sequences before anyone proceeded to the *Titanic* site.

"There are certain shots that can't be done on the site," Stephen told me. "It's impossible to photograph two and a half miles down—like close up shots of the outside of the submersible, the lights, the portholes, the actual sub coming to rest on the bottom. These have to be done in shallow water."

Once these shots were concluded, the second leg— the *Titanic* leg—followed.

In June, the expedition sailed from Bermuda to the *Titanic* site on the world's largest oceanographic vessel, the *Akademk Keldysh*. Four hundred and forty-two feet long, this Russian ship carried one hundred and thirty people, had eighteen laboratories and a data acquisition system with nineteen different outside sensors to measure temperature, salinity, depth, sound velocities and water currents. It also carried the world's most advanced submersibles, *Mir I* and *Mir II,* first launched in 1987 and designed to withstand pressures of nine thousand pounds per square inch—more than enough for the two and a half mile descent to the *Titanic.*

Unlike my 1987 expedition, Stephen had no intention of bringing artifacts to the surface. He only wanted to photograph them and have the pictures speak for themselves. This eliminated all controversy, and I felt relieved.

The horror of dealing with Don's character assassination was also counteracted by watching Kevin. I could see he worshiped Stephen, and was studying his every move. My teenaged son had a naturally creative mind, and he wanted to know how Stephen had achieved the amazing underwater sequences for his former IMAX film, *Beavers.* He was eager to find out how Stephen had been able to fly so close to migrating geese in *Skyward,* and admired Stephen for being a pioneer, a creator on the cutting edge, since *Skyward* was the same story as the later feature film, *Fly Away Home.* "He's amazing," Kevin said. "He knows so much—and he's a nice guy to boot."

The first dive of the 1991 expedition took place on June 30 with Emory, Al Giddings and Anatoly Sagalevitch, head of manned submersibles of the Shirshov Institute. That dive had to be cut short when *Mir I's* main propulsion unit jammed, and *Mir II* snapped its starboard HMI light bar.

Ralph and Paul Mockler, the other expert undersea cameraman on the expedition, were expected to figure out what was on the wreck.

"I was in one sub," said Stephen, "and I radioed Ralph

to describe the scene. "He'd say, 'Oh, you're outside the captain's bedroom. Look in there and you'll see the bathtub.'"

Four years had passed since our 87 expedition, and we were all surprised by the amount of corrosion that had formed. When we saw Emory's history-making photographs, and compared them with photos he had taken in 1985 and 1986, the extent of decay was shockingly evident. The amount of rusticles hanging off the bow had accelerated; they were dramatically longer and larger. Rusticles blocked portholes that had once been entirely visible. The stream of rust that was just a few feet from a cast iron deck bench now began to touch and encircle it.

The sense of how ephemeral life was accosted me—the rusticles which were actually bacteria could eat away and destroy steel; mollusks could eat and destroy the wood; and other marine creatures could destroy carpeting, drapery and clothes. Nothing on earth was indestructible; we were all part of a cycle that ended and kept repeating.

These electrifying images of the beautiful but deadly rusticles gave solid support to the words of our marine engineering geologist and chief scientist, Steve Blasco. "Two processes—chemical and biological—are corroding the *Titanic* at a substantial rate. However, it looks like the biological—bacteria metabolizing the iron, producing rusticles—is more dominant. Myriads of rusticles, shaped like icicles, dangling from all parts of the ship, piles of fallen rusticles on the seabed adjacent to the hull, rivers of rust flowing from the wreck and across decking and plating, coated with rust, combine to create this first impression."

To my horror I could see that the *Titanic* was disintegrating, and would eventually dissolve and disappear.

Other important scientific discoveries were made. Dr. Lev Moskalev with his mass of black hair, was fifty-six years old. Known as Big Lev, he was our marine biologist, and the chief scientist at the Shirshov Institute in Moscow. Moskalev specialized in invertebrate zoology and studied the distribution of animals at the bottom of the sea. He became animated, his eyes popping out of his head, when he enthusiastically described the characteristics of marine creatures.

"The environment is dynamic and biologically active. Twenty-four invertebrate species of animals and four species of fish inhabit the wreck site, including three foot long rat tails, coral, crabs, shrimp, anemones and starfish. All of which will still be there when the *Titanic* ceases to exist."

As the dives continued, many under the capable piloting hands of Evgeny Chernjaev, the hovering dangers that *Lloyds of London* had feared, dangers that had been ever-present on my *Nautile* dive; always threatened to pin the pilots and passengers down—in the form of cable and twisted metal.

"One submersible got hooked on some cables on the *Titanic* deck and another almost got stuck in a hole while trying to shoot the lower decks inside the hull," Ralph reported. "The pilots skillfully maneuvered the submersibles out of danger."

The submersible also had a tremendous capacity for hiding things, said Bill Reeve, Supervisor of Camera Development Research and Development.

"When you're inside a six foot diameter sphere, you would think you'd be able to locate just about anything. But when you want a roll of tape or your Swiss army knife, or if you dropped something, you'll never find it because there was *so much equipment in there.* You can't really appreciate the frustration of dropping a screw and being scared of not being able to get it back again."

Above all, said Stephen, "extreme caution was taken to prevent the powerful HMI lights from imploding. The time limit for burning the HMI lights was twenty minutes, followed by a ten minute cool down. A stop watch on the four lights and traveling in the dark solved this dilemma."

The *Titanica* expedition offered the pilots and passengers far more time on the bottom than we had experienced on *Titanic* 87—eighteen hours from the time the pilots climbed into the hatch to the time it was opened up. The launch procedure took about thirty minutes before the submersible started its descent. Once on the sea bottom, the crews functioned up from twelve to fourteen hours. Seventeen dives were made in all.

Stephen would succeed in his goal "to take people where they would otherwise not be able to go, like into outer space, and in this case the inner space of the *Titanic,* sitting at the bottom of the sea." Later, on the large-screen, he would show survivor Eva Hart and penetrate to her deepest emotions, to illuminate recollections of her father carrying her from her berth to the boat deck to place her on a lifeboat along with her mother.

"I was seven years old," Eva would relate, "and now I'm the last survivor of the *Titanic* who can remember it clearly, and am still able to get about.

"I had an enormous teddy bear my father had bought for me the Christmas before we went away. It was almost as tall as I was. I loved it and I used to play with it on the deck with my father, and the captain stopped several times and commented on my teddy bear and spoke to my father, who was delighted with him... I wanted to go back for my teddy bear when my father was carrying me out of the cabin to take me up to the boat deck. I remember saying, 'I want my teddy bear.' He didn't say anything. He just continued to carry me. I never had another teddy bear—I never wanted another one." Those words still resonate in my heart, even though Eva Hart died in 1995.

To the end, Don Barkham continued his campaign to oust me, but, anchored by Peter and Stephen's belief, I stayed with *Titanica*. In the ensuing battle, I learned how vulnerable a person is when someone decides, with methodical dedication, to destroy them. Policemen know that if someone decides to kill someone else, there's little that can be done until a crime has been committed. Unseen enemies, operating by darkness, can do irreparable damage.

The only defense is to fight back, and even more crucial, to wait the enemy out. Enemies always count on one thing—that you'll cave in, back off when the heat blazes too intensely. Most of the time they're right; all people have limited reserves. After that the seams tear, the walls crumble and they crack. But there are rewards if you can dig your heels deep in the ground and hold on under the most unbearable circumstances. And if you have people like Stephen and Peter to offer the backup you need.

Since then, I've worked with both of them steadily. I'm still working; I haven't been destroyed; and I have an added sense of pride, knowing I fought my way through the battle and emerged bloody but unbroken.

When *Titanica* was unveiled, the press hailed it as

a masterpiece, the kind of treatment a legendary ship deserved. I met James Cameron at the premiere and watched his hypnotic concentration. Cameron, who subsequently wrote, edited and directed *Titanic*, studied Stephen's film carefully, already conceiving the idea of doing his own *Titanic* story.

I've now worked on two more IMAX projects for Stephen Low and Peter—*Across the Sea of Time* and *Mark Twain's America*. Both men continue to be my greatest inspirations. They've entrusted me with great responsibility, and I've done my best to never let them down.

I admire Stephen and Peter so much because they dare to dream big. Their thinking is larger than life, and they encourage the people around them to strive for goals that seem unattainable.

George Tulloch is another one of the dreamers, and as a result his group has become RMS *Titanic* Inc., a company awarded the status of salvor-in-possession by the United States District Court Judge J. Calvitt Clarke, Jr. To date, thousands of artifacts have been brought up from the wreck and these are being guarded and restored with extreme care by Tulloch's organization. No one else has the right to salvage the *Titanic*, and in return for this absolute control, Tulloch is legally bound to protect the artifacts and keep them from ever being commercially sold.

Hundreds of *Titanic* relics have been conserved and exhibited worldwide. There have been displays in Paris, Stockholm, Malmo and Goteborg, Sweden and Oslo, Norway. The 1994 National Maritime Museum in Greenwich, England, drew over seven hundred thousand people when they featured a *Titanic* exhibit; and exhibitions have drawn enthusiastic crowds in Hamburg, Germany,

Memphis, Tennessee, Los Angeles at the Queen Mary, and
St. Petersburg, Florida.

The *Titanic* legend is composed of so many events
and people. I'm one participant in that legend and I take
pride in it. With the exception of my husband and children,
those incomparable moments at sea and on the ocean floor
are the most meaningful highlights of my life.

Through the years, I've watched, admired and
worked with great women adventurers—Beverly Johnson,
Valerie Taylor, Eugenie Clark, Sylvia Earle—and it's
heartening to me that opportunities continue to grow for
women to explore and be key figures in the world of adventure. These women have proven themselves as strong and
as resourceful as their male counterparts when faced with
the same life-threatening dangers and challenges. In the
process, they've forged a special bond with men. I'm proud
to be in their company, and excited that so many others are
joining our ranks.

Miraculously, through all my physical and emotional voyages, I've landed on my feet. I admit I've stumbled and made mistakes, been tactless at times, come on
too strong or said too little. I let myself be brutalized in my
first marriage and accepted second place in other relationships. Because my father was an abstraction, a stranger living under the same roof, I never had a male role model. I
had to improvise.

But I've learned that improvising is at the heart of
all living, all relationships. There are no fixed road maps,
no matter how many self-help or counselors' books protest
differently. From my point of view, there are only two mind
sets: believing things will work out or believing they won't.
Dreams don't even have to be well-defined at first, or realistic. How realistic was it for a bank teller to imagine she

would someday establish a connection with the *Titanic*—
or travel the globe as a scuba diver, a skydiver and a filmmaker? Or, for that matter, for someone who had been so
hurt by an abusive relationship to love someone as much as
I love Joel, a love that only grows with time.

Being open to experience, saying yes to life when
everything in you is afraid, is the key—or at least it's the
key I have utilized to unlock the door to excitement and
fulfillment. I've tried to give that sense of meeting life
head-on to my sons. To grip fear by the throat and strangle
it until it doesn't overwhelm you anymore.

I was certainly afraid when Westgate said, "Will
you be expedition leader?" I quaked inside when Captain
Nargeolet said, "You will dive to the *Titanic*." And yet the
moment the invitation came, I fought back the butterflies
and soon afterward climbed into the *Nautile*.

I know that God presents us with tests and trusts
us to handle them. I haven't always welcomed those tests,
but I'm grateful now that they were given to me.

As a result, I've been blessed—I've gone where few
ever go, and I hope *Titanic* 87 and *Titanic* 91 are only two
of many unforgettable experiences.

Yet unforgettable as these new vistas may prove to
be, nothing will ever match the moment when I went down
to the ocean's depths and saw the magnificent ruins of that
great ocean liner, flooded by artificial light, as real to me as
if it had been raised and lying on the surface. So real, that
it was impossible to fathom the danger of being 12,500 feet
below the sea. So real, that I had the impulse to open the
door of the *Nautile* and swim out to greet it, swim inside its
mysterious openings, up the grand stairs, into its ghost-like
staterooms.

How I wished I could survive in that 6,000 pounds per square inch pressure, so I could explore the wreck safely and forge an even more intimate bond with the ship.

Only a person with *Titanic* fever—a person with awe of its beauty, awe of its power and respect for its memory—would ever write that scene in her imagination. And it's a scene I envision, even now, in my dreams. For the *Titanic,* lying silently below the sea in a waiting game with extinction gave me, paradoxically, a new sense of the meaning of life.

REFERENCES

Archibold, Rick, text, Dana McCauley, recipes, *Last Dinner on the Titanic*. New York: Hyperion, 1997.

Ballard, Dr. Robert D., "How We Found Titanic." *National Geographic*: December, 1985.

Ballard, Dr. Robert D., "A Long Last Look at Titanic." *National Geographic*: December, 1986.

Beebe, William, *Half Mile Down*. New York: Harcourt Brace and Company, 1934.

Bonsall, Thomas E., *Titanic - The Story of the Great White Star Line Trio*. New York: Gallery Books, 1987.

Boyd-Smith, Peter. *Titanic from Rare Historical Reports*. Southhampton, England: Steamship Publications, 1994.

Buckley, Jr., William F. "Down to the Great Ship." *The New York Times Magazine*: 18 October 1987.

Brown, Rustie. *The Titanic, the Psychic and the Sea*. Lomita, California: Blue Harbor Press, 1981.

Bryceson, Dave. *The Titanic Disaster as Reported in the British National Press, April-July 1912*. New York: W.W. Norton and Company, 1997.

Burgess, Robert F., Ships Beneath the Sea - A History of Subs and Submersibles. New York: McGraw Hill, 1975.

Carter, Jennifer. *Daily Diary and Faxes from the Nadir*. Titanic Site: 1987.

Davie, Michael. *Titanic*. New York: Alfred A . Knopf, 1987.

Earle, Dr. Sylvia A. and Giddings, Al, *Exploring the Deep Frontier*. Washington, D.C.: The National Geographic Society, 1980.

Earle, Dr. Sylvia, A. *Sea Change - A Message of the Oceans*. New York: G. P. Putnam's Sons, 1995.

Eaton, John P. and Haas, Charles, A. *Titanic: Triumph and Tragedy*. New York: W. W. Norton, 1994.

————. *Titanic: Destination Disaster*. New York: W. W. Norton, 1987.

Ellis, Richard. *The Book of Sharks*. New York: Grosset & Dunlap, 1975.

Ellis, William S. Photographs by Emory Kristof. "Loch Ness, the Lake and the Legend." *National Geographic*: June, 1977, p. 759-779.

Gannon, Robert. "What Really Sank the Titanic." *Popular Science*: February, 1995, p. 49-55.

Gracie, Col. Archibald. *The Truth About the Titanic*. New York: Mitchell, Kennerley, 1913.

Gracie, Archibald and Thayer, John B. *Titanic: A Survivor's Story and the Sinking of the S.S. Titanic*. Chicago: Academy Chicago Publishers, 1998.

Hardy, Kevin. "Return to the Titanic - The Third Manned Mission." *Sea Technology*: December, 1991, p. 10-19.

Hart, Eva. M.B.E., J.P., as told to Ronald C. Denney. *Shadow of the Titanic*. Dartford, Great Britain: Greenwich University Press, 1995.

Hoffman, William and Grimm, Jack. Beyond Reach: The Search for Titanic. New York: Beaufort Books, 1982.

Hutchinson, Gillian. "Titanic Today." *USA Today*: March 1995.

————. *The Wreck of the Titanic*. Greenwich, England: National Maritime Museum, 1994.

Jessop, Violet. Introduced, edited and annotated by John Maxtone-Graham. *Titanic Survivor*. Dobbs Ferry, New York: Sheridan House, Inc., 1997.

Johnson, Rebecca L. *Diving Into Darkness*. Minneapolis: Lerner Publications Company, 1989.

Kotsch, William J. *Weather for the Mariner*. 3rd ed. Annapolis, Maryland: Naval Institute Press, 1983.

Lemonick, Michael D. "Tempest Over the *Titanic*." *Time*: 3 August 1987.

————. "Treasures Reclaimed from the Deep." *Time*: 2 November 1987.

Lord, Walter. *A Night to Remember*. New York: Holt, Rinehart and Winston, 1955.

————. *The Night Lives On*. New York: William Morrow, 1986.

Lyons, Dr. Walter A. *The Handy Weather Answer Book*. Detroit: Visible Ink Press, 1997.

Muckelroy, Keith, ed. *Archaeology Underwater*. New York: McGraw-Hill Book Company, 1980.

Lynch, Don, text and Marschall, Ken, paintings. *Titanic - an Illustrated History*. New York: Hyperion/Madison Press, 1992.

Mackal, Roy P. *The Monsters of Loch Ness*. Chicago: The Swallow Press, 1976.

Montlucon, Jacques and Lacoudre, N. *Les Objets du Titanic - La Memoire des Abimes*. Paris: Admitech, 1989.

Murphy, Jamie. "Down into the Deep." *Time*, 11 August 1986.

Murphy, Joy Waldron. "The Search for the Titanic is Over." *Smithsonian*, August, 1986.

Potter, Jr., John S. *The Treasure Diver's Guide - Revised*. New York: Bonanza Books, 1972.

Reader's Digest. "The Unsinkable Titanic." Pleasantville, New York, 1986.

Renaldi, Brigitte. *Memoire du Titanic*. Versailles, France: Editions des 7 Vents, 1990.

Report on the Loss of the S. S. Titanic. New York: St. Martin's Press, 1990.

Rubin, Sydney. "Treasures of the Titanic." *Popular Mechanics*, December, 1987.

Sweeney, James B. *A Pictorial History of Oceanographic Submersibles*. New York: Crown Publishers, Inc., 1971.

Sylvester, Shaune. "Titanica takes IMAX into New Waters." *American Cinematographer*, January, 1995, p. 32-36.

U.S. Senate, Subcommittee Hearings of the Committee on Commerce, 60 second Congress. *Titanic Disaster*. Washington, D.C.: Government Printing Office, 1912.

Wade, Wyn Craig. *The Titanic: End of a Dream*. New York: Rawson, Wade Publishers, Inc., 1979.

Wangemann, Garth W. Reva Web Productions, 1998.

Wels, Susan. *Titanic - Legacy of the World's Greatest Ocean Liner*. New York: Time-Life Books, 1997.

Whipple, A.B.C. *The Editors of Time-Life Books*. Alexandria, Virginia: Time-Life Books, 1983.

Wincour, Jack, ed. *The Story of the Titanic as told by its survivors*, Beesley, Lawrence, Gracie, Archibald, Commander Lightoller Charles, Bride, Harold. New York: Dover Publications, 1960.

Wreck Commissioners' Court, Proceedings Before the Right Honourable Lord Marsey, on a Formal Investigation Ordered by the Board of Trade into the Loss of the S.S. Titanic.